Fire at Sea

Other Naval History Titles from Potomac Books:

USS Los Angeles: *The Navy's Venerable Airship and Aviation Technology*
William F. Althoff

USS Ranger: *The Navy's First Flattop from Keel to Mast, 1934-46*
Robert J. Cressman

The Liberty *Incident: The 1967 Israeli Attack on the U.S. Navy Spy Ship*
A. Jay Cristol

Cold War Submarines: The Design and Construction of U.S. and Soviet Submarines
Norman Polmar and K. J. Moore

War in the Boats: My WWII Submarine Battles
William J. Ruhe

Fire at Sea

The Tragedy of the Soviet Submarine *Komsomolets*

D. A. Romanov
Edited by K. J. Moore
Translated by Jonathan E. Acus

Potomac Books, Inc.

Washington, D.C.

Library of Congress Cataloging-in-Publication Data
Romanov, D. A. (Dmitrii Andreevich)
[Tragediia podvodnoi lodki "Komsomolets". English]
Fire at sea : the tragedy of the Soviet submarine Komsomolets / D.A.
Romanov ; edited by K.J. Moore ; translated by Jonathan E. Acus.— 1st ed.
p. cm.
Includes bibliographical references and index.
ISBN 1-57488-426-3 (alk. paper)
1. Komsomoleëi (Submarine) 2. Submarine disasters—Norwegian Sea. I. Moore,
Kenneth J., 1942-

VA575.K66R6613 2006
910.9163'24—dc22

2005054496

Printed in the United States of America on acid-free paper that meets the American National Standards Institute Z39-48 Standard.

Potomac Books, Inc.
22841 Quicksilver Drive
Dulles, Virginia 20166

First Edition

10 9 8 7 6 5 4 3 2 1

Contents

Illustrations

Editor's Preface

Fire at Sea is more than a review of the events leading to the loss of a nuclear submarine. It is more than a series of arguments presented by a ship designer in defense of his work. It is more than a sequential set of case studies that demonstrate the risk incurred when procedure is not well-established and operator training is not a sufficient priority. It is more than an examination of the confused and split responsibilities of a Ministry of Defense and a Ministry of Shipbuilding. It is more than the accusation that a bureaucracy was intent on obfuscating facts to avoid personal responsibility and that it did so without concern for the reoccurrence of such tragedies. In the aggregate, this book addresses the responsibility and risk incurred when operating at the frontiers of technology. History has demonstrated that accidents—whether related to a bridge, a space shuttle, or a nuclear submarine—can provide the insight necessary to enhance the safety and performance of current and subsequent designs. To squander such opportunities is to condemn future generations to further failure. Indeed, in his prophetic postscript to the first edition, the author warned that people would continue to die and ships would continue to sink unless the Russian Navy faced up to its responsibilities.

It is arguable that the success of the bureaucracy to obfuscate the poor level of training focused attention away from this important aspect of safe operations. While the loss of *Komsomolets* was a series of events initiated by an electrical fire, the loss of the cruise missile submarine *Kursk* eleven years later (July 2000) was apparently initiated by the crew's handling of a torpedo with a potentially unstable propulsion system. Events on the *Kursk* proceeded rapidly in comparison to the *Komsomolets*. But loss of the *Komsomolets* in 1989 could have been a useful warning that training aboard Soviet nuclear submarines was not always up to the level necessary for safe operation. Unbiased reviews of past accidents must address the operation as well as the design of technically demanding systems. The inability to address both the man and the machine simultaneously can condemn an organization to continued catastrophes. This book is replete with descriptions of crew responses that demonstrate a lack of knowledge of critical ship systems, including the life-saving equipment. But the apparent unwillingness to address these training issues squandered an eleven-year opportunity to aggressively improve the training and performance level of the crewmen tasked with the safe operation of submarines.

Romanov is not alone in his frustration with the lack of continuous training and qualification, particularly for newer crewmembers, i.e., those not trained during the construction and acceptance of the ship. During personal discussions, designers from other bureaus and high-level technical naval officers often vent their frustration with regard to the crew's unfamiliarity with equipment, including safety circuits and emergency procedures. To them, the solution is to remove the crewmen from the loop completely. On the other hand, the U.S. Navy looks to the crew to improve safety. As Romanov points out in his conclusion, the U.S. Navy openly states that training is its number one priority.

While less obvious, failure also offers the opportunity to recognize more successful approaches. Successful approaches rarely draw the attention that failure brings. Indeed, success can often result in relaxing well-established and proven standards—in both man and technology—to the point that a failure occurs in what once had been a well-tested and well-operated system. Thus, it is just as important to recognize successful systems and insist that the designs and organization not be altered to the point that success can no longer continue.

The U.S. Navy's nuclear submarine program is an example of such a success. Navy nuclear trained personnel and, in particular, naval nuclear submariners, are certainly among the best technically trained personnel in the world. The legacy of Admiral Hyman G. Rickover is a self-regulating, introspective organization that has responsibility for the safety, development, operation, and security of naval nuclear reactors. In this case there is no division of responsibility. The integration of man and machine is a continuous and centralized process controlled by personnel who have a lifetime of experience in and commitment to all aspects of the program. The importance and value of such an organization often goes unrecognized, even after the occurrence of the tragic events presented in this text.

The real value of *Fire at Sea* may be to underscore the importance of successful organizations and to appreciate the value of a society that allows such open examination of technological failures, as demonstrated by the recent investigations into the loss of the space shuttle *Columbia*. For these reasons, we applaud the openness of the People's Republic of China in announcing the death of the seventy-man crew of a MING-Class diesel submarine. It is with sincere concern for all brother submariners that we hope tragedy is being followed by an objective examination of possible failures in both design and training, which then leads to meaningful improvements in crew safety for all cutting-edge manned platforms.

                                                                                                    K. J. Moore

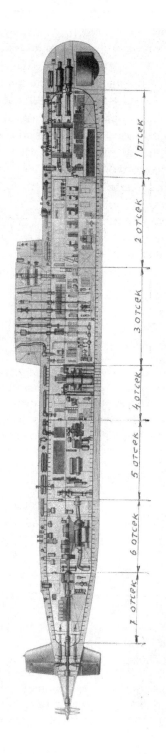

Drawing of the ill-fated *Komsomolets* showing the submarine's seven compartments.

Preface

On April 7, 1989, an accident occurred aboard the Soviet nuclear-powered submarine *Komsomolets* in the Sea of Norway. As a result of that accident, the submarine sank, and a large part of its crew, including many who survived the initial accident and had made it to the surface, tragically perished.

A state commission that was created to reveal the causes of the accident consisted of representatives both from the USSR (Soviet) Navy and from the Ministry of Shipbuilding Industry. In the course of the commission's work, members of its working group from the shipbuilding industry who directly participated in the submarine's construction—chief delivery agent V. N. Chuvakin, delivery mechanic E. P. Leonov, and assistant chief designer D. A. Romanov—arrived at an opinion regarding the causes of the accident and the loss of the submarine that differed from the opinion of other members of the working group who represented the Soviet Navy. However, these differences in opinion were not reflected in the documents of the commission's working group. This compelled the members from the shipbuilding industry to write a letter to the chairman of the State Commission, CPSU Central Committee Secretary O. D. Baklanov; but even after this, the opinion of the shipbuilding engineers had only an insignificant degree of influence on the official conclusion of the State Commission regarding the causes of the accident and loss of the submarine.

Appeals by the author of this book in the newspapers *Izvestiya*, *Literaturnaya Gazeta*, *Komsomolskaya Pravda*, *Krasnaya Zvezda*, *Sovetskaya Rossiya*, and *Smena* and in the journals *Ogonek* and *Morskoy Sbornik* regarding certain aspects of the tragedy were fruitless as well. Thus, the opinion of the workers of the shipbuilding industry regarding the causes of the tragedy of the submarine *Komsomolets* never was brought to the awareness of the people, which is what compelled the author to write this book. Questions that had not been clarified to one degree or another by the working group of the State Commission are addressed in this book on multiple occasions. The lack of addressal by the commission was not because the questions could not be clarified; they had not been clarified due to active opposition of the naval representatives who dominated any discussion, simply because they made up the absolute majority of the commission.

This documentary narrative *The Tragedy of the Submarine* Komsomolets cannot be considered to be the labor of a single author. Many specialists of the shipbuilding industry and the Navy took part in the examination of the tragedy and the causes leading up to it, and in the analysis of the events and of the actions of the personnel in the fight for the ship's survival. The author analyzed the results of their work, and used them in the book.

The author is deeply grateful to Sevmashpredpriyatiye Production Association workers V. M. Chuvakin, E. P. Leonov, and V. A. Vybornykh (the enterprise's assistant chief designer), and to the designers and sector and division chiefs of the Rubin Central Design Office of Marine Engineering for their active support and invaluable assistance in writing this book.

The author is also grateful to his numerous opponents, whose arguments, even when specious or technically incorrect, promoted a more careful examination of all aspects of the tragedy. This examination made it possible to confirm the conclusions presented herein and document the details needed for the judgment of readers.

D. A. Romanov, 1993

Introduction:

Looking For Truth

Different hypotheses regarding the causes of the tragedy of the Soviet nuclear-powered submarine *Komsomolets* have been stated in numerous articles published in a number of newspapers and journals by representatives of the Navy. Their essence reduces to the following:

> a fire occurred as the result of an electrical equipment fault; thereafter, the leakage of the air systems during the fire (hence the introduction of additional oxygen) predetermined the high intensity and swiftness of the fire's development, which, in turn, rendered fire-extinguishing resources ineffective.

The opinion of the representatives of the Soviet Navy as to the cause of the accident is reflected by the following statement of the Main Naval Staff: "As far as causes bringing about the accident are concerned, numerous technical imperfections in the submarine's various systems should be named first. These imperfections may be attributed entirely to things left undone by the designers and shipbuilders, and to the impermissible liberalism displayed during the ship's acceptance trials."[1] They concluded, "Despite the self-sacrificing and technically competent actions by the personnel, it was impossible to save the submarine."

Any remarks critical of the actions of the personnel and their professional training were met "with bayonets" by the Navy's "royal host," which, unfortunately, was not averse to falsifications and obvious slander.

Soviet and foreign experience in designing advanced technical systems shows that there is no such thing as absolutely safe equipment, and, unfortunately, its operation is always associated with the probability of accidents, unpredictable in many cases. Throughout all time, military systems have been created on the basis of the latest scientific and technical accomplishments, and naturally they unavoidably fell within the zone of maximum technical risk. Nuclear-powered attack submarines are the most complex, potentially dangerous, and vulnerable objects in this respect. The especially high danger of fire they present is a consequence of the high levels of power flowing through the compartments, the proximity of combustible materials and fluids to the equipment, imperfections in systems-monitoring conditions in the compartments, and the limited possibilities of fire-extinguishing resources available to a submarine.

At the same time, we cannot agree with N. Cherkashin's assertion[2] that the fire and explosion danger of submarines corresponds to locating a powder magazine in a gasoline storage area, and that submariners live in an environment in which death awaits them at any second. There is no need for extremes either in embellishing the life of submariners or in inflating the horror. Service aboard submarines is harsh and difficult even without these horrors. And no rest areas, swimming pools, canaries, and artificial grass can do anything to make it significantly easier.

Designers creating and testing submarines are constantly concerned with improving the equipment, raising its reliability, and reducing the degree of technical risk, but it is impossible to totally remove the probability of accidents. Under these conditions, the theoretical training and practical skills of every crew member—that is, the professionalism of the people operating the complex and potentially dangerous equipment—have always had the decisive role, and will continue to do so. It is the professionalism of the crew that actually influences the situation and events in a submarine's compartments before and during an accident; prevents or, contrariwise, promotes the advent and development of an accident situation; and determines the effectiveness of the actions in recovering from the accident. Captain 2nd Rank (Reserve) V. V. Stefanovskiy, the former chief engineer of a naval ship repair plant and currently the senior watchman of a gardening cooperative, was right a thousand times over when he said, "Competent seamen can deal with an accident. Responsible seamen won't let one happen."[3] For this truthfulness, Vladimir Vladimirovich should not have had to make a career change.

The submarine *Komsomolets* did not differ in any way from modern Russian submarines currently in operation in terms of the composition of combat and technical resources, including its control systems and its damage control systems. It was accepted in 1983, and in August 1984 it was commissioned.

1. "Roll out" of the *Komsomolets*

"After its commissioning, the submarine underwent experimental operation for several years. The reliability of the design concepts and the correspondence of its operating characteristics to its predicted performance parameters were validated during this period. The trials were carried out intensively in the most varied navigational conditions, including totally self-contained navigation. As with any other trials, certain problems did occur, but not a single serious breakdown ever occurred. The submarine crew gave a high evaluation to the submarine's operating properties on the basis of their navigational experience."[4]

We should add to this that all of the trials, as well as experimental operation and subsequent patrol duty, were carried out by the first crew under the command of Captain 1st Rank Y. A. Zelenskiy. During the stage of experimental operation, the first crew was supported by the participation of a group of specialists from the USSR Ministry of Shipbuilding Industry. In 1988 the submarine was recognized as an outstanding submarine, and it was awarded the name *Komsomolets*. Captain 1st Rank Y. A. Vanin's crew was the second crew of this submarine, and the cruise that began on February 25, 1989, and ended in the tragedy on April 7, 1989, was their first independent cruise.

First, while giving credit to the individual heroism and bravery of the crew members, we need to objectively evaluate their actions, as a crew, during the accident. This is imperative if repetition of such tragedies are to be avoided in the future. Wrong and biased conclusions based on imaginary or real imperfections of a submarine will only obfuscate the real issues. In this case I must agree with Vice Admiral Y. D. Chernov's opinion[5] that any distortion or toning down of information, even out of the most humane motives, is immoral in relation to submariners, who, now and in the future, are called to serve patrol duty.

Second, we also need to objectively examine the "numerous technical imperfections" alleged to be present in this submarine and, in the opinion of the naval leadership, helped to bring about the accident. And third, we need to describe what measures are being undertaken or should be undertaken to raise the reliability of submarines currently in operation.

1.

Crew Readiness

According to the detail design, the submarine *Komsomolets* was intended to be manned by highly qualified specialists from among officers and warrant officer technicians. According to the manning table approved in 1982 by the general staff of the USSR Ministry of Defense, the submarine's crew was fifty-seven persons (twenty-nine officers with rank not below senior lieutenant, twenty-six warrant officer technicians, and two compulsory-service petty officers). In this case, the engineering department (identified as BCh-5) should have consisted of ten officers and ten warrant officer technicians.

However, the crew was increased later to sixty-four persons without industry's consent. Further, warrant officer technicians were replaced by compulsory-service seamen, supposedly because of difficulty in manning crews with warrant officers, as well as for the purpose of economizing resources. This automatically reduced the crew's potential in terms of its combat and occupational training. This change in the crew's qualitative composition had an especially great effect on the damage control and electrical engineering divisions of BCh-5, which are the principal subunits to be engaged in fighting for the ship's survival. Thus, although the total manning in the damage control division was increased by two seamen, one of three warrant officer technicians was replaced by a compulsory-service seaman. In the electrical engineering division, while the manning was kept the same, two of the four warrant officer technicians were replaced by compulsory-service seamen.

This reduction of professional level, "rationalized" by the Navy's elite, affected not only the crew of the submarine *Komsomolets* but also of all other submarines. Note that this "rationalization" by the naval leadership was neither reflected nor evaluated in the documents of the State Commission. It would have been naive to expect such objectivity, since the "Combat Training" section of the State Commission Working Group, which addressed this issue, consisted entirely of fleet representatives who were to one degree or another accessory to such foolish bungling—bungling that may border on the criminal.

Great was the price paid by the country for such "economy"! For whatever reason, it was not until after the loss of the submarine *Komsomolets* that the Main Naval Staff came to understand that "the crews of ships of this type should be manned only by officers and warrant officers, because compulsory-service seamen and petty officers lack the means to adequately master operation of a submarine in such a short time."[1]

The circumstances of the submarine accident were investigated in the following manner. The members of the State Commission subjected sixteen members of the crew that participated in the cruise to only an initial interrogation. In this case, most of the members of the working group were present, but for practical purposes they did not take part in the interrogation. And only once did a narrow circle of persons from the working group visit the hospital—and only for a short time—to officially interrogate crew members. Unofficially, however, without the knowledge of the members of the working group who represented industry, fleet representatives visited the hospital several times, where they talked with the crew and exerted certain pressures upon them. This is why the explanatory reports of some of the crew members differ considerably from what they previously had said to members of the State Commission. "The survivors talked a great deal in the beginning, but then they bit their tongues."[2]

There is a basis to contend that, up to the time of the interrogation by the State Commission, the surviving members of the crew remained subject to influence from the leadership of the Northern Fleet and that they had received direction from that leadership that "industry is always responsible." And it is absolutely clear that Captain 1st Rank S. I. Bystrov was totally inconsistent with reality when he asserted, "surviving *Komsomolets* crew members were questioned in a faultfinding manner by the State Commission, which also contains representatives of industry. All unanimously marked the high level of special knowledge of the submariners."[3]

The working group has a tape recording of the interrogation of submarine personnel by members of the State Commission, the explanatory reports of the surviving members of the crew, extracts from the ship's log, and extracts from the control log of the main propulsion unit. However, interrogation of personnel during visits to the hospital was not documented.

From the very beginning, naval representatives did everything to prove that the submarine was prepared well for the cruise, that the personnel were excellently trained, and that the actions of the ship's attack center and the leadership of the Northern Fleet were the right ones; and, if the submarine sank and the greater part of the crew perished, it was at the fault of the designer and industrial workers.

An extensive campaign to publicize the "competent" actions of the crew was begun in the press under the leadership of the Fleet Command long before the initial conclusions were reached by the State Commission. The campaign was also directed at concealing serious shortcomings associated with manning and training the crews, with servicing the submarine, and with solving social problems. Its purpose had nothing in common with real concern for people, or with the objective of raising the fleet's combat readiness.

The administration of the CPSU Central Committee also voiced its opinion. A news brief appeared in the May 13, 1989, edition of *Pravda* regarding decoration of the crew of the submarine *Komsomolets*. The assessment of the crew's professional actions had already been made. "In a critical situation the crew acted with maximum bravery and technical competency, fighting to save the ship and render it safe." Thus, the administration of the CPSU Central Committee confirmed and approved the actions taken by the naval leadership to conceal the true causes of the accident. These same objectives were also pursued by the State Commission.

But let's return to Captain 1st Rank Y. A. Vanin's crew. It had undergone combat training, passed all of the tests, and was brought out to the first line[4] by September 1987. Under a point-scoring system, the crew was fourth (out of five) in the division, and it had not participated in a single independent combat patrol. The assertion that this was "one of the strongest crews one could imagine"[5] was quite significantly exaggerated. In 1988 the crew underwent retraining at the training center, and in September it was certified with an unsatisfactory score in ship damage control (as reported in a letter from submarine commanders of the Northern Fleet's First Flotilla sent in August 1989 to CPSU Central Committee Secretary O. D. Baklanov). According to documents, the average score received by the crew in work on damage control problems was only 2.7 on a five-point scale. But this fact is not contained in materials of the "Combat Training" section of the State Commission Working Group, which consisted of naval representatives only. This fact does appear, in distorted form, in N. Cherkashin's articles[6] as: "And in the training center where both of the crews had been 'perfected,' they hastened to write an unfavorable performance report on Vanin, the deceased commander of the *Komsomolets*, second-guessing the usual course of thinking of the supreme leadership: 'criminal negligence.'"

In the letter mentioned above from the submarine commanders, it is asserted that the crew had corrected the shortcomings revealed in work on damage control problems, and completed them with a good grade. But knowing the make-up of the command of the division to which the submarine *Komsomolets* belonged, one can assert that none of the division's flag officer specialists were sufficiently versed in the matériel of this submarine to rule adequately on performance in damage control problems.

2. Raising the Navy flag on *Komsomolets*

"In early January 1989 a conflict occurred among the crew during the submarine's preparation for patrol duty. The conflict arose because of the crew's work on ship damage control problems, which was being evaluated during an emergency party meeting,"[7] and it ended with Captain 3rd Rank A. S. Ternovskiy, the submarine deputy commander for political affairs, being sent to the hospital. "It so happened that the crew of the *Komsomolets* would not accept the former deputy commander for political affairs, and did not wish to go out to sea with him," is the "spin" N. Cherkashin put on this event.[8]

Let's return to the act drawn up by the "Crew Political Morale" section of the State Commission Working Group: "Captain 3rd Rank Y. I. Maksimchuk was transferred to crew 604 on temporary duty for the time of patrol duty on 16 January 1989 in place of the regular political worker, Captain 3rd Rank A. S. Ternovskiy. Captain 3rd Rank A. S. Ternovskiy was not allowed to serve patrol duty for health reasons. Prior to patrol duty he visited the hospital twice for treatment from 12 January to 27 January 1989 with a diagnosis of a 'neurological condition, not sharply pronounced, situationally predicated' and from 16 February to 28 February 1989 with a diagnosis of 'an asthenic state, moderately expressed.'"

The places of the cause and effect were deliberately changed here. The deputy commander for political affairs wound up in the hospital as a result of a confrontation and his suspension from patrol duty, and not vice versa, as the working group section tried to portray. One need not be a great expert in medicine to understand that this "cause" of Ternovskiy's replacement was clearly fabricated. The members of the section also understood this—that could be the only explanation for the following supplement to the act: "In resolving the matter of suspending [Now he's suspended, although previously it was said that he was disallowed.—D. R.] Captain 3rd Rank Ternovskiy from patrol duty, it was also considered that he was unable to carry out his duties in full volume." As a result of the conflict, Captain 1st Rank Y. A. Vanin's crew was broken down into opposing groups and was practically demoralized. Besides that, in order to delay departure of the crew into combat service until a healthy environment was created, the political organization decided to "strengthen" the crew with the chief of the political department of the division. And the question stands: would the tragedy have occurred if the political organization of the Navy objectively investigated the conflict? So what was the reason for Ternovskiy's suspension? Illness, or his "inability to carry out his duties in full volume"? The section members never did get around to attentively analyzing this conflict, and they didn't talk with Ternovskiy. Obviously, they only tried to show that there are no shortcomings in the work of the Navy's political organs, and that there couldn't be any.

By the beginning of the cruise, the crew consisted of sixty-four persons: thirty officers, twenty-two warrant officers, and twelve compulsory-service petty officers and seamen. In this case, eight of the officers were lieutenants—that is, 25 percent of the officers had served aboard a submarine for about a year after graduating from school, and their rank (and consequently their level of occupational training) did not correspond to the approved table. It should also be noted that damage control division commander, Captain 3rd Rank V. A. Yudin, possessed the specialty of a turbine engineer—in no way corresponding to the position he occupied—and had served in this position for only about a year, while the division's second officer was a lieutenant and also lacked sufficient experience. Moreover, one of the two warrant officers in the division (Warrant Officer Y. P. Podgornov) was unable to pass the tests, and he was not certified for independent control, while two of the three seamen were in their first year of naval service.

It is clear from the above that, prior to the ship's departure for sea, the crew lacked a damage control division as a full-fledged combat unit. Thus, the requirements of the "Manual of Submarine Damage Control" (identified as RBZh-PL-82) were violated:

> RBZh-PL-82, Article 173: Departure for sea is prohibited . . .
> when a full complement of trained personnel is lacking.

The fact that the requirements of the manual were violated was not reflected in the documents of the State Commission.

Unfortunately, this was not the only violation. As it became known later, Warrant Officer S. S. Bondar, Warrant Officer Y. F. Kapusta, and others were not certified for independent control. Neither they, nor the assistant commander of the division, Captain 1st Rank B. G. Kolyada, nor the head of the political department of the division, Captain 1st Rank T. A. Burkulakov, knew the layout of the submarine *Komsomolets*. Also, the assistant commander in the political section, Captain 3rd Rank Y. I. Maksimchuk, did not know the layout of the submarine, and part of the crew did not pass exams involving damage control.

Due to objective causes, the submarine crew could not have possessed high professional skill and experience in operating the matériel, which ultimately affected the outcome of the crew's fight for the submarine's survival. This was not so much the fault as the misfortune of the crew.

There should be concern regarding the quality and rigor of the curriculum provided submarine crews at training centers. The quality of the training is extremely unsatisfactory, because it is carried out sporadically, with emphasis on theory, and without relevance to a particular submarine, especially when it comes to carrying out general damage control exercises aboard ship. Also, the centers are poorly supplied with trainers and training displays.

The Navy also lacks a system of occupational selection of submarine crew members on the basis of psychological stability in extreme situations. "We aren't cosmonauts," one highly placed official from the Navy commented. Does he really believe that a combat patrol by a submarine under fully self-contained conditions is any less complex and dangerous a mission than a flight into space?

Submarine crews are perpetually diverted from combat training for garrison duty, for housekeeping work, and for other incidental duties; this occurs both during construction and testing of a submarine and during patrol duty.

Training complexes are absent from the permanent home port of submarines. Because submarines are provided an unsatisfactory supply of electric power and working power production units, it is impossible to organize high-quality crew training aboard the submarine itself.

The prestige of serving aboard nuclear-powered submarines dropped dramatically in the last two decades, because such service involved continual relocations, absence of housing, the unsettled daily life of the families of submariners, and the difficulty of the work itself. Also, there are no prospects for providing housing to them upon completion of service. The possibility for promotions in rank (and consequently pay raises) are limited when a submariner serves permanently in a single position. All of this results in high turnover of seagoing personnel and limits the possibilities for growth of professionalism. The second crews of submarines, which are deprived of the possibility for learning from the experience of qualified industrial specialists, and upon whom all of the above factors act to a significantly greater degree, find themselves in an especially difficult situation. Consequently, it is no accident that most of the worst accidents aboard submarines happen with the second crews.

2.

Preparations for the Cruise

Routine inspection, maintenance, and work to correct existing faults were carried out prior to the forthcoming cruise of the submarine *Komsomolets* in accordance with regulations. Considering the complexity and intensity of the work, and according to the technical design documents, it should have been carried out by a special technical crew with the help of highly qualified specialists from the Navy's ship repair plants. The trial run of the submarine *Komsomolets* demonstrated the need for assembling such a crew, but one was not provided.

In order that the full schedule of routine inspection and maintenance be carried out within the established time aboard a *Komsomolets*-class submarine, no less than 200 to 250 highly qualified specialists should be used. The Navy's repair bases do not have such a large number of specialists, and they do not participate in routine maintenance and inspection. The entire burden of this work is laid upon the submarine crews.

"A ship's officer is responsible for the good working condition of his matériel, and must do everything to restore it in the event of breakdown," declared Navy Commander-in-Chief V. N. Chernavin, apparently feeling that there are no problems in repairs, routine maintenance, and inspection in the fleet that cannot be addressed by ship's officers.[1]

In reality, submarine crews are physically unable to carry out the full volume of routine inspection and maintenance with acceptable quality within the forty days allowed. Consequently, they are forced to compromise with their conscience and carry out routine inspection and maintenance principally only on equipment that failed or was placed on report during the last cruise. The submarine fleet has even evolved a system of "failure-to-failure" equipment operation. Unsatisfactory maintenance of matériel, and late and poor quality inspection and maintenance, resulting from the absence of specially trained, highly qualified technical crews and from imperfections in the Navy's repair service, are recorded aboard all submarines of the Navy, especially after expiration of the warranty period.

Further, as a result of the limited availability of pierside electric power and power generators of acceptable quality at naval bases, submarines moored at those bases must generate their own power and thereby expend the life of ship equipment (to avoid malfunction of electronic equipment).

These factors, coupled with the lack of a system for documenting and certifying completion of routine inspection and maintenance in the Navy, render it practically impossible to conduct the required maintenance and verify the completeness and quality of such work.

Every issue identified above applied to the submarine *Komsomolets* as well. Moreover, the difficulties of routine inspection and maintenance aboard this submarine were aggravated by the absence of a set of documents concerning refits between cruises. An order of the Main Naval Command placed the responsibility of drafting these documents on a specialized naval department, but the order was not carried out.

None of these issues were reflected in the published findings of the State Commission. This omission could be expected because Vice Admiral V. V. Zaytsev, who, as the chief of the Navy's Main Directorate for Operation and Repair, was responsible for the unsatisfactory equipment of submarine bases and the quality of repairs and routine maintenance and inspection, was appointed chairman of the "Operation and Damage Control" section of the State Commission's working group.

Being aware that the situation concerning routine inspection, maintenance, and repairs by Navy personnel was so unfavorable, the workers of the shipbuilding industry suggested in their letter to CPSU Central Committee Secretary O. D. Baklanov, cited above, that the industry should service submarines over the course of the entire submarine cycle. This proposal was shamelessly distorted in the August 8, 1989, edition of *Krasnaya Zvezda*, in which the need for industry service was suggested as being related to the low quality of submarine construction.

But let's return to the submarine *Komsomolets*. As is confirmed in the joint act of two sections of the State Commission Working Group—the "Operation and Damage Control" and "Shipbuilding" sections—the *Komsomolets* set out to sea for patrol duty in serviceable condition. A question not clarified by the working group regards the extent to which this assertion, in serviceable conditions, corresponded to reality. The work order for refitting of the submarine *Komsomolets* between cruises, which was signed off by Division Commander Rear Admiral O. T. Shkiryatov and approved by Flotilla Deputy Commander Rear Admiral L. B. Nikitin, foresaw the need to repair the closed circuit television system equipment (one of the television cameras of this system was in compartment seven of the submarine) and the oxygen gas analyzer for compartment seven (items 7 and 71 of the work order). No documents attesting to completion of these repairs were presented. According to a statement by naval representatives, the repairs were carried out in floating ship repair drydock number seven, but they were unable to say who carried them out, and who accepted the equipment after repairs. However, the joint act of the two working group sections, mentioned above, states: "The sensor of the MN-5134 automatic oxygen gas analyzer of compartment seven failed on the tenth day of the cruise," and "the television system failed during the navigation period prior to the submarine's accident."

The question arises as to whether these multiple failures are a chance occurrence or a definite pattern. There are certainly grounds for suggesting that the submarine set out on its cruise with a faulty gas analyzer and a faulty television system. In any case, no measures were undertaken to clarify the circumstances associated with repair of this equipment. Neither section chairman Vice Admiral V. V. Zaytsev, nor members of the section representing the Navy's Main Directorate for Operation and Repair were interested in clarifying these issues, because then all of the shortcomings in the organization of ship repair, for which these same people were personally responsible, would be revealed.

And this was apparently not the only equipment that was faulty prior to the cruise. During the work of the State Commission in the city of Severomorsk, at my request, Captain 1st Rank M. V. Petrovskiy, chief mechanical engineer of the Northern Fleet, telephoned the hospital to ask Lieutenant A. V. Zaytsev by specifically what means (batch [portsionnyy] or emergency) the end groups of ballast tanks were blown. Lieutenant Zaytsev replied that emergency blowing was carried out, because the batch blowing system was "not in operation." It follows from this reply that the submarine went to sea with a faulty system for the batch-blowing of ballast tanks.

An examination of the submarine *Komsomolets* with deep-sea submersibles in August–September 1991 revealed that it lacked an aft outboard television camera. Review of videotape showing the location at which this camera is secured permits a categorical conclusion—the television camera had been removed from the submarine at the base prior to its cruise. Such are the facts. Eventually, in 1993, it became clear that the oxygen gas analyzer in compartment seven had been faulty in 1988, and practically all that year the submarine operated with a faulty oxygen gas analyzer. Thus, one may maintain that the submarine *Komsomolets* went into combat service with an inaccurate oxygen gas analyzer in compartment seven and without its complement of television cameras.

> RBZh-PL-82, Article 173: Departure for sea is prohibited . . .
> in the presence of faults in the hull, technical equipment, or rescue devices.

It is difficult to say how much a working television system could have helped the submarine's attack center to correctly estimate the situation in compartment seven and adopt the necessary damage control decisions, but one thing is clear—there is no doubt that its breakdown played a negative role. The role the oxygen gas analyzer played in creating the accident situation in compartment seven will be discussed later.

Prior to this cruise, the submarine *Komsomolets* had already operated for more than five years. During that time the reactor worked more than fourteen thousand hours. The other equipment of the main energy installation had operated the corresponding number of hours. Continually running the equipment practically exhausted the automation system's resources (consumable materials) completely. Also, all automated gas oxygen analyzers, having the resources for twelve thousand hours, were in need of repair or needed to be replaced.

From all this data it follows that the assertion of the report by the State Commission Working Group that the submarine *Komsomolets* entered into combat service in a serviceable condition, as published in the sections "Operating and Damage Control" and "Shipbuilding," does not correspond to the facts.

Prior to the patrol, the *Komsomolets* took aboard stores of provisions, bed linens, underwear, warm clothing, and other gear and supplies for sixty-nine persons intended for full self-sufficiency. Part of these provisions and supplies (including bread) were stored in compartment seven, even though storage in that compartment is not foreseen by the design documents. Such compartments are intended to be kept clear to avoid unnecessary hazard. Despite this, the State Commission Working Group failed to establish either the assortment or the quantity of provisions and gear in compartment seven. The joint act of the two sections simply states: "The following may be noted among conditions contributing to fire in compartment seven: . . . presence of 500 kg of bread, for which alcohol is used as a preservative, during the cruise in compartment seven." We should add to this that in the initial stage of the commission's work the figure was 1,000 kilograms of bread. But by calculation of the use-note, there should have been not less than 2,000 kilograms of bread in compartment seven at the moment of the accident.

It was revealed during investigation of the accident's circumstances that in accordance with a decision of the corresponding higher "father-commanders," chocolate in the emergency rations was replaced with sugar. It was unpleasant to listen to the childish prattle of admirals attempting to justify this outrage by claiming a chocolate shortage. It is true that Russia is living through hard times. But there is no shortage of this kind, and there cannot be one when the discussion turns to submariners, and all the more so to emergency rations for them. But the shortage of conscience and responsibility revealed itself fully. It is shameful to write about this, but it must be done—otherwise next time the "geniuses" in the Navy will put sugar coupons in the emergency ration instead of chocolate, and will then justify this by the long lines at the stores.

Such was the "readiness" of the submarine *Komsomolets* for the difficult cruise as reflected by the facts made available to the State Commission Working Group. However, since that time, additional information has come to light. As background, on February 21 and 22, 1989, Navy specialists conducted a readiness test of the crew for combat service. According to the results of the test, the crew received an unsatisfactory appraisal. Neither the leaders of the division nor the leaders of the Navy did anything to address the conclusions of this test.

Before the combat cruise, the submarine *Komsomolets* performed a test cruise. On this cruise the submarine seemed to be on the verge of a disaster. As the head of the chemical department, Captain Lieutenant V. A. Gregulev states that as a result of his "dawdling" the composition of oxygen in the atmosphere in compartment seven rose to 30 percent. Only by pure coincidence did a fire not spring up in that compartment. And even after this extraordinary event, the Navy and the commander of the division did not arrive at the obvious conclusions and make the necessary decisions. The crew was not kept from combat service.

By not recognizing the situations, the impression was created that some type of evil fate fell upon the crew of Captain 1st Rank Y. A. Vanin leading to a disaster.Maybe it was not the result of "evil fate" but the result of real people and of matériel circumstances. The authors of the "matériel" version maintain that the combat cruise of the crew was planned in the Moscow circles of the Navy, in coordination with their preference to transfer Vanin to the central apparatus of the Navy. Independent of whether this version is real or not, one thing is clear—the green light to the disaster of the submarine *Komsomolets* lit up the leadership of the 6th Division and the 1st Submarine Flotilla of the Northern Fleet.

In 1994 the "Unification Report *Bellona* Version 1" was published. In the article Thomas Nelson and Niles Bemer put forth the following statement from Captain Lieutenant I. S. Orlov from a conversation that was held February 22, 1992. "At 1103 in the seventh compartment at the stern of the nuclear submarine a fire broke out in the electrical panel, which caused a series of short circuits throughout the entire ship. The emergency defense system for the most part did not work and on board there were a few centers where fire formed. At 1700 the nuclear submarine sank. Forty-two members of the crew were killed. Before the cruise in the beginning of 1989, the nuclear submarine *Komsomolets* went through an emergency defense system's test, which showed it was not in a satisfactory condition. For this reason, it was planned to delay the cruise of the *Komsomolets*; however, it all the same went out to sea."

The statement of Captain Lieutenant Orlov provides important insight to the readiness of *Komsomolets*. Of course, the fire did not break out in the electrical panel. Rather, the electrical panels seemed to be in the area of the fire. It is also not true that the hot spots of the fire in the third, fourth, and fifth compartments were formed due to "a large part of the emergency defense system not working." All of this will be discussed further. As to the unsatisfactory state of the emergency defense system of the *Komsomolets* before the cruise, no one from the crew, including Orlov himself, said anything to the State Commission. Instead, many of them maintained that the submarine was well prepared for the cruise. The State Commission was not provided any type of data about the unsatisfactory condition of the automation system and the emergency defense system.

3.

The Cruise

And so, on February 28, 1989, the submarine *Komsomolets* set off on its cruise.

On August 8, 1988, the naval command and the USSR Ministry of Shipbuilding Industry adopted a joint decision to use the *Komsomolets* purposefully, in a special scientific research program. This program was developed and forwarded to the Northern Fleet and to the naval leadership for coordination and approval. But to satisfy its own internal plans, the command of the Northern Fleet tasked the submarine for ordinary patrol duty, which could have been carried out by any of the dozens of other submarines in the fleet. Thus, highly scientific research, including research of a defensive nature, would be interrupted by ordinary patrol duty. When this question was brought up at a meeting of the State Commission with the press on December 28, 1989, Division Deputy Commander Captain 1st Rank B. G. Kolyada suddenly announced some sort of "second program of all kinds of tests" supposedly being carried out by the fleet since August 1988.[1] Vice Admiral V. V. Zaytsev, the chief of the naval Main Directorate for Operation and Repair, had something somewhat different to say about this. In his conclusion to the "Analysis of the Personnel's Damage Control Actions Aboard the Submarine *Komsomolets*," which was an analysis carried out by a group of specialists from the Kuznetsov Naval Academy, imeni [named for] N. G. Kuznetsov, under the leadership of Vice Admiral Y. D. Chernov, he stated: "the mission posed for this patrol duty [that is, the submarine's last cruise—D.R.] was to carry out scientific research together with

15

hydrographic research vessels from 14 April to the end of May 1989." In confirming this, Captain 1st Rank Kolyada and Vice Admiral Zaytsev apparently
forgot, and perhaps did not even know, that official documents exist saying the
opposite. Northern Fleet chief of staff Vice Admiral Y. N. Patrushev communicated in letter No. 47/0220 dated February 17, 1989, that the scientific research program "cannot be carried out in 1989 because the plan for utilization
of ships in 1989 approved by the Naval Commander in Chief did not foresee
use of the submarine *Komsomolets* in a special program." Chief of the main
naval staff Fleet Admiral K. V. Makarov confirmed the decision of the command of the Northern Fleet to carry out scientific research beginning in 1990
in his directive No. 725/559/KP dated March 7, 1989. Such are the myths and
realities regarding the goals of the last cruise of the submarine *Komsomolets*.

According to Division Deputy Commander Kolyada, during the cruise
there had been no remarks regarding the condition of the matériel, with the
exception of one breakdown of the rudder control system (for depth and course
control) because the fuse burned out. This fault was quickly corrected. In addition, the television system broke down on the thirteenth and fourteenth days
of the cruise, and never was fixed.

In regards to the television system, everything is clear. The system

3. *Komsomolets* on patrol

most probably was faulty from the very beginning of the cruise. Regarding the breakdown of the steering system, it is necessary to speak in more detail. As is told by the remaining members of the crew, Senior Warrant Officer V. V. Tkach, who was training Seaman V. F. Tkachev, happened to "arrange" a short circuit, with the intent of affecting the steering. As a result, the safety device burned up and the rudders shifted for surfacing. The submarine began to surface with a large trim difference to the stern. In the mess room, the dishes flew from the tables onto the deck. The emergency alert "rudder jam" was not announced. Everything ended with a light fright. Seaman Tkachev was replaced for a week by Seaman A. U. Koritov, who had been taken on from the first crew in the capacity of an orderly.

There is still one event the members of the second crew also talk about. In March 1989, during a communication drill, several tons of seawater were noticed in the hold of the submarine. It is not clear what exactly happened, as the people who talk about this are not from the electro-mechanic combat section. Warrant Officer V. S. Kadantsev and Lieutenant A. V. Zaytsev say nothing about it. The emergency signal "Entrance of sea water in the compartment!" was also not announced. Crew members said nothing during their interrogation by the State Commission about this fact or the time of breakdown of the oxygen gas analyzer in compartment seven. This was revealed only during a visit to the hospital, but the date of its breakdown never was ascertained. And it is understood, as was mentioned earlier, the oxygen gas analyzer was out of commission in 1988.

On the evening of April 6, 1989, Warrant Officer S. I. Chernikov became ill. The warrant officer was in charge of the electro-mechanical air regenerating system. The system remained in the care of the head of the chemical department, Captain Lieutenant V. A. Gregulev.

April 7, 1989 rolled around. If we are to believe the ship's log, the submarine was traveling at a depth of 386 meters at a speed of eight knots, or if we believe what was said by Division Deputy Commander B. G. Kolyada and Remote Control Division Commander Captain Lieutenant I. S. Orlov when they were interrogated by the State Commission, the submarine was at a speed of six knots. Captain 1st Rank B. G. Kolyada (interrogation tape recording):

> I relinquished the position of watchstander to the Commander when the speed was up to 6 knots and then left the Main Command Center. . . . At 10:00 I returned to the Main Command Center and ascertained the conditions of the ship's position from the Commander. We were twenty-three miles ahead of schedule,

and we had reached a speed of six knots following along a zigzag course. I then went to rest.

Based on this recording, it appears that Captain 1st Rank Kolyada gave the watch to the commander of the ship at 0747, which agrees with the notes in the ship's log. Before this, at 0738, the submarine changed speed. The main engine was running at 70 rpm. This corresponds to a submarine speed of eight knots, not six knots as Kolyada states. The speed did not change until the accident. The discrepancy between the notes in the ship's log and the testimony of Kolyada could be considered a misunderstanding if it were not for the evidence of Orlov, who, at the time of the accident, increased the speed of the submarine as ordered.

Captain Lieutenant I. S. Orlov (interrogation tape recording): "I began to increase shaft rotation to the upper limit of the allowed speed. I could control its increase up to 70 to 80 rpm."

From this information it follows that before the accident the engine was doing less than 70 rpm; that is, the submarine was going at a speed less than eight knots. The speed of the submarine before the accident is a point of discrepancy between the notes in the ship's log and testimony from the members of the crew.

According to entries in the ship's log, the compartments were inspected at 1100, and no remarks were entered. In accordance with the ship regulations and RBZh-PL-82, compartments must be inspected every half-hour during a cruise, and the inspection results must be entered in the ship's log in the control room.

> RBZh-PL-82, Article 183: During inspection of compartments the correspondence of the condition of the hull, weapons and technical resources to requirements of the guidelines must be meticulously verified, and the presence or absence of signs of emergency situations and conditions for them must be verified.

Watch duty is actually lax aboard many submarines—compartments and equipment are not inspected, and compartment and inspection reports are made only as a formality. The submarine command is fighting this attitude toward duty, but without results as yet. One cannot conclude that this was the way things were in Captain 1st Rank Y. A. Vanin's crew also, but that this was the situation cannot be excluded.

Such discussion will likely bring the disdain of defenders of "clean uniforms" and the accusations of slander against the Navy and of other mortal sins. This whole set of standard accusations has been voiced many, many times in our press. But there is something to respond with to this.

A so-called "Compartment Readiness Command and Information System" (KISGO) is installed in submarines built in recent years. In addition to standard items, this system contains control buttons, which are installed in different locations in each compartment. The number of buttons in a compartment depends on the size of the compartments to ensure that the entire space of a compartment is covered by these buttons. The compartment inspection report is accepted by the watch mechanic only if the compartment watchstander first presses all of the buttons in succession. It is assumed that as he successively presses the buttons, the compartment watchstander will look around and thus "carry out inspection of the compartment." That's how far our glorious Navy has gone!

The submariners know this, and the command knows it; they know it, and are quiet about it, which is no less shameful than this fact that such a system is necessary to ensure the integrity of the compartment watchstanders.Consequently, it is not to them that this book appeals. It appeals to the mothers and fathers, to the wives and children, to the sisters and brothers of submariners. Ask your sons, husbands, fathers, and brothers how they managed to get to a point in their lives where submarine designers are compelled to create an "electronic cattle prod" to force the submariner to do something upon which his life and the welfare of his relatives and family depend.

4.

Fire!

And so, an inspection of the compartments was conducted at 1100. From the ship's log:

> 1100—rudder 5 degrees port. Course—222 degrees. Compartments inspected. No remarks. Oxygen concentration 0.2 percent [*sic*]. Battery ventilation system in "hydrogen combustion" mode. Vacuum equals 35 mm H_2O.

And suddenly: "1103. Course—222 degrees. Deliver LOKh to compartment seven!"[1]

What happened within these three minutes of ship's log time? How do they correlate with real events and temporal parameters?

Let's review the "Extract From the Draft Ship's Log of the Nuclear-Powered Submarine *Komsomolets*" authenticated by the Fleet Chief of Staff Vice Admiral Y. N. Patrushev. The first conclusion: Two types of ship's logs exist in the fleet—draft and final. The successes of ship crews in combat and political training are evaluated on the basis of the final copy, while the draft copy reflects the actual level of these successes. This double "bookkeeping" does nothing to improve the discipline of the crew during watch duty, it doesn't nurture the personnel's ability to maintain the ship's log with the needed completeness and quality, and it doesn't raise the sense of responsibility of command personnel for their decisions. On the contrary, it creates good soil for slovenliness and falsification.

So what are we told by the entries in the ship's log for April 7, 1989, from midnight to the time when the command "Deliver LOKh to compartment seven!" resounded like a shot? There are no entries in the ship's log for compartment inspections at 0800 and 1000. Signatures attesting to the relief of the second watch section from watch and to the assumption of watch by the third watch section are absent.

All of this gives no indication of a high level of professional training and work discipline in Captain 1st Rank Y. A. Vanin's crew.

A system automatically documenting commands from the attack center and messages from the duty stations would have been a great help in clarifying the circumstances of the first minutes of the accident. Such a system is present aboard submarines, although it is very imperfect. There was one aboard the *Komsomolets* as well. However, as a rule, submarine crews do not make a practice of using this system in their day-to-day activities, and they do not use it at times of accidents.

So at what time was compartment seven actually inspected and was there a report of its inspection? It does not seem possible to answer this question categorically. During the interrogation by the State Commission, Captain Lieutenant S. A. Dvorov and Lieutenant K. A. Fedotko said that they had personally heard a report from the watchstander for compartment seven, Senior Seaman N. O. Bukhnikashvili, regarding inspection of the compartment, and they cite a time of 1058 and "around five minutes before all of it began." Lieutenant A. V. Tretyakov believes that the report was at 1100. All of this information is made doubtful by the following responses from the senior watch officer, Captain Lieutenant A. G. Verezgov, to questions of the State Commission (interrogation tape recording):

> Question: Did you hear the report from compartment seven that everything was well?
>
> Answer: I didn't hear this report personally. The fact is that the watch officer's console or, more accurately, desk is located a slight distance away from the command post of BCh-5. Therefore, when he receives reports, the watch mechanical engineer reports to me. He reported to me that the submarine had been inspected, without remarks, somewhere around 1100. As a rule, the watchstanders make their reports (well, that's the way we did it) five minutes before the scheduled time.
>
> Question: Are these messages transmitted by loudspeaker?
>
> Answer: That's right, they're transmitted by the "Listvennitsa"[2], from the compartments.

Question: And you didn't hear a single report?

Answer: The fact is that he [the watch mechanical engineer—D.R.] keeps the volume down a little. He makes it so that only he could hear, not so that it would be silent, but so that only the watch mechanic could hear, without distracting the rest of the personnel serving watch at other stations.

Captain Lieutenant Verezgov, who was the watch officer, was closest of all to Captain 3rd Rank V. A. Yudin, who received the compartment inspection reports. Still, he did not hear the reports from the compartment watchstanders. Captain Lieutenant Dvorov and Lieutenant Fedotko heard these reports, although they were farther away from the watch mechanic.

Thus, we did not receive a consistent answer to the question concerning the inspection by the watchstander of compartment seven. We shall attempt to ask that question from another angle.

So when did the fire start? One thing is clear: This happened before 1103, when the command to deliver LOKh to compartment seven was given.

Here is what participants of the tragedy have to say about the 1100 inspection in compartment seven:

Warrant Officer V. V. Gerashchenko:

Around five or ten minutes before 1100 the lights, especially the incandescent lamps, began blinking in the gyro-compass room. I went up to the monitoring equipment of the "Mindal" power supply system. It was my duty to check the power supply parameters once every four hours. I checked them. All of the parameters seemed to be normal. The blinking lights were powered by the ship's general power network. My instruments have their own power supply.

And then Lieutenant Fedotko, who was the navigator, said: "Vasily, how are things? Something is happening in the electrician's station."

This was apparently the first indication of the beginning of the fire. The approximate time was no later than 1055. From this it follows that the fire in compartment seven began before 1055; that is, before the time when the watchstander gave his report about the inspection. This adds doubt to the confirmation by Captain Lieutenant Dvorov and Lieutenant Fedotko in that they personally heard the report of the watchstander concerning compartment seven.

Captain Lieutenant V. A. Gregulev:

The technician said that voltage drops had been observed before the accident, which was noticeable from the sound of the fan—that is, power was fluctuating two or three minutes before the alarm.

Lieutenant K. A. Fedotko:

I was the engineer of the electronic navigation group. I was at my console, on watch in the control room. When Yudin said that the temperature in compartment seven was over seventy degrees Celsius . . .

Question: You heard that yourself?

Answer: Yes, I did. Senior Lieutenant Markov was sitting at the "Onega" console. He looked troubled. I used the "Listvennitsa" system to report to the gyro-compass room that the electricians might be switching the systems. I told the warrant officer in the gyro-compass room to turn his attention to the work of the navigation system.

Was discovery of the fire reported to the attack center, and when? Let's listen to the crew members:

Lieutenant A. V. Zaytsev (explanatory report):

When I heard the alarm signal l went from my cabin to the "Molybden" control console. I relieved Captain 3rd Rank Yudin, the Damage Control Division Commander, at the console. I heard him say to Captain 2nd Rank [V. I.] Babenko, the BCh-5 commander: "There's a fire in compartment seven." Bukhnikashvili reported the fire, after which two thuds could be heard, like the sound of air-lock doors closing.

Captain 1st Rank B. G. Kolyada (interrogation tape recording):

I believe that at one minute before 1100 Seaman Bukhnikashvili reported that compartment seven had been inspected, that there were no remarks, and that the gas composition of the air was 20 percent oxygen. Literally, just a few minutes later, a report was transmitted from compartment seven: "Damage control alarm fire in compartment seven," but none of the survivors heard this.

A few comments on Kolyada's statement. This captain is the only surviving crew member who recalls information on the oxygen concentration in compartment seven in the watchstander's report, even though he was not present in the attack center during the reports of the watchstanders. Moreover, the value he gives for the oxygen concentration in compartment seven is significantly below the permissible norms (21.5 to 23 percent), which, in practical terms, could not have been correct. There's an obvious discrepancy here, which makes us suppose that during his interrogation by the State Commission, Captain Kolyada concealed the possible cause of the fire. Significantly later, Lieutenant Tretyakov said that near 1100 the left instrument 101 of the combat information control system broke. He unplugged it. At this time, Senior Lieutenant S. Y. Markov was working behind the control panel of the electro-energy system, and Captain 3rd Rank Yudin said to someone in a loud speaking voice: "What, are you late . . . ?"

With whom did Yudin speak and what did he ask the interlocutor about? The answer becomes apparent. He may have been speaking with the watchstander of compartment seven, Senior Seaman N. A. Bukhnikashvili, and asked him why he was late with the report concerning the inspection of the compartment. Bukhnikashvili's answer is clear. Relying on the evidence of Lieutenant Zaytsev and Captain 1st Rank Kolyada with regard to the afore-cited information of Tretyakov, we can assume that the watchstander for compartment seven reported the fire before 1103. This absolutely refutes the official version of the Navy concerning the compartment fire, which was presented later in a joint order of the USSR Minister of Defense and the USSR Minister of Shipbuilding Industry. And so a metamorphosis occurs: "The fire in compartment seven began with an explosion, and consequently it would be blasphemous to accuse deceased Senior Seaman N. Bukhnikashvili of acting in a manner different from his actions in training exercises. He was stunned, killed in the very first seconds of the accident," declared Kolyada in the January 15, 1990, edition of *Izvestiya*.

As far as I know, no one has ever accused Senior Seaman Bukhnikashvili. On the contrary, his actions during the accident were apparently fully competent: He reported the fire, fought the flames using an air-foam fire extinguisher, and he perished in this fight. But then, we can ask Kolyada an impartial question. When was he speaking the truth, before the State Commission or when he was being interviewed by the writer N. Cherkashin? The answer to this question is clear. Kolyada's entire interview, beginning with incompetent notions regarding an "experimental vessel" and ending with the shameful assertions that the crew had dealt with the fire with minimum sacrifices (apparently, the loss of a submarine and forty-two crew members is a minimum sacrifice!), was false and unobjective.

The joint order cited above states that "at 1103 the compartment became fully involved with fire of great intensity, causing a leak in the high-pressure air system, which brought about a rapid increase in pressure and temperature in compartment seven." There are no grounds for such an assertion. As was mentioned earlier, a command to use the fire extinguishing system had already been given at 1103, meaning that the fire had only started at this moment. Certain conditions had to exist in the compartment for it to become fully involved: flammable materials had to be distributed throughout the entire compartment (spilled or sprayed oil, fuel, etc.). Consequently, the compartment could not have been "fully involved" right from the start. It became fully involved later on. This logical conclusion is reinforced by entries in the ship's log and the testimony of surviving members of the submarine crew. Technical calculations show that if compartment seven had in fact become fully involved from the very beginning, the consequences of the accident would have been minimal.

Why did naval representatives find it necessary to "condense" the initial stage of the fire's development, and invent a story about a fully involved compartment "rapidly causing a leak in the high-pressure air lines"? There was but one goal—to justify the delay and the incompetent actions of the submarine's leadership in the initial period of the accident, to prove that it was impossible to save the ship, and that the crew could not have taken any more radical actions in the fight for the submarine's survival. This point of view was advantageous to the bureaucratic command system of the military-industrial complex. This deception was also aided by the unprincipled, conniving policy of the leadership of the design office.

Be that as it may, what might have caused the fire? The joint order cited above states that "a fire in electrical equipment at the pump-starting station of the rudder hydraulic system or in the oil separation system, which was due to maladjustment of controlling devices and this equipment's safety system, was the possible primary cause of the submarine's disaster." As a reluctant concession to opponents, it was added that "this may have been promoted by a possible increase in the oxygen concentration in the compartment's atmosphere above the permissible level." But in the State Commission's report there is absolutely no mention of oxygen as one of the possible causes of the tragedy that occurred aboard the submarine. The "royal host" of the Navy won the battle!

But why did the State Commission select these versions as the possible primary causes of the accident? According to these versions, it appears at first glance that there are no clear culprits for the fire, which suited the naval leadership and the party apparatus, and it didn't hurt the USSR Ministry of Ship-building Industry very much—that is, it suited everyone.

The 'Pump' Version

It is assumed that as a result of breakdown of automatic system components, rapid spontaneous switching on and off of the starting stations of one of the hydraulic system pumps (a so-called "bell" effect) began, which caused burning of contacts, the appearance of an arc discharge, and ultimately a fire in the compartment. However, an experiment conducted by the State Commission Working Group on the work of a starting station in "bell" mode produced a negative result even when the oxygen concentration in the atmosphere was high. In real conditions, work of the starting station of the hydraulic system pump aboard the submarine in "bell" mode would have been noticed by the operator at the "Molybden" console, and the faulty pump would have been disconnected with no consequences to the compartment. Moreover, the pump's malfunction would have also been detected by the watchstander for compartment seven, and it could have been contained there as well.

Crew testimony revealed that the warning signal "Temperature in compartment seven above 70 degrees Celsius" lit up first, and only after that or simultaneously with it did the warning signal "Low insulation resistance" light up. This alone completely excludes the version suggesting that the fire in compartment seven had an electrical cause. The State Commission Working Group established that it was most probable that the fire began in the forward section of compartment seven, on the port side—that is, away from the location of the hydraulic system pump starting stations. In short, the State Commission Working Group had no objective data of any kind to substantiate this version.

The 'Separator' Version

The oil separation system contains an electric oil heater. It is suggested that oil overheated in the oil heater while the separator was not working, resulting in boiling of the oil, followed by a flash and a fire (oil in a working separator would not become overheated to the flash point). An experiment confirmed the possibility of such ignition of the oil heater over a period of about fifteen minutes. The oil heater was located in the fore section of compartment seven, on the port side—that is, within the zone of the supposed initiation of the fire. However, the oil separation system was disconnected early in the morning on April 7, and it was not working before the accident. The oil heater connecting circuit is interlocked with a pressure relay (the oil heater can be switched on only when the separator is operating) and with a temperature relay, which turns off the oil heater when the oil temperature exceeds the permissible limit.

This version may be accepted if we allow the following assumptions:

1. The pressure relay and the temperature relay failed simultaneously (which is practically excluded), or they were deliberately blocked and were in the "on" position.

2. The watchstander for compartment seven deliberately turned on the oil heater without turning on the separator, which is prohibited by the operating instructions.

3. The watchstander for compartment seven left the compartment after turning on the oil heater since, according to the experiment, intensive production of smoke from the oil heater began in the eighth to tenth minute, which the watchstander would certainly have noticed, and he would have switched off the oil heater.

4. The operator at the console of the main propulsion unit paid no attention to unsanctioned engagement of the oil heater.

Thus, if we assume that this version is possible, we would have to say that the fire in compartment seven arose due to the personnel's grossest violations of instructions and manuals on equipment operation, or due to deliberate sabotage. In promoting this version as the primary cause of the accident, the State Commission Working Group shamefully remains silent about its preconditions.

Neither of these versions explains the high intensity with which the fire developed in the initial stage or the fable that the compartment became fully involved right from the very beginning. And in order to complete the analysis of these versions, tone should review Captain 1st Rank Kolyada's statement (interrogation tape recording):

A telegram reporting an accident aboard the submarine "B-354"—a distribution panel catching fire—was received on the fourth [The reference is to April 4, 1989, three days before the accident.—D.R.]. The fleet commander ordered an inspection of all cable routes, and of the condition of distribution panels and electrical equipment. I gave the command to inspect all of the electrical equipment that day. On the fifth at 2100 the commanders of all departments reported that the electrical equipment had been inspected. There were no remarks.

Industrial members of the State Commission Working Group sitting in the "Operation and Damage Control" section rejected both of these versions as implausible, and they felt that the primary cause of the fire was the creation of a fire hazard in compartment seven due to uncontrolled delivery of oxygen into the compartment. This cause is so obvious that you would have to deliberately shut your eyes not to see it.

The 'Oxygen' Version

As was said earlier, the oxygen gas analyzer was not working in compartment seven aboard the submarine. Its functions are to constantly monitor the percent oxygen concentration in the compartment's atmosphere, and to control the automatic engagement and disengagement of the oxygen dispenser. A fault in the gas analyzer was the first objective precondition for creation of a fire hazard in the compartment.

How was oxygen delivered to compartment seven during the cruise in the presence of a nonworking gas analyzer? "At the stern, oxygen was being dispensed automatically," Captain Lieutenant V. A. Gregulev, chief of the chemical service, answered in the interrogation tape recording. Gregulev confirmed the same thing in the hospital when he was visited by representatives of the State Commission Working Group. Only significantly later did he clear up how he understands the distribution of oxygen by the automatic system. In compartments five and seven, the automated oxygen supply valve (oxygen distributor) was continually open. The supply of oxygen in these compartments was provided by the periodic opening of the corresponding valves in the oxygenated collector of the electro-laser in the electromechanical air regenerating system located in the second compartment. What conclusions may we make from this clarification by Gregulev?

First, on the submarine *Komsomolets* there were two faulty oxygen gas analyzers at the time of the last combat cruise—one each in compartments five and seven. There is no information regarding the time of the breakdown of the gas analyzer in compartment five.

Second, the instruction by the head of the chemical service to inject a supply of oxygen in the compartment is not stipulated by the operating instructions of an electro-chemical air regenerating system. According to the instructions, during a breakdown of the oxygen gas analyzer, the supply of oxygen into the compartment is entrusted to the watchstander of the compartment. In accordance with the RBZh-PL-82 (appendix 15), the watchstander of the compartment must control the content of the oxygen in the atmosphere of the compartment no less than six times a day by the use of a portable apparatus, independent from the condition of the automatic means of control. Thus, during the fulfillment of the instructions relating to the exploitation of the electro-chemical air regeneration system, the supply of oxygen into the compartment and the control of its percentage content is entrusted to one in the same person (the watchstander). According to Lieutenant Gregulev's scheme, the supply of oxygen in compartment five and in compartment seven was carried out by the chemical service and the percentage content in the atmosphere of the compartment was controlled by the watchstander of the electro-mechanic combat section; that is, there was a division of one process between two services of the ship. A violation of operating instructions was the second precondition, and this time a subjective one, which led to creating a fire danger in the compartment.

A fire aboard the submarine was likely inevitable as a result of these two preconditions.

One must conclude from the explanations given by Captain Lieutenant Gregulev to the State Commission that the operating instructions for the electro-chemical air regenerating system were violated during the cruise with the sanction of the submarine's leadership, and that an oxygen concentration above permissible limits was maintained in the atmospheres of compartments two and three.

Was there too high an oxygen content in the atmosphere of compartments five and seven before the accident? Yes, there was. Answering to the State Commission, Lieutenant S. A. Dvorov and Seaman Y. V. Kozlov spoke about a flare-up in the fifth compartment that they characterized as a flash or a blue flame. A blue flame is one of the signs of too high an oxygen content. There are other direct and indirect confirmations that oxygen had accumulated in compartments five and seven before the accident. These will be discussed later.

What was the oxygen content percentage in the atmosphere of compartments five and seven before the accident? Not knowing the duration of each effort to supply oxygen into the compartment and which productivity (volume rate) was used for the distribution of oxygen, it is impossible to calculate. However, with a large degree of certainty one may lay a path of logical reasoning. As mentioned earlier, at the time of the submarine's departure trial, the oxygen content in the air of compartment seven rose to 30 percent. Calculations show that for an oxygen distributor set to a productivity (volume rate) of one/hour (as is stated in the instructions and calibrated during construction), the achievement of a 30 percent oxygen content in compartment seven requires nearly one hundred hours of uninterrupted supply; while for a distributor that is fully opened (relative to other compartments), nearly twelve hours is required. From these calculations it follows that at the time of the test, the submarine's oxygen distributor was capable of too large a productivity, since during the time of the test cruise (less than three days) it would have been impossible to reach an oxygen content of 30 percent in compartment seven while observing the operating instructions. This gives one the basis to assume that, at the time of the combat cruise, the oxygen distributors in the fifth and seventh compartments were capable of a significantly large productivity, quite close to their maximum level.

At the time of the test cruise, no fire occurred in compartment seven; however, the oxygen content in its atmosphere was equal to 30 percent. This allows us to reason that the oxygen content in the atmosphere of compartment seven before the accident was also no less than 30 percent. The oxygen content in the air of the fifth compartment (it is two times larger by volume than compartment seven) at that time was perhaps near 27 percent. This completes our chain of a logical argument regarding the sickness of Warrant Officer Chernikov, which left the electro-mechanic regenerating air system practically "unmanned" for no less than twelve hours. During that period, the oxygen produced could have been released continuously into the fifth and seventh compartments.

The reader asks, "but how could that be?" In accordance with Appendix 15 of RBZh-PL-82, the watchstanders of the compartments are required to measure the oxygen content in the atmosphere of the compartment by use of the portable gas analyzer no less than six times a day; that is, every four hours. Even if the oxygen distributor were fully open, then one would have to include in the report three more times that the content of oxygen in the compartment was high. The procedure is correct. Then it must be the training and responsibility of the submarine's crew. However, remember the test cruise of the submarine. There was 30 percent oxygen content in compartment seven, but there were no reports about the high oxygen content. To this, one can add that in March 1988 there were two other incidents according to the head of the chemical service, Lieutenant Gregulev, when the oxygen content in compartment seven went up to 27–30 percent. And at these times no report was made! This speaks about the degree of training and responsibility of Captain 1st Rank Y. A. Vanin's crew. Even the faulty portable gas analyzer (which is not to be excluded) may not serve as justification for this irresponsibility.

One should also consider the relationships between BCh-5 and the chemical service of the crew. The small number in chemical service (two people)

must provide a constant watchstander at the ship's main control panels where all gas analyzers, for controlling the gas composition of the air in all compartments, are connected and their output is evident. This gave the head of the chemical service reason to believe that the gas analyzers did not fall under his management. The commander of BCh-5 thought that the guarantee of the proper gas composition of air in the compartments was the responsibility of the chemical services; so naturally, the gas analyzer was the responsibility of this service. Hence, the responsibility of the gas analyzer seemed to be a "bone of contention" between the BCh-5 and the chemical service. This discord appears to have been the reason that the submarine *Komsomolets* went into combat service with faulty automation and a faulty portable gas analyzer.

What could have caught fire in compartment seven when the oxygen content in the atmosphere was near 30 percent? With such a percent oxygen concentration, a fire could have arisen in the compartment as a result of any cause, even the most harmless under ordinary conditions (heating of some piece of equipment, for example, a soldering gun, a tea kettle, an oily rag, static electricity, etc.).

What was a more probable cause of the fire? In order to answer this question we must examine the difference in the conditions of compartment seven during the test cruise and during the combat cruise. There is one distinction. During the test cruise there was no distribution of rations or supplies in compartment seven. The distribution of rations and supplies in compartment seven, which was a link that led to the chain of the events in the accident, was the most probable cause. However, contrary to the obvious facts, the naval leadership and the USSR Ministry of Shipbuilding Industry believed that the cause of the fire was associated with some mythical "series-manufactured models of electrical equipment developed in the 1970s which were insufficiently reliable in terms of fire safety." So that we won't have to come back to the oxygen question again, I need to say this: The oxygen concentration in the atmosphere of the compartments of nuclear-powered submarines is maintained between 21.5 and 23 percent—that is, 0.5 to 2 percent higher than in the terrestrial atmosphere—on the basis of a requirement of the Navy. In other words, an elevated danger of fire aboard our submarines was in a sense "preplanned" by the Naval Institute No. 1, which developed these requirements. And it was only after the loss of the submarine *Komsomolets* that the compartment oxygen concentration norms were changed in 1991—to between 19 and 21 percent.

But let's return to the fire. Where was the watchstander for compartment seven at the moment the fire started?

Warrant Officer V. S. Kadantsev (interrogation tape recording):

The watchstander for compartment seven entered compartment six, took measurements, returned, and reported from compartment seven only the load of the turbo-generator and the insulation resistance at the turbo-generator itself, which he read from the panels. There was no report of a fire from compartment seven. We saw what was happening from instruments of the "Molybden" system—the "70 degrees Celsius" warning signal lit up, after which the commander sounded the damage control alarm.

Question: When did the watchstander enter compartment six?

Answer: Fifteen minutes to eleven. Usually the inspection reports come in at five minutes before eleven.

It is not understood why the watchstander of compartment seven had to go to the sixth compartment and measure the load of the turbo-generator. The load of the turbo-generator and resistance of its insulation may be called up at any time on the information table by the operator of the panel controlling the electro-energy system. Besides that, these parameters are automatically noted by the systems documenter. Together with the information from Kadantsev, it follows that, at the moment the fire started, the watchstander may have been in compartment six and, upon returning to compartment seven, he discovered the fire already in an advanced stage of development. In this case, there may not have been a report of the compartment's inspection at 1100. Moreover, Warrant Officer Kadantsev fails to confirm the statement by Captain 1st Rank Kolyada and Lieutenant Zaytsev regarding the watchstander's report of the fire.

Captain Lieutenant S. A. Dvorov (interrogation tape recording):

At 1100 there was a report from Warrant Officer [V. V.] Kolotilin of the fifth compartment. "The compartment has been inspected, nothing observed." And around 1100 Seaman Bukhnikashvili from compartment seven, "The compartment has been inspected, nothing observed" (around 2 minutes to 1100). . . . At 1105 or 1106—I can't say exactly, that the first unification of reports occurred—working together was an alarm on the "Molybden" panel "The temperature is higher than 70 degrees Celsius in compartment seven," and practically simultaneously the "Onega" panel burned the warning "low resistance of the insulation in the shield of compartment seven." . . . The commander of the ship, Captain 1st Rank Vanin, ran to the "Molybden" panel. . . . On the

"Molybden" panel watchman Engineer-Mechanic [V. A.] Yudin was on duty. At once they tried to bring up the connection with compartment seven. Compartment seven did not come up. I yelled, "Sound the emergency alarm!" The Commander gave the command, "Sound the emergency alarm!"

Unfortunately, in the version of the circumstances given by Dvorov, no annotation of the command at 1103 concerning the introduction of LOKh into compartment seven was found. One thing is clear —if his assertion concerning the start of the fire at 1105 or 1106 and the high temperature alarm and the indication of low electric insulation in compartment seven corresponds with reality, then it means one may maintain that the command at 1103 to supply LOKh in compartment seven was given according to the report in the ship's log. Further, according to the report of Dvorov, there was large invisible tension provoked by the indecisive commander of the submarine, which was conveyed (in violation of subordination and ethics) by the subordinate Dvorov's cry, "Sound the emergency alarm!"

And so, at 1103 the command "Deliver LOKh to compartment seven!" was given. What is the main command post supposed to do the moment a fire is discovered?

RBZh-PL-82, Article 89: Mandatory initial actions of the main command post in the event of a fire: Sound the bell alarm and announce a damage control alarm over the ship's general broadcasting system, indicating the place and nature of the accident.

This was not done.

5.

"Damage Control Alarm!"

From the ship's log:

> 1106—Damage control alarm! Rise to a depth of 50 meters.
> LOKh delivered to compartment seven.

This entry requires some comments. "LOKh delivered to compartment seven" may also be read as "Deliver LOKh to compartment seven" because the suffix was not clearly written in the ship's log.

Let's listen to the explanations by the tragedy's participants.

Captain 1st Rank B. G. Kolyada (in a report to the Northern Fleet commander):

> At 1105 a "damage control alarm" was announced aboard ship. On reaching the GKP [Main command post —D.R.], I found everyone at their places carrying out their duties. BCh-5 commander Captain 2nd Rank Babenko tried to raise compartment seven with the loudspeaker communication system, but there was no answer. On my advice the commander gave the command: "Dispense LOKh into compartment seven."

Lieutenant A. V. Zaytsev (interrogation tape recording):

> At the moment of the alarm I was in my cot. I dressed and ran

up to the control room. Damage Control Division Commander Captain 3rd Rank Yudin yielded his place to me at my console. The compartment seven warning light was on—"Temperature above 70 degrees Celsius." The BCh-5 commander tried to raise compartment seven, but there was no answer. Then the report from compartment six: "Smoke leaking into the compartment." The command "Dispense LOKh into compartment seven from compartment six" was given. There is a telegram transmitting system on our "Molybden" console. I composed a telegram. A bell was ringing in the compartment from which the LOKh was to have been delivered. A "Revun" siren was wailing in the compartment into which the LOKh was to be delivered. I pressed the telegram transmit button and checked the monitoring parameters.

Captain 3rd Rank Vladimir Ivanovich Yelmanov and captain lieutenants Dvorov, Y. N. Paramonov, and I. V. Kalinin, and lieutenants A. L. Stepanov and A. V. Tretyakov, who were in the control room, also confirmed that after the alarm was announced, a command was transmitted to compartment six to deliver LOKh from it into compartment seven. There are no grounds for disbelieving them. Thus, the entry in the ship's log for 1106 can be read only as a command: "Deliver LOKh to compartment seven," which was given to the watchstander for compartment six. And it follows from this that there were no entries in the ship's log regarding execution of the command to deliver LOKh into compartment seven.

The damage control alarm was announced, but for some reason the place and nature of the accident were not indicated, as is required by Article 89 of the RBZh-PL-82. This can be explained either by careless maintenance of the ship's log, or could it be that sounding of the damage control alarm disoriented the submarine personnel?

Warrant Officer V. S. Kadantsev (interrogation tape recording):

The alarm was announced. I was resting in my cabin in compartment two. I'm the chief of the mechanics' crew, and all of the general ship systems are under my management. A training damage control alarm was sounded. I immediately arrived at the TsP [Control room—D. R.]. My seamen immediately arrived in the hold. I reported to the TsP: "The third's ready for action." After this the submarine began to surface. They began blowing the tanks of the central group twice. The seamen asked me what happened, but I couldn't tell them anything. Then came the announcement: "Damage control alarm! Fire in compartment seven!"

The approximate time of the second blowing of the central group of ballast tanks was 1112.

Lieutenant A. V. Tretyakov (interrogation tape recording):

I was standing watch in the third watch section in the control room. A report arrived from Seaman Bukhnikashvili, the watchstander for compartment seven, at 1100: "The compartment has been inspected. No remarks." At 1112 Senior Lieutenant Markov reported: "Short circuit in so: [R]ShchNo.12." The temperature sensor was activated: "Over 70 degrees Celsius in compartment seven." The commander announced: "Damage control alarm!"

Captain 3rd Rank V. I. Yelmanov (explanatory report):

I, Captain 3rd Rank Vladimir Ivanovich Yelmanov, was in my cabin at the moment the damage control alarm was announced—I was resting after my watch. At 1115 I arrived at the control room in response to the damage control alarm, and I began directing the work of the observation and data processing stations in order to ensure safe surfacing of the distressed submarine. At this time the fire was raging in compartment seven. I heard Warrant Officer Kolotilin's report from compartment six: "The temperature of the bulkhead of compartment seven is 90 degrees Celsius, gas leaks have been stopped, the situation in compartment six is normal."

1. The alarm was announced at 1106. Warrant Officer Kadantsev says that this was a training alarm, and it was not until later that the damage control alarm was announced.
2. Lieutenant Tretyakov and Captain 3rd Rank Yelmanov believe that the damage control alarm was announced at 1112 and 1115, respectively. Most of the rest of the crew put the announcement of the alarm somewhere between 1103 and 1110.
3. At 1106 a command to deliver LOKh to compartment seven was transmitted to compartment six. It is unknown to whom the command to deliver LOKh was given at 1103.

There are no grounds for not believing Warrant Officer Kadantsev. The conflicting testimony of crew members concerning the time of the alarm's announcement confirms his story to some degree. In the first meeting of the State Commission in Severomorsk on April 9, 1989, Division Commander Rear Admiral O. T. Shkiryatov gave a report on the accident of the submarine *Komsomolets* on the basis of the information he received from Captain 1st Rank B.G. Kolyada. He reported that at 1100 a training alarm was announced aboard the submarine, and that the warning signal "Temperature in compartment seven above 70 degrees Celsius" lit up at 1103. In this case he stated that the training alarm was sounded supposedly to awaken the personnel (he was given a blistering scolding for this by his superiors). But Captain 1st Rank Kolyada said nothing about a training alarm in either the report or in the interrogation by the State Commission. Nor did other members of the crew say anything about this. Still, there are indirect confirmations in both the testimony and the actions of the submarine's personnel that a training alarm may have been announced.

Captain Lieutenant S. A. Dvorov (interrogation tape recording):

> Compartment seven commander [Captain Lieutenant Nikoli] Volkov and I ran to compartment six. We ran through compartment four where [Lieutenant A.V.] Makhota and [Warrant Officer M. N.] Valyavin were. When they looked at me in astonishment, I said: "The fire's real," and told them to seal off the compartment behind me, because I was running and I didn't have time to shut the doors.

Every submariner knows that if an emergency occurs during a training alarm, all commands, reports, and messages associated with the accident must be given together with the word "actual," in order to distinguish actual events and actions from training. Moreover, what would one find astonishing about a person running at breakneck speed to his action station in response to a real damage control alarm? Now, if he had been running like this for a training alarm, then you would certainly drop your jaw in astonishment. Thus, Captain Lieutenant Dvorov's report indirectly confirms Warrant Officer Kadantsev's report that a training alarm was announced aboard ship, in response to which Lieutenant Makhota and Warrant Officer Valyavin arrived in compartment four knowing nothing of what happened. This is obviously the only explanation for the fact that they arrived in compartment four "traveling light," without any kind of individual protective equipment, like to a picnic. One must believe that they would have been carrying both an IP-6 self-contained breathing protective tank and an IDA-59 self-contained breathing apparatus in a real damage control alarm.

Let's leave the question of a training alarm aside for awhile. At precisely what moment in time in the interval from 1103 to 1115 was the damage control alarm announced? If this happened at 1106 or earlier, then it is incomprehensible that compartment six commander Captain Lieutenant Dvorov and compartment seven commander Captain Lieutenant Volkov were unable to get into compartment six with their men. Dvorov explains this by a fire in compartment six, which was discovered in an attempt to open the bulkhead door. But there was no fire in the compartment, at least before 1114! This is confirmed by entries in the ship's log concerning Warrant Officer Kolotilin's report at 1110 and the submarine commander's decision to establish the line of defense[1] at the aft bulkhead of compartment five at 1113. The last report from Warrant Officer Kolotilin was received around 1114, after which communication with the stern was severed, as was recorded in the ship's log at 1116. Thus, there was more than enough time between 1106 and 1114 to reach compartment six in response to the alarm. How do we evaluate the actions of captain lieutenants Dvorov and Volkov in this case? However, if it was not until 1112 that the damage control alarm was announced, in this case they may in fact not have been able to reach compartment six.

There is no testimony by the participants of the tragedy regarding the command to deliver a fire extinguisher into compartment seven, given at 1103. Considering the testimony of Captain 1st Rank Kolyada and Lieutenant Zaytsev on the fire report of the watchstander for compartment seven, we can assume that the command to deliver freon into compartment seven was given to the watchstander for compartment seven—that is, he was ordered to deliver LOKh onto "his own position" and abandon compartment seven. This can explain the entry in the ship's log: "Bukhnikashvili tentatively in compartment six," made at 1325. However, for some reason the watchstander for compartment seven was unable to fulfill this command (most probably because of the fire).

Now it is time to talk about the version that was given, by those who are alive today, at the very beginning of the investigation concerning the circumstances surrounding the accident. The advocates of this version maintain that the rough draft of the watchstander's journal was falsified, that it was rewritten with the corresponding corrections while the crew survivors were on the cruiser *Kirov* or in the hospital. Based on their version, they offer the following facts: the presented falsified journal began at 00 hours April 7, 1989 (that is, from the day of the accident), and this falsified journal was checked and strengthened by the seal of the first crew but not the second crew of the submarine. During this process it was firmly established that the expert's graphology was done inaccurately.

As far as the realism of the version? Only with the support and active collaboration of the leaders of the division and the Navy would it be possible to falsify the rough draft of the ship's log. Unfortunately, such collaboration could have occurred (remember the guidance "industry is always responsible"). There remains a number of inconsistencies between the surviving members of the crew about the first minutes of the accident. They also speak in favor of this version. Nevertheless, it was impossible to write a completely new scenario about the accident in the falsified journal. One could only change a few time parameters of a few events at the beginning of the accident, excluding or adding separate episodes. With regard to what was said, the supposed rough draft of the ship's log is considered to be a farce. To this we can add that, in practice, the authority over the false and real ship's log is the VMF (Navy) who has the responsibility not only to report the results of such versions, but also if a falsified ship's log exists.

Why was the fire in compartment seven not extinguished by the LOKh system? Before answering this question, let's listen to the participants.

Captain 1st Rank B. G. Kolyada (interrogation tape recording):

> LOKh was dispensed into the compartment at approximately 1105. Compartment six was queried. Six replied: "Dispensing LOKh into compartment seven." On the console I observed the signal indicating delivery of LOKh to compartment seven. Pressure in compartment seven was normal. . . . Delivery of LOKh could be heard over the loudspeaker communication system. . . . After the LOKh was dispensed, a report came in from compartment six: "LOKh dispensed."

If we remove from the quotation the "story" that Kolyada could hear LOKh being delivered into compartment seven over the loudspeaker communication system, everything in this explanation by the captain 1st rank would be plausible, were it not for one "but." . . . As the reader may remember, Lieutenant Zaytsev transmitted the command to use the LOKh system. Let's listen to the lieutenant.

Lieutenant A. V. Zaytsev (interrogation tape recording):

I pressed the telegram transmission button, and checked the monitoring parameters. I did not see a signal indicating that the LOKh was on its way. The BCh-5 commander, the damage control division commander, and Captain 1st Rank Kolyada, the division deputy commander, said that the light indicating delivery of LOKh to the compartment went on, but I was looking in another direction.

This creates a paradox—the chiefs saw the signal indicating delivery of the LOKh, while for some reason the console operator didn't. Even so, Lieutenant Zaytsev's explanation about some "other direction" in which he was supposedly looking may have been given credence, were it not for one circumstance: The warning system is set up in such a way that once the LOKh delivery light goes on, it cannot go off on its own. It has to be deliberately turned off. Moreover, when the light goes on, a sound signal occurs. Thus, if Lieutenant Zaytsev had not seen the light and had not heard the signal, then this would mean that these things did not happen, and that a fire extinguisher had not been delivered to compartment seven.

But what do the other members of the crew say? Captain Lieutenant A. G. Verezgov (interrogation tape recording):

> Question: Did you hear the command to dispense LOKh from compartment six into compartment seven when you were in the control room?
> Answer: No. The commander was busy with surfacing, and I was monitoring the underwater situation with the sonar operators.
> Question: But did you hear the reply regarding delivery of the LOKh?
> Answer: No.
> Question: Who could have heard it?
> Answer: Dvorov.

Warrant Officer Kolotilin's report that the LOKh system had been activated could have been received by Lieutenant Zaytsev—the operator of the "Molybden" console, and by Captain Lieutenant Dvorov, or by his replacement, Captain Lieutenant Orlov—the operators of the main propulsion unit's console. However, during their interrogation by the State Commission, none of them said that they received a report that the fire extinguisher had been delivered to the distressed compartment. And yet, although sonar specialists

Captain Lieutenant Y. N. Paramonov and Captain Lieutenant I. V. Kalinin were checking on the underwater situation together with Captain Lieutenant Verezgov, in contrast to him they did hear Warrant Officer Kolotilin's report that the LOKh system had been activated. Lieutenant A. L. Stepanov, the navigator, also heard this report.

This creates another paradox. People directly involved in the delivery of a fire extinguisher to the distressed compartment did not hear Warrant Officer Kolotilin's report, while people having no relationship to this procedure mention it.

For the sake of fairness we should add that references to an LOKh delivery signal lighting up and to Warrant Officer Kolotilin's report did suddenly appear in Lieutenant Zaytsev's explanatory report, submitted two days after the interrogation: The influence of superiors, discussed earlier, had its effect.

Where was Warrant Officer Kolotilin, the watchstander in the energy compartment, when the alarm sounded?

Captain Lieutenant S. A. Dvorov (interrogation tape recording): "At 1100 there was a report from Warrant Officer Kolotilin in the fifth compartment, 'The compartment has been inspected, nothing observed.'"

Not excluding the assumption that, at the time of the first indication of the emergency, Warrant Officer Kolotilin was in the fifth compartment, this reflects on the response to the command to supply the gas fire extinguisher to the seventh compartment. Significantly later, this assumption was confirmed by Lieutenant A. V. Tretyakov when he reported that the commander of the BCh-5 gave the command to Warrant Officer Kolotilin to supply LOKh to the seventh compartment, but only after he had received the authority to turn on the IDA-59 apparatus, because as reported, it was hard to breathe in the sixth compartment. The time of the report concerning the difficulty of breathing in the sixth compartment was fixed at 1100. The authority to turn on the IDA-59 apparatus was received by the warrant officer after 1114, which agrees with the information given by Captain Lieutenant I. S. Orlov. Before that time Warrant Officer Kolotilin simply could not have supplied LOKh to the seventh compartment.

There is still one unclear question in connection with the LOKh system. In the united act sections, "Operation and Damage Control" and "Shipbuilding," of the State Commission Working Group the following statement is made: "The LOKh fire extinguishers were replenished (Freon 114B$_2$ GOST 15899-70) during the period of examining the submarine in 1983. Replenishment of the gas fire extinguisher reservoirs (Freon 114B$_2$ is a product of Japan having qualitative indices consistent with GOST 15899-70 and certified under import certificate No. 426) were carried out to standards in December 1988." At first glance there is nothing unusual in these notes. The fire extinguisher's reservoirs were replenished to standards and there were no problems. But the fact is that when the LOKh system broke down it failed to transfer the gas fire extinguisher from the reservoir into the emergency compartment. Immediately the question arises: how was the replenishment of the reservoir with freon performed, and in which compartment was this process conducted? What quantity of the fire gas extinguisher was added to the reservoir? How was the hermitization (gas-tight integrity) of the LOKh system ensured after the replenishment of the reservoirs? To all of these questions there are no answers. And no answer to the basic question: To what degree do these efforts reflect on the results of battling the fire in the seventh compartment?

And how did the submarine's leadership view the matter of delivering LOKh to compartment seven at the time of the accident?

Warrant Officer V. F. Slyusarenko (interrogation tape recording):

> I ascended to the control room. The senior watch officer said that people were needed to deliver LOKh from compartment six to compartment seven. Consequently, it was not known whether or not LOKh was being dispensed into compartment seven. I volunteered to go, because I was feeling good and I was wearing an IP-6 self-contained breathing protective mask. Yudin and [A. A.] Grundul were supposed to make their way into compartment six, and I was the safety man at the bulkhead between compartments six and five together with Lieutenant Tretyakov. We were unable to budge the rack-and-pinion[2] on the bulkhead leading from compartment five to compartment six. Yudin sent Grundul off to open the clack [check] valve to equalize the pressure. He couldn't do it. It was hard working in an IP. The entire floor of compartment five was covered with a brown liquid—maybe hydraulic fluid, or maybe VPL[3] used to put out the fire. We left compartment five and reported that it was impossible to get into compartment six because the bulkhead couldn't be opened. Then the executive officer ordered Yudin to dispense LOKh into six out of five.

This patrol of the damage control team into compartment six was entered in the ship's log at 1356 without indicating its goal.

There is one other circumstance relating to a certain degree to the question of delivery of LOKh into compartment seven.

Captain Lieutenant S. A. Dvorov (explanatory report):

> I surrendered my watch to Captain Lieutenant Orlov. On or-
> ders from the BCh-5 commander, Captain 2nd Rank [V. I.]
> Babenko, I was to leave for compartment seven with two IP-6
> self-contained protective breathing masks and carry Senior Sea-
> man Bukhnikashvili into the airlock between compartments six
> and seven, and if he was unconscious, to connect him up to an
> IDA-59."[4]

It follows from this that the submarine's leadership did not believe that compartment seven was fully involved. Moreover, it believed the fire to be small, and supposed that the watchstander was not only alive but may also have not lost consciousness. The possibility is not excluded that the attack center had information on the nature of the fire. But that's not the question. How do we explain that two mutually exclusive decisions are made at practically the same time—first, sealing off compartment seven and delivering LOKh into it, and second, unsealing the compartment with the purpose of rescuing the watchstander? According to RBZh-PL-82, Article 99, when the LOKh system is used to put out a fire, the distressed compartment may be opened not earlier than thirty minutes after the fire extinguisher is delivered into it. The explana-tion for this may be as follows: Either the submarine's leadership was not unani-mous in its opinion and actions in fighting the accident, or what is more prob-able, the decision to send Captain Lieutenant Dvorov with his men into com-partment seven was made later (tentatively at 1112), after it already became known that the fire extinguisher had not been delivered to compartment seven. The latter hypothesis is confirmed by the following entries in the ship's log: at 1113 on designation of the lines of defense in compartment six, and at 1114 on closure of the LOKh valves in compartment six to avoid any surprises.

Let's summarize. All of the objective data indicate that freon was not delivered to compartment seven. Again, there are no records of this in the ship's log.

Experiments confirmed the fire-extinguishing characteristics of the freon used in the LOKh system. Delivery of freon guarantees extinguishment of a fire at any stage of its development within around sixty seconds at normal pressure and normal oxygen concentration in the compartment atmosphere. The fire would have been extinguished even in the presence of a high oxygen concentration in the compartment, because the concentration of freon that would have been delivered to compartment seven exceeded the minimum necessary concentration by almost two times.

The following question naturally arises: Why all of these conjectures about the first minutes of the accident? Wouldn't it be simpler to ask the participants in the tragedy who were in the attack center in the first minutes of the accident about these events? In an open letter published in *Morskoy Sbornik* (No. 2, 1990), Captain 1st Rank Kolyada, speaking on behalf of the surviving crew members, even invites us to go to him first to get "information that is in fact truthful."

Unfortunately, one must say that many of the members of the crew, especially the officers, were not sincere during the investigation by the State Commission and attempted to present the accident in an advantageous light for the crew. This effort continued in the press. Therefore, there was no reason to expect candid answers to unclear questions.

Why did the crew decide to rise to a depth of fifty meters, rather than to the surface itself, which is what the above-cited Article 89 of RBZh-PL-82 states as the primary course of action? This is a very serious question, and it has far-reaching consequences, because the choice of the surfacing procedures depends on the decision reached. Rising to a depth of fifty meters would be possible only with ship's power; at the same time that surfacing could be accomplished by three different methods: with ship's power, by blowing the middle group of ballast tanks, and by using powder gas generators—or by any combination of these methods. The assertions of naval representatives that the decision reached—rising to a depth of fifty meters—was dictated by navigation safety are absolutely unfounded because the submarine was not in an area of intensive shipping and, moreover, the situation around the ship was known to a radius of dozens of nautical miles.

Captain Lieutenant Y. N. Paramonov (interrogation tape recording):

> I am the commander of the sonar group. I was on watch. There was a group target left of our bearing. It was apparently the tender *Khlobystov*. The group target was classified as fishing trawlers. The horizon was clear. After this I heard the "Onega" system squeal out its warning signal. Then the damage control alarm was announced.

The distance to the tender *Aleksey Khlobystov* and the fishing trawlers was over fifty nautical miles.

There could be only one explanation—the submarine command un-

derestimated the full seriousness of the accident, and adopted a halfway decision that had fateful consequences.

What optimum sequence of decisions should the submarine have
adopted after receiving notice of the fire in compartment seven?

1. To announce an "actual" damage control alarm, with an indication
of the place and nature of the accident (this was done after a delay).

2. To designate the lines of defense and supervise their establishment
(this was done with a delay, and not completely).

3. To ensure delivery of fire extinguisher into compartment seven (this
was apparently not done for the reasons indicated above).

4. To make the decision to surface the submarine, and to surface by blowing the middle group of main ballast tanks with air from high-pressure air
cofferdam ("banks") No. 4 located in compartment seven, completely
using up its air reserve, and then stopping the main propulsion unit
and completely sealing off compartment seven (this was not done).

5. To shut off the air and hydraulic pipelines passing into the distressed
compartment (not done).

6. To select the main focus of submarine damage control measures,
and then make adjustments to it as the accident situation developed
(also not done).

7. To monitor fulfillment of measures to seal off the compartments
by personnel of these compartments (not done).

It would have taken not more than five minutes to carry out all of
these actions, and rescue of the submarine and the crew would have been guaranteed.

"Now, in smoke-filled rooms, having sorted through all of the options
for putting out the fire with the assistance of their own and foreign experience,
critics of the second crew are eager to throw stones at Vanin's back: 'He did this
wrong, he didn't give that order, while he could have done such and such, and
then . . . ,'" says writer and seascape painter N. Cherkashin.[5]

"Of course, in a calm situation, when time is not sharply lacking, and
with the help of the most competent specialists in different fields of science
and engineering, and of the most experienced practical experts, decisions and
actions aboard a ship in distress that are somehow more effective or prudent
could be proposed. Especially when the outcome is known"—these are the
words spoken by Vice Admiral V. V. Zaytsev, deputy commander in chief and
chief of the Navy's Main Directorate for Operation and Repair, and repeated
after him by Captain 1st Rank B. G. Kolyada.[6]

But what is forgivable to a certain degree in a writer and painter of seascapes is unforgivable in an admiral.

These recommendations are appropriate for any kind of fire in compartment seven of the submarine *Komsomolets* and they follow from the requirements of Articles 21, 38, 59, 90, 91, 121 of the RBZh-PL-82, the principal document on submarine damage control. And the concrete actions to be taken by the crew in response to accidents and combat damage are spelled out in the "Manual on Combat Use of Technical Resources (RBITS)," which is written for each submarine design. The "Emergency Bill" is drawn up and plans for conducting ship exercises to work on submarine damage control problems are drawn up on the basis of these documents. The standard problem "Fire in Compartment Seven" should have been practiced within the framework of crew training until the actions of the crew were automatic. But if during an emergency a crew were to begin inventing "decisions that were somehow more effective or prudent," it would probably be destined to defeat. This had to be known by Vice Admiral Zaytsev and Captain 1st Rank Kolyada.

And when the industrial representatives in the "Operation and Damage Control" section attempted to analyze how Captain 1st Rank Vanin's crew trained and what the training objectives were in the work on submarine damage control problems, they found that a "Manual on Combat Use of Technical Resources" had not been written for the submarine *Komsomolets*, even though the basic data for this end were provided by the design office back in 1983. Five years were not enough for the Navy to draw up, "in a calm situation, when time is not sharply lacking, and with the help of the most competent specialists" the main document on damage control, which was supposed to have fleshed out the general requirements of the RBZh-PL-82 as it applied to the submarine *Komsomolets*.

The "Manual on Combat Use of Technical Resources" is part of the set of combat documents on submarine survivability. Without this document the crew was not supposed to have taken the test in ship damage control, and the submarine itself was not supposed to have been allowed to sea. But as we can see, the law was not written for our naval commanders.

It follows from this that Captain 1st Rank Vanin's crew did not have the theoretical foundation for competent study of damage control problems, which was a crucial factor in the accident. The crew found itself hostage to the criminal irresponsibility and devil-may-care attitude of the naval leadership toward the needs of submariners.

Also, the plans for ship damage control exercises were not furnished to the State Commission.

None of this was reflected in the materials of the State Commission that investigated the accident aboard the submarine *Komsomolets*. The reason is simple: Those who were personally responsible for the incident—Naval Institute No. 1 chief, Vice Admiral M. N. Budayev, and Naval Main Directorate for Operation and Repair chief, Vice Admiral V. V. Zaytsev—were the chairmen of the sections of the State Commission Working Group. The investigation of the accident was conducted not by an impartial commission, but by a kangaroo court.

6.

Surfacing

From the ship's log: "1106—Damage control alarm: Rise to a depth of fifty meters. Deliver LOKh into compartment seven."

What were the actions of the attack center upon the alarm's announcement? Or more accurately, inactions? They did not announce the place and nature of the accident, they did not designate lines of defense, they did not make a decision to take damaged propulsion equipment off line, they did not determine the main focus of submarine damage control, they did not give orders to shut off the sections of the high pressure air and hydraulic systems passing through the distressed compartment, and they did not make the decision to surface the submarine.

And what should the personnel have done after the damage control alarm was announced?

First, they should have taken their places in accordance with the "Emergency Bill." For some unknown reason, personnel assigned to compartments six and seven were not even able to get into compartment six under the leadership of their commanders, and they were stopped in compartment five. Personnel of compartment four arrived without individual protective equipment, which predetermined all of their subsequent actions.

Second, they should have sealed off the compartments. Analysis of the subsequent events of the accident showed that this was not done in compartments six, five, three, and two. The [piping and ventilation] lines or "mains"emerging from compartment seven were not cut off until the loss of the submarine itself. Smoke made its way through these mains into compartments three and five, which complicated damage control efforts. The operator at the main propulsion unit console failed to shut the Kingston valve of the cooling system for the stern-tube gland. Later, flooding of compartment seven began through this Kingston valve.

It must be said for the sake of fairness that the designer did make a mistake: The suction system and seals of the turbo-pump in compartment five did not permit closure of the line from the direction of this compartment, which could have complicated the submarine damage-control efforts, had they been carried out. However, this single design error was transformed later into "numerous technical imperfections in the submarine's various systems," which "may be attributed entirely to things left undone by the designers."[1]

How do we explain the fact that steps were taken in practically none of the compartments to seal them off—that is, to do what was supposed to have been done without orders (Articles 90 and 91, RBZh-PL-82)? It is difficult to believe that the personnel were so poorly trained. It is more likely that announcement of a training damage control alarm in the initial stage of the accident introduced disorganization into submarine damage control efforts.

At the same time the impression is created from an analysis of tape recordings of the personnel's interrogation and of their explanatory reports that, for most of the crew members, sealing off a compartment meant battening down only the bulkhead doors and the bulkhead ventilation closure valves. Thus, it would seem that what they did in training is exactly what they did in a real accident. Few knew that when a fire occurs, the valves on the *main* pipelines have to be closed, and consequently these lines were left open during the accident.

The submarine began rising under its own power. The fire continued.

"1108—Seaman Bukhnikashvili is in compartment seven."

What did they mean by this entry? Was this just the assertion of a fact, or something else? In light of it, how do we interpret the 1325 entry? Bukhnikashvili is tentatively in compartment six.

In the meantime, the consequences of the fire made themselves known. The automatic intersectional circuit-breaker that isolates the disconnectable load section of the No. 1 main distribution panel tripped. Pump No. 1 of the steam-generating unit in the first cooling loop automatically switched to low speed. Captain Lieutenant Orlov, who relieved Captain Lieutenant Dvorov at the main propulsion unit console, switched pump No. 2 of the first loop to low speed as well. The power output of the main propulsion unit was limited then to 30 percent. At this power output, it is not necessary to cool the stern-tube gland [where the propulsion shafting penetrates the hull], but Captain Lieutenant Orlov did not shut the Kingston valve of the stern-tube cooling system. Captain lieutenants Dvorov and Volkov ran to their compartments. The command "engines 150 rpm ahead" was given. Because of the limit on power output (now 30 percent), Orlov was unable to fulfill this command. Then followed the command "Squeeze out everything you can!"

Captain Lieutenant I. S. Orlov (interrogation tape recording):

> I began increasing the rpm above the limit. I could monitor its increase to 70-80. Then the rpm signals disappeared, because the rpm sensors were in compartment seven. Signals indicating the work at the turbine disappeared. The submarine began to shudder. I realized that the turbine was beginning to increase its rpm. There were no signals indicating activation of the turbine's emergency safety system at the initial moment in time.

But in an explanatory report submitted three days later, Orlov now asserted that at the moment of his arrival in response to the damage control alarm, there were no shafting line rpm or turbine operation signals on the console of the main propulsion unit. Hence, as one can see, the pressure of the naval leadership upon the personnel of the submarine manifested itself here as well.

From the ship's log: "1110—Left the Greenland Sea. Prepare a damage control party of eight men. Hard to breathe in six. Two . . . scouts."

A report was received from Warrant Officer Kolotilin in compartment six that it was hard to breathe there. This meant that the fire in compartment seven was still burning, pressure generated by the heating of the air in the compartment was growing, and hot air was getting into compartment six together with combustion products. Compartment six air was becoming fouled because the bulkhead between it and compartment seven was not sealed as a result of the operation of the shafting. There was no report that a fire extinguisher gas had been delivered to compartment seven. A fire was not yet burning in compartment six, and Captain Lieutenant Dvorov and his men were still running toward it in order to assume their stations for the alarm, which had been sounded four minutes previously. The interpretation of the last phase in the 1100 log entry is not possible due to the illegible report. However, one may speculate about the meaning of the entry.

Lieutenant A.V. Tretyakov (interrogation tape recording):

> In my opinion we were already on the surface when the commander of BCh-5 gave the command to prepare a reconnaissance group to go into the sixth compartment. Lieutenant Captain Volkov and Lieutenant Captain Dvorov were appointed to the reconnaissance. I don't remember which one was the safety man.

From the information Tretyakov gave, it follows that the notes in the ship's log must be understood as orders concerning the reconnaissance groups. Incidentally, we find that Lieutenant Captain Dvorov and Lieutenant Captain Volkov did not run "like mad" in order to take their stations during the alarm, but somehow found themselves in the main command post. At a depth of around 150 meters the steam turbine unit emergency safety system activated. The submarine lost its propulsion.

Captain Lieutenant I. S. Orlov (interrogation tape recording):

> Then the AZ GTZA [The emergency safety system of the main turbogear unit.—D. R.] activated in order to reduce pressure in the regulating system. Two pumps of the oil system of the GTZA regulating system stopped right away.

The starting stations of these pumps were in compartment seven.

Lieutenant Zaytsev received orders to blow the middle group of ballast tanks, and so he did, delivering air into these tanks twice—at a depth of 150 and then between one hundred meters and seventy meters. At this time, in the words of Warrant Officer Kadantsev there came the announcement "Damage control alarm! Fire in compartment seven!" This happened at 1112. It was also at that moment that a signal indicating a short circuit in distribution panel RShchN No. 12, located in compartment seven, lit up on the electric power unit console.

There could no longer be any talk of rising to a depth of fifty meters. The submarine surfaced. In this case the middle group of main ballast tanks (MBT) was blown from high-pressure air "cofferdam" (bank) No. 2—that is, as in normal surfacing. Had the tanks been blown from high-pressure air cofferdam No. 4, another objective besides surfacing would have been reached—

purging the air reserves from the cofferdam in the fire zone. In that case, not a single pipe of the air supply system would have been additionally charged with high pressure in compartment seven. The resources available at that time would have permitted complete monitoring of the blowing of the middle group of main ballast tanks from cofferdam No. 4. In addition, high-pressure air, the principal damage control resource of the submarine, would have been saved. However, the absence of a "Manual on Combat Use of Technical Resources" predetermined the wrong actions of the attack center.

It should be noted that there were no entries in the ship's log concerning activation of the emergency safety system of the main turbogear unit, the short circuit in distribution panel RShchN No. 12, the decision to surface, or the emergency blowing of the middle group of main ballast tanks.

"1113—Oil pumps stopped. Pressure in six rising. Lines are at the aft bulkhead of three, and the fore and aft bulkheads of compartment six."

The fire in compartment seven continued to burn, and pressure in it grew. Air was entering the compartment from the air-foam fire extinguishing system, and possibly from the medium-pressure air system, the fittings of which have rubber seals. Combustion products passed into compartment six, in which pressure increased as well. There was no fire in it yet, and captain lieutenants Dvorov and Volkov were still running to this compartment. The submarine commander was seven minutes late in designating the lines of defense, including in compartment six. He believed in this case that Dvorov and Volkov were already in compartment six with their men, since otherwise it would be difficult to explain how Warrant Officer Kolotilin could hold the line of defense alone simultaneously at two bulkheads. At this time the submarine was rising swiftly to the surface.

"1114—Shut off the LOKh in six!"

What made it necessary to give this command at the most critical moment of surfacing, and to enter it in the ship's log?

Lieutenant A.V. Zaytsev (interrogation tape recording):

During surfacing, somewhere near fifty meters, I completely opened the alarm and the controls of the sixth and seventh compartments according to the general ship systems "Molybden." How could I be sure of this? The command to deliver "LOKh" stood. The command could not be rescinded. They read on the "Molybden": "Faulty electromagnetic lines" and "Reserve feeding."

An insufficient knowledge to fully explain the material parts did not allow the lieutenant to correctly classify the casualty according to the information he indicates. Simply, one may only confirm that the breakdown was due to a short circuit, resulting from the fire, in the "telegram feeding" lines for opening the LOKh system in the sixth and seventh compartments. A short time went by and, from the control panel of the "Molybden" system, Lieutenant Zaytsev opened the valve for blowing the stern group of main ballast tanks located in the seventh compartment. At 1134 he repeated this operation. From this information it also follows that the lieutenant was no longer "looking in another direction," as he testified elsewhere, and yet he still could not see the indicator showing that fire extinguisher had been delivered into compartment seven. Moreover, the command at 1114 meant nothing other than recision of the command at 1103 to deliver a fire extinguisher into compartment seven. The motives behind this command are clear as well—Captain Lieutenant Dvorov had been given the assignment of evacuating the watchstander from compartment seven.

Summarizing the actions of the crew in the time from 1112 to 1114, we can assert that during this period the attack center had finally begun carrying out the mandatory primary actions in response to a fire, as prescribed by Article 89, RBZh-PL-82: It made the decision to surface the submarine; it designated the lines of defense; and it made the decision to evacuate personnel from the distressed compartment. These actions by the attack center confirm the statements of Warrant Officer Kadantsev, Lieutenant Tretyakov, and Captain 3rd Rank Yelmanov that the damage control alarm was announced at 1112. Unfortunately, these actions by the submarine command were incomplete, and considerably late.

From the ship's log: "1114—Rising to the surface. Raise the 'Bukhta' [radar] and periscope. Blow the main ballast tanks. Rudder under manual control. Blowing the main ballast tanks."

So came the culmination of the initial stage of the accident.

Lieutenant A. V. Zaytsev (explanatory report):

Having been ordered to blow the middle group, I started blowing at a depth of 152 meters. I fed air in again at seventy to one
hundred meters, and when the submarine came to the surface, I
blew the end groups of the main ballast tanks. After I blew the
end groups of the main ballast tanks, list and trim were equal to
zero degrees. Pressure[2] in cofferdams one, three, and four was
around 150 to 200 kg/cm^2 Ten minutes later the pressure gauges
in compartments six and seven read a pressure of 6 kg/cm^2, and
it was growing; pressure in cofferdams one, three, and four was
falling simultaneously. Immediately after surfacing, list and trim
were equal to zero degrees, but literally one to two minutes later
there was a starboard list of four to six degrees.

Captain Lieutenant I. S. Orlov (explanatory report):

Then I heard the commander order "Surface, blow the ballast." The submarine surfaced. A report by Warrant Officer
Kolotilin [the roving watchstander for the aft compartments] came
in from compartment six: "Hydraulic fluid is leaking onto the
left turbo-generator, and onto the turbine also, permission to get
into my IDA." Then there were no more reports received, despite our queries.

Captain Lieutenant Yu. I. Paramonov (explanatory report): "As we were
surfacing, the chief boatswain's mate reported that control of the rudder and
then the aft hydroplanes was lost."

What happened during this time period? Let's try to sort it out.
When the main ballast tanks are blown, air at high pressure—around
200 to 250 kg/cm^2—enters pipes leading to each tank. In the absence of any
information on the fire in compartment seven, the decision to blow the aft
group of main ballast tanks was the next serious mistake by the submarine's
leadership, since the blowing introduced high pressure into pipes that could be
in the fire zone. The objective data indicate that at the moment the blowing of
the aft main ballast tanks began, the pipe used for emergency blowing of the
port main ballast tank [No. 10] ruptured. This pipe was located in compartment seven. Practically all of the air intended to blow tank No. 10 wound up in
compartment seven, which transformed a local fire into a compartment-wide
fire. The pressure in compartment seven rose abruptly to 5-6 kg/cm^2. Air and

combustion products entered the circulating oil tank of the main engine, located in compartment six, through seals of the main thrust bearing and the oil drain pipe. The pressure of the circulating air rose, the turbine oil along the port line went in the opposite direction and streamed copiously into the compartment and onto surrounding equipment. Only seconds remained before compartment six would become fully involved. It was at this moment that the control room received the last report from Warrant Officer Kolotilin.

The construction of the submarine *Komsomolets* did not guarantee a hermetic closure between compartments six and seven during the operation of the line shaft or when there was an emergency (high) pressure in compartment seven. The representatives of the BCh-5 consider that construction a shortcoming. The inappropriateness of such an assertion is discussed at great length in Peculiarity 2 of Appendix II "Design Peculiarities of the Submarine *Komsomolets*." We address that here. We will look at an alternative scenario of the accident for the case of guaranteed hermetic closure of each of compartments six and seven when the line shaft is working and during emergency when the pressure is abnormally high. As a guide, calculations show that, after 1114, the pressure in the compartment seven would have risen to 8 to 10 kg/cm^2 and at 1120 it would have reached 15 to 20 kg/cm^2. The transversal bulkhead between the sixth and seventh compartments was designed to collapse at a pressure of 10 kg/cm^2, and the fire would have spread into compartment six. Not to exclude the fact that the resulting shockwave would also collapse the bulkhead between compartments six and five. It is hard to predict what the consequences would have been if the bulkhead between compartments six and seven would have collapsed. They may have been just as tragic, right up to the destruction of the waterproof hull and the sinking of the submarine before 1200. Thus, in this situation, it was the failure to take the primary measures of damage control and the construction of the submarine, which did not guarantee the hermetic closure between compartments six and seven when the line shafts were operating. Hence during the emergency, the high compartment pressure allowed the boat to stay on the surface for nearly six hours.

The State Commission Working Group conducted calculations and experiments to determine the temperature conditions under which the pipe of the emergency main ballast tank blowing system could rupture. The results show that rupture is possible when the pipe is heated to between 650 to 700 degrees Celsius. It is difficult to imagine that the pipe could have heated to such a temperature in the presence of a fire in a compartment having a limited quantity of air with a normal oxygen concentration. This is possible only in an atmosphere with an elevated oxygen concentration.

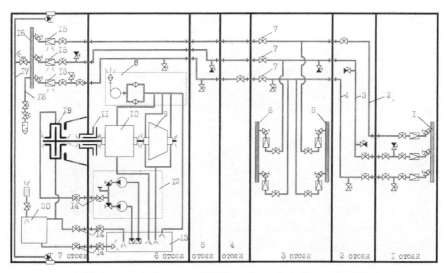

4. High pressure air system (VVD) to the main ballast tanks (MBT)

Captain Lieutenant S. A. Dvorov (interrogation tape recording):

I ran through compartment five and heard the door closing behind me. Compartment five was sealed off. I ran to the aft bulkhead and began opening the rack-and-pinion between compartments five and six, releasing a billowing cloud of black smoke. The door was latched. I shut the door and raised the control room with the loudspeaker communication system; communication was still possible then.

It follows from this information that Dvorov reported the fire in compartment six to the control room (TsP) through the loudspeaker communication system and that he was in compartment five. There is no basis for not believing the captain lieutenant. Still, there is not even a hint of receipt of a report on the fire in compartment six in the materials from interrogation of the personnel by the State Commission, in the explanatory reports, in the ship's and control logs, or in the subsequent actions of the submarine's leadership.

Let us try to establish by indirect evidence the time at which Captain Lieutenant Dvorov attempted to get into compartment six (interrogation tape recordings):

I raised the TsP and reported that it was impossible to enter compartment six, there was a fire there, and what was I to do? I got nothing from the TsP—I knew that they could hear me, but they were unable to transmit anything. I raised them on the emergency telephone. Communication was poor, after that the loud-speaker communication system and the telephone failed. I sent Volkov to the compartment five bulkhead to establish communication with compartment four by tapping on the wall.

Lieutenant A. V. Makhota:

I was in communication. The rack-and-pinion began to open from the direction of compartment five. The TsP called compartment five. At this time the starting station for the loop 1 pump in our compartment caught fire, and a huge sheaf of sparks began flying out and smoke billowed from it.

It follows from these statements that Captain Lieutenant Volkov was trying to open the bulkhead door leading from compartment five into compartment four. This was before 1121 (the time the starting station of the loop one pump caught fire is documented in the ship's log). A report of a fire in compartment six was not received, because communication was interrupted at 1116, which was also noted in the ship's log. Thus, there are full grounds for supposing that the earliest Captain Lieutenant Dvorov tried to get into compartment six was 1115. A fire was already in fact burning in compartment six by this time. It took Captain Lieutenant Dvorov around ten minutes to make his way from the control room to the bulkhead door leading into compartment six in response to the damage control alarm. Later Lieutenant Captain Dvorov had to confirm that at the time of Warrant Officer Kolotilin's report about the turbine oil entering into the 6th compartment (after 1114), he was still located at the main command post. Thus, the question arises, if the emergency alarm was not sounded at 1106, how could that time and event have been entered into the ship's log and be affirmed by the majority of surviving crew members? And how could Lieutenant Captain Dvorov's delay have been assessed? Why did the Assistant Commander of the Division, Head of the Political Division, and the Commander of the Submarine quietly look at an apparent violation of the war oath and soldiers' duty?

What is the purpose of this question? Any reader asks this. What would change if a few more men were killed with Warrant Officer Kolotilin? Let us analyze this. Life is not as the rough draft journal of the Navy. It cannot be rewritten. One cannot exclude the possibility that the timely arrival of Lieutenant Captain Dvorov in the sixth compartment would not have stopped the development of the accident. However, with a large degree of certainty one may assert the opposite. And here's why: the log states that at 1106 the alarm sounded. When did Lieutenant Captain Orlov arrive at the Main Command Post in order to relieve Lieutenant Captain Dvorov?

Captain Lieutenant Orlov (tape recording of the investigation):

Question: "How long after the alarm did you arrive at post?"
Answer: "Well, maybe between 15 and 20 seconds.

Thus, Lieutenant Captain Dvorov, in reality, could have been in compartment six within one to two minutes after the sounding of the purported alarm, that is, at 1108 and in compartment seven for five to six minutes before the blowing of the main ballast tank. This may have radically changed the emergency situation on the submarine and excluded any possibility of her sinking.

Why was the steering lost? There are two reasons: a short in the electric wiring control panel from the fire and the loss of the hydraulic fluid in the steering system.

Warrant Officer V.S. Kadantsev (interrogation tape recording):

I went down to the hold. The hydraulic system for steering was disconnected resulting in an uncontrolled rudder. The usual tem-

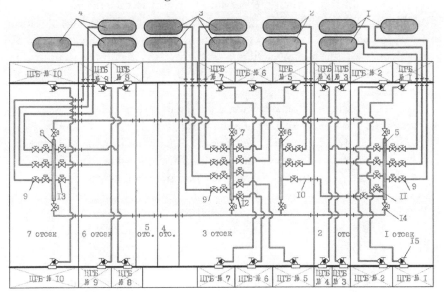

5. Sources of air pressurizing Compartment Seven

perature of the ship's general hydraulic system is 18 to 20 degrees Celsius. The ship's general hydraulics returning from circulation was already hot. The Commander of BCh-5 ordered: to go topside and prepare the lower fin [sail] hatch of the rescue chamber and the fore chamber hatch to be opened.

Question: How many minutes after the alarm sounded did you notice the heightened temperature?

Answer: It was literally within five to six minutes. Our depth was 310 meters.

Obviously, the Warrant Officer's information does not correspond with the ship's log. Five to six minutes after the alarm, that is, after 1110, the submarine was located at a depth near 150 meters and not 310 meters. Besides that, Warrant Officer Kadantsev was mistaken maintaining that the "hydraulics are circulating." At that time the critical mechanisms of the ship's main hydraulic systems were not working and there could be no circulating liquid. This only means that due to the fire, the hydraulic flow of the ship's main system lost its pressure and gas entered into it, which raised the pipe line temperature to between 55 to 60 degrees Celsius. This was not within five to six minutes after the alarm, but later. The port main hydraulic system has a breast-valve regulating the pressure to 2 kg/cm^2; therefore, the circulation of the gases in the main flow was possible only when the pressure in compartment seven was higher than 2 kg/cm^2, that is, after blowing the end ballast tanks. Therefore, the ship's main hydraulic system lost its pressure [integrity] after 1114. One may assume the hydraulics of the steering system also lost its density before this time. The steering was lost earlier than 1114, which allows us to consider the short circuit in the steering as a more probable cause for the breakdown.

The heating of the ship's main hydraulic system meant a loss of the working fluid and was a signal for action. Unfortunately, it was not understood. It must be said that, concerning the scheme of the main hydraulics aboard the submarine *Komsomolets*, damage control was insufficient to address an intense fire.

As a designer, the following is my interpretation of the development of events aboard the submarine in the first minutes of the accident, based on the voluminous, but often contradictory testimony from the tragedy's participants.

During the evening of April 6, 1989, as was already discussed, Warrant Officer S. I. Chernikov, who had been servicing the electro-mechanical oxygen regenerating system, became ill. Before this, he or Lieutenant V. A. Gregulev may have opened the valves of the oxygen dispenser that supplied oxygen to compartments five and seven. Neither the watchstander of compartment seven nor the mobile watchstander of the stern compartments measured the oxygen contents with the portable gas analyzer, nor was it done formally. Being alone, Lieutenant Gregulev either forgot, or maybe did not know about, the open valves supplying oxygen to the compartments five and seven. April 7, 1989, arrived. The fire began fifteen to twenty minutes before 1100 in compartment seven. At this time the watchstander was located in compartment six (compartment six of the submarine *Komsomolets* was more comfortable in comparison with other compartments and the watchstanders liked to go there). It was nearing 1100. It was time to prepare to report on inspection of the compartment. Arriving in compartment seven the watchstander discovered the flame and began to extinguish it using the VPL system. Near 1100, not having a report about the inspection of the seventh compartment, the commander of the damage control division managed to get in touch with the watchstander of the compartment to question him about the lateness of the report. At that time he received information about the fire. Having learned of the fire, a "quick conference" was apparently held in the control room, after which the watchstander for compartment seven was ordered to turn the LOKh system "on his own position" and move into compartment six—this command was documented in the ship's log at 1103. The watchstander for compartment seven was unable to fulfill this command, and he died fighting the fire.

Several questions must have been considered in the control room. What to do? Sound the alarm or not? Previously, there had been an incident (the steering was jammed, and sea water was entering the compartment), but trouble had been evaded. Maybe it would happen this time also?

At this time warning signals indicating the temperature in compartment seven and the low insulation resistance appeared at the control consoles. A damage control alarm was announced, a training one in all probability. Upon arriving in the control room Captain 1st Rank Kolyada advised delivering a gas fire extinguisher into compartment seven. A decision was made simultaneously to raise the submarine to a depth of fifty meters. The time was 1106. They began trying to make contact with Warrant Officer Kolotilin, the watchstander for the power compartments, in order to instruct him to turn on the LOKh system for compartment seven out of compartment six. The personnel assumed their stations as for the training alarm; the men of compartments 6 and 7 waited for their commanders, Lieutenant Dvorov and Lieutenant Volkov, and did not hurry to their compartments. But their commanders were in the main command post participating in the "working conference" on what to do next in fighting the fire. Lieutenant Zaytsev composed and transmitted a command to compartment six to deliver a gas fire extinguisher with the LOKh system into compartment seven, after which no one was to be admitted into the compartment until the proper time. Warrant Officer Kolotilin was in compartment five, but the men subordinate to Dvorov and Volkov waited for their commanders. Only after 1110 did Warrant Officer Kolotilin, having arrived in compartment six, receive the order to supply LOKh to compartment seven, but he could not fulfill the order. Receiving no "scenario inputs," the personnel of the other compartments remained ignorant of the events. It was only after loss of power and rudder control that a damage control alarm may have been announced that provided an indication of the place and nature of the accident. The time was 1112. At about that time Dvorov and Volkov received the command to make their way into compartment seven and evacuate Senior Seaman Bukhnikashvili. However, they were not even able to get into compartment six.

And what about the ship's log? It is apparent that the log entries during the initial period of the accident were not made and the events after 1103 were entered into the journal later.

As for how this corresponds to reality, it's not for me to judge. Members of Captain 1st Rank Vanin's crew could have aided in establishing the truth, but the keepers of the "real truth" are silent. Why?

Completing our examination of the first minutes of the accident and the actions of the attack center, we need to summarize the results:

■ A delay, in no way justified, in announcing the damage control alarm was permitted, making it impossible for the personnel of compartments six and seven to take their places according to the "Emergency Bill." This in all probability was why the gas fire extinguisher was not delivered by the LOKh system into compartment seven.

■ The decision to raise the submarine to a depth of fity meters was the wrong one, making it impossible to seal off the aft bulkhead of compartment six and bleed overboard the high pressure air reserves in "cofferdam" No. 4, which was located in compartment seven.

A command was not given to shut off the high-pressure air and hydraulic lines leading into the distressed compartment seven, which intensified the fire and resulted in the loss of ship air reserves and the breakdown of the ship hydraulic system.

■ The decision to blow the aft main ballast tanks with high-pressure air was wrong, causing the fire in compartment seven to intensify and a fire to break out in compartment six. The air-tightness of the bulkheads of all compartments was not checked, which subsequently led to penetration of smoke into compartments two, three, and five, and complicated submarine damage control efforts.

Signal No. 6 [Distress Signal]

From the ship's log:

> 1115—Close shut-offs 1, 2 on aft ring.
> 1116—"Listvennitsa" communication with stern out. Switched to reserve. Depth twenty meters.
> 1116—Rose to surface. Periscope raised. No communication with stern. Hydrophone operator. System deenergized.

The command to prepare for use of the aft ring of the ship's general ventilation system was given. The submarine rose to the surface with the starboard No. 10 main ballast tank partially blown and the port tank not blown. Hot gases entered only the starboard No. 10 main ballast tank from compartment seven through the damaged emergency blowing pipe, purging this tank. This is the only explanation for the list to port immediately after surfacing, and for the subsequent peeling of the lining plates (tiles) on the outer hull only on the starboard side. Only this can explain the air bubbles coming out of the starboard No. 10 main ballast tank. For what amount of time could the starboard side of the No. 10 main ballast tank be blown through the ruptured piping system? Calculations show that ten to twelve minutes is sufficient when the pressure in the accident compartment is equal to 6 kg/cm^2.

Captain Lieutenant A. G. Verezgov (interrogation tape recording):

Sheets of the lining material were swaying with the waves. They began to come off. Then the ship began listing to port.

Question: When did this begin?

Answer: Around five, six minutes after surfacing.

Question: Was air being released from the stern?

Answer: Initially there was none. But later air began coming out, as if starboard No. 10 was being blown. A huge bubble came out of the right side.

The port main ballast tank No. 10 never did get blown. There may be different reasons for this, and it is difficult to attach a preference to any particular one. The emergency blow pipe for the starboard tank No. 10 may have been plugged up by partially burned remains of provisions and supply items. It is possible that the side valve for blowing the tanks remained closed either after the completion of the possible repair work conducted before the combat cruise, or it just happened to be closed during the loading of provisions and supply items into compartment seven. While the side valve is closed, the emergency pipe for blowing the port side No. 10 main ballast tank may fail if the temperature is reduced below freezing, due to the so-called "blind effect."

6. *Komsomolets'* superstructure over Compartment Seven

The periscope was raised. The "Bukhta" radar mast was probably raised, although there are no entries to this effect in the ship's log.

The nuclear reactor's emergency shielding was activated at this time. The automatic section switching system deenergized the disconnectable load section of the No. 2 main distribution panel. All systems using electric power supplied by the nondisconnectable load sections of the main distribution panel were switched to storage batteries. The sonar complex was deenergized.

The system of loudspeaker communication with the stern failed. Communications! They are hardly noticed when they are there, and we find ourselves totally helpless when they're not. It is impossible to overstate the harm done to submarine damage control by the absence of communications, and how it influenced the making of particular decisions. Consequently, we need to discuss communications in greater detail.

The Naval Communications Directorate holds a monopoly on all forms of communications, including shipboard. The submarine designer is deprived of the possibility for independently selecting or ordering the form of communications he requires. He is compelled to take what is prescribed to him by this naval directorate. This brings events of almost twenty years ago to mind. Designers were actively opposed to installing the "Listvennitsa" loudspeaker communication system aboard submarines. It was pointed out in this case that the "Kashtan" loudspeaker communication system used earlier was more flexible in control and more dependable in operation, while the new "Listvennitsa" system had practically no advantages. Nonetheless, with some arm-twisting the Naval Communications Directorate forced the designers to accept its newborn "retard" for submarines. The accident aboard the submarine *Komsomolets* provided an evaluation of this system. It showed that even highly reliable two-way telephone communication is not much use in a fire. Numerous short circuits in most of the varied electric circuits create a large level of interference, and for practical purposes, put the system out of commission. The submarine *Komsomolets* was supplied with three portable "Prichal" radio sets in accordance with naval norms, but it is impossible to establish communication among seven compartments with three radio sets. Moreover, as a rule they are stored not where they would be needed, but from where they cannot be stolen. This is not slander but bitter reality.

The question that naturally follows is this: Was it really not until the accident aboard the submarine *Komsomolets* that the complete unreliability of shipboard communication during a fire revealed itself? The answer is no.

Decision No. 702/41/003855 was adopted on August 25, 1983, by the Navy and the USSR Ministry of Shipbuilding Industry after one of a number of submarine accidents. Item 20 of Attachment No. 1 to this decision reads: "To make official the decision of the Navy and the USSR Ministry of Communications Equipment Industry to develop a special intercompartment radio communication station out of the 68RTN-2-4m radio station with devices making it possible to use the radio station while wearing self-contained breathing masks. Responsibility shall be borne by the Naval Communications Directorate, and the deadline shall be the fourth quarter of 1983."

This is something needed by submariners because when they wear breathing masks today they are practically mute and deaf. But nine years have passed, and the bureaucracy is still going around in circles about it. Moreover, the problems of creating a new shipboard loudspeaker communication system based on fiber technology had to be dealt with, though this was after the loss of the *Komsomolets*. Now, agreement has been reached with a certain production association to develop this system. Use of such a communications system would have made it possible to exclude interference and significantly upgrade the quality and reliability of communications, especially during fires. The Naval Communications Directorate became an insurmountable obstacle on the path of creating this shipboard communication system. The Directorate leadership ordered installation of a new shipboard communication system that was already being designed on the basis of an order from the Navy. They are not concerned that the "new system" they proposed is being created out of old components, and that it will have the same deficiencies as the "Listvennitsa" system. And if a shipboard communication system that is highly reliable in the presence of fire comes into being, it will do so not owing to, but despite the efforts of the Naval Communications Directorate.

Where are you, Captain 1st Rank S. I. Bystrov, editor of the naval department of the newspaper *Krasnaya Zvezda*? Where is that photograph of the deceased signalman of the submarine *Komsomolets* you carried in your March 15, 1990, edition of the newspaper with the following text, addressed "to a certain interested party unfortunately standing in opposition to the Navy": "Those who are attempting to cover up their mistakes at the price of accusing the submariners of poor occupational training need only look into the eyes of the deceased"? Send it, please, to the Naval Communications Directorate, and ask the workers of this directorate to look into the eyes of the deceased, and answer this question: When will submariners be supplied with reliable shipboard communication resources?

How did the submarine's leadership react to the abrupt pressure increase in compartment seven and then in compartment six, to Warrant Officer Kolotilin's last report, to the listing to port, to the fall in pressure in the high-pressure air tank groups, to the bleeding of air out of the starboard No. 10 main ballast tanks, and to sloughing off of the lining tiles on the starboard side in the vicinity of this tank? Weren't they able to put all of these processes together to make the appropriate conclusions, to work out, and then to implement the necessary damage control measures? All of these questions have to be answered in the negative.

Throughout the entire time of the accident, the three valves in compartment three that shut off the air lines passing into compartment seven were never closed—that is, the primary step identified in case of fire by Article 59 of the RBZh-FL-82 was not carried out. The requirement of Article 21 of the RBZh-FL-82 to bleed air overboard from a damaged high-pressure air cofferdam was not carried out. The decision to change the lines of defense was not made. No attempt was made to establish the cause of listing to port.

How is all of this explained? The only explanation is the combination of insufficient effort by the crew on damage control problems in the absence of the "Manual on Combat Use of Technical Resources," the crew's poor knowledge of the submarine's equipment, and the low level of crew occupational training. Everyone in BCh-5 saw and heard that air was bleeding into compartment seven, everyone was talking and reporting this to one another, but no one did anything to stop the bleeding. The impression is created that there was not a single person in the entire BCh-5 who knew about the high-pressure air system to even the minimally necessary level.

"We went through the full course of combat training, we prepared several years for our first independent major cruise, we studied at the training center and completed the course problems with good and excellent grades, and we carried out combat exercises. Training was carried out in full correspondence with the guidelines," declared Captain 1st Rank Kolyada in a letter published in the journal *Morskoy Sbornik* (No. 2, 1990). What can be said about this declaration? If people who have undergone the full course of combat training, and who have completed course problems with good and excellent grades, turn out to be so defenseless and incapable of active struggle in the face of an accident, then this means that the course itself, the crew manning system, and the course grading system do not satisfy the necessary level of submariner occupational training. Unfortunately, the naval leaders responsible for crew combat training say everything is all right with the training. They say the crew was trained as it should have been and all pieces of paper confirming this are present. Obviously, in order to change the crew combat training situation we will have to start by replacing the people responsible for this training.

Something should also be said here about the "Submarine Damage

Control Manual" (RBZh-PL-82), the principal document on maintaining the viability of submarines. This "manual," and especially its section on firefighting, is written with an eye on the actions to be taken by personnel in response to a small "clean" accident, that is, without other emergencies superimposed over it. The personnel turn out to be unprepared for complex emergencies. Every submariner knows the golden rule: "If a fire starts, expect an increase in pressure in the compartment; and if pressure begins to fall in a compartment, expect water to flood in." Unfortunately, this rule is not reflected in the RBZh-PL-82, nor does it contain any radical recommendations on forestalling the possible consequences of an accident, including the case of a rise in pressure in a compartment and entry of water into it.

From the ship's log: "1117—Prepare the diesel generator. Telephone communications being established."

The attack center was trying to establish communications with the stern. Compartment six was silent. There was no news from Captain Lieutenant Dvorov.

The command to prepare the diesel generator was given simultaneously. A diesel generator with an emergency starter was installed aboard the submarine *Komsomolets*. In the absence of electric power and high-pressure air, with the hydraulic system not working and with low temperature in the compartment, one person can start up the diesel generator and supply power in not more than ten minutes. It took the crew two hours and sixteen minutes to start up the diesel generator and begin supplying power. And this was with all forms of electric power and high-pressure air available, with the hydraulic system working, and with a normal temperature in the compartment. This fact alone says something about the level of combat training of the crew, and about the quality of the submarine damage control problems in which they had been trained.

From the ship's log:

1118—Man the radar watch. Raise the "Anis," "Kora," "Sintez."
Prepare Signal No. 6. Signal No. 6 ready. Periscope deenergized.
1120—Rescue chamber hatch opened.

The conning (fairwater) hatch and the hatch in the rescue chamber were opened. The time in the ship's log noting when the hatch of the rescue chamber was opened did not coincide with the time of blowing the aft ballast tanks (1114) according to this log. A six-minute difference is too large a difference and cannot be explained. The hatches were opened by the senior member of the hold (below decks) command team, Warrant Officer V. S. Kadantsev. Therefore, here is the time to look at the actions of the senior member of the ready command and his damage control people in compartment three of the submarine. The emergency alarm sounds. What should the personnel of the compartment do?

> RBZh-PL-82, Article 22: The personnel, except for the people located in the casualty compartment, should quickly proceed to their command and combat posts in accordance with the damage control schedule and carry out damage control action, without orders, under the leadership of the Main Command Post.

Warrant Officer V. S. Kadantsev (explanatory note):

> When the emergency alarm sounded, I went to the middle panel in compartment three, surveyed it, and accepted the reports about combat readiness from the hold from Seaman [R. K.] Filippov and from Seaman [A. V.] Machalev. I then reported the compartment's combat readiness to the main command post.

And that's all. Not a word about fulfilling actions without orders as stipulated in Article 91, RBZh-PL-82. What else can a sergeant of the hold command do?

Warrant Officer V. S. Kadantsev (explanatory note):

> By order of the main command post, I arrived at the hatch of the fore chamber and, at a depth of 270 meters, I began opening the hatches of the fore chamber and the lower hatch of the rescue chamber. After rising to the surface, the commander's assistant opened the upper hatch of the rescue chamber in accordance with directions. It was located at the footway. I looked over the submarine and spotted blistering in the region of compartment seven. I received the order to cast off the containers with the rafts from the commander's assistant. At that time Lieutenant Kalinin came to the top [bridge] and said that the "Korund" in the TsP (control room) was burning. Ten to fifteen minutes later I went below.

From Warrant Officer Kadantsev's explanatory notes, it follows that from practically the time of the alarm signal to at least 1132, the sergeant of the hold command and the only damage control specialist in the division knowing the ship's system, was occupied with everything except the damage control of the submarine. This is one of the reasons why full measures were not taken to close off the compartment, as stipulated by Articles 89, 90, 91, and 120 of RBZh-PL-82. Beyond that, the information from Warrant Officer Kadantsev does not coincide with the notes of the ship's log at 1120, which again returns us to the question of a false ship's log or about entering notes that do not correlate with time parameters and factual events.

The submarine was now in cruising position. The radar station was on. Because the disconnectable sections of the main distribution panel were deenergized, there was no power to the periscope turning gear. The radar station cooling system was not working for the same reason. No steps were taken to support its operation. An order was given to raise the communication antenna, but there is no entry in the ship's log of the time at which it was raised. The mechanical raising time is less than one minute. A coded distress signal was prepared for transmission, but it was not transmitted. The distress signal was not transmitted until 1137—that is, twelve minutes after it was prepared.

"Well, here is what I have to say about that," said one person in an anonymous interview with the writer N. Cherkashin. "It was he [division political department chief Captain 1st Rank T. A. Burkulakov—D.R.] who insisted that the message about the fire should be radioed immediately. He's not one of those who always believes that something that might prove embarrassing shouldn't be broadcast over the air waves. The fact that he did not delay with the report is what saved everyone taken off of the raft."[1] It follows from this that the delay in transmitting the signal about the accident may have been even longer. But Captain 1st Rank Kolyada believes that everything was done properly: "If the commander had lost it [composure] or issued incorrect orders, I as the senior officer aboard would have been obligated to assume command. . . . There was no need for such actions: Vanin made good decisions. In any case, the same ones I would have made. Therefore, my participation in ship damage control was limited only to advice."[2] However, Captain 1st Rank Kolyada asserts in a report sent to the commander of the Northern Fleet that the distress signal was transmitted at 1120. This is inconsistent with reality, and says something only about the absence of any justifiable motives for delaying transmission of the distress signal. It would not make any sense to go into the moral side of the issue again.

When was the distress signal received and fully decoded?

Fleet Admiral V. N. Chernavin:

I was suddenly summoned and told that the headquarters of the Northern Fleet and the Main Naval Staff received a signal from the submarine at 1141. It was highly distorted, making it difficult to sort it out. However, it was already clear that some sort of misfortune had occurred. . . . At 1219 a clear signal was received from it, after which it became immediately clear as to what submarine this was, its location, and that there was a fire aboard it."[3]

Such is the official time the Navy received and fully decoded the distress signal.

How truthful are these data?

Lieutenant A. V. Zaytsev (explanatory report):

> We managed to open the fittings of the ventilation system by means of the hydraulic system, and raise the retractable "Kora" and "Anis" devices, but we were unable to raise the "Sintez" system completely.

Captain 1st Rank B. G. Kolyada (interrogation tape recording):

> The communications antenna was raised, but the hydraulic system began losing pressure right then. We managed to transmit the "sixth" signal three times with the "Kora" antenna.

Captain Lieutenant A. G. Verezgov (interrogation tape recording):

> There is another thing I remember about surfacing: We were listing to port, and the antennas began sagging under their own weight; it was apparent that the hydraulic system pumps had stopped. I asked if communication was still open so that I could bring up the emergency radio set in time.

Warrant Officer V. S. Kadantsev (explanatory report):

> At this time I saw from the warning signals on the "Molybden" console that the signal indicating the minimum level in the tank of the ship's hydraulic system lit up, indicating a loss of hydraulic fluid. On orders from the commander of BCh-5, I descended to the pumping unit and saw through the peephole that the tank was empty. I closed the starboard and port pressure valve switches.

I ascended to the attack center and reported fulfillment of the order. At this time the radar operators inquired as to the position of their retractable devices. At my suggestion the commander of BCh-5 gave orders to close the manual valves on the retractable devices, which is what I did.

It was in this way that hydraulic fluid was lost from the ship's hydraulic system because of the attack center's failure to implement the primary measure in a fire—shutting off the hydraulic lines leading into the distressed compartment (Article 89, RBZh-PL-82).

As was mentioned above, the distress signal was not transmitted for the first time until 1137. At this time the communication antennae began sagging, and this may have been why the distress signal was not fully decoded the first time around. It was only after the eighth transmission of the distress signal (the eighth!), at 1219, that it was decoded. Thus, the submarine's leadership made yet another fateful mistake, which placed the lives of most of the crew in jeopardy. How can the delay in transmitting the distress signal be justified? It is impossible to justify it.

We could have ended our discussion of signal No. 6 with this, but . . .

The operations duty officer for the Northern Fleet's command post, Captain 1st Rank V. I. Goncharuk, said, "At 1141 the ship's command transmitted the distress signal, which was received by the fleet's command post without delay."[4] And not a single word about the incompletely decoded signal. It follows from this report that the distress signal was received immediately and completely, without distortion.

There is still more evidence that the emergency signal was immediately received without distortion.

"1154—The crew of Major Gennady Petrogradsky rose to the alarm. It was announced to use all the rescue strength of the air Navy, but first this crew had to get into the air. On the KP [control panel] the task appeared: In the region of Medvezhi Island a fire has erupted on a Soviet submarine."[5] Maybe the atmosphere conditions hindered the passing of the signals? No, it was not hindered.

"The day before it had been very hard to receive signals. But now all is normal. The connection from the shore is reliable."[6]

Who in the naval leadership will shed some light on this question?

What was the subsequent course of events in organizing the rescue of the submariners? It was not until 1242—one hour and twenty-four minutes after signal No. 6 was ready to be transmitted—that the operations duty officer of the Northern Fleet queried the Sevryba Association for information on the location of the fishing vessels. Nothing is known about what the command of the Northern Fleet did from 1219 to 1242 (and perhaps from 1141 to 1242). A fateful mistake was superimposed over fateful irresponsibility. Had this not been the case, the tender *Aleksey Khlobystov* may have begun moving one hour and twenty minutes sooner, and reached the accident site before the submarine's loss. The lives of most of the submariners would have been saved.

In light of these facts, what is the worth of the assurances and promises of the Naval Command that all measures to rescue the submariners had supposedly been implemented? Given such irresponsibility, neither Norwegian nor any other foreign rescue services can help us. We need to clean up our own act first.

8.

"Connect Up to the Stationary Emergency Breathing System!"

From the ship's log: "1121—Fire in compartment four. Pump starting station burning. Sparking and smoking. Deenergized. Smoke concentration and gas content in compartment four normal."

What happened in compartment four? Lieutenant A. V. Makhota (explanatory report):

> I heard the control room try to raise compartment five by telephone. The rack-and-pinion turned from the compartment five side, and [M. N.] Valyavin took hold of it. It was at this moment that a sheaf of sparks flew out of the starting station at the No.1 pump of the first loop, and dense white smoke billowed out. I reported the fire in the compartment to the control room, after which communication was broken, but they managed to receive my report and deenergize the starting station. The fire stopped, but the compartment was extremely smoky. It was then that I gave the command to prepare to abandon the compartment, and then to abandon it for compartment three (this is what we did in practicing damage control in case of fire in compartment four because of the absence of individual protective equipment). Upon opening the bulkhead door leading to compartment three, we saw through the airlock porthole that there was a fire in compartment three as well (it was smoky in there). We returned to com-

partment four, and I gave the command to enter the instrument
enclosure, in which we sealed ourselves. We remained in the instrument enclosure for about an hour.

From the regulations:

> RBZh-PL-82, Article 23: No one shall have the right to aban-
> don a distressed compartment independently. Personnel shall be
> moved out of a distressed compartment only on orders from the
> control room into the compartment designated by it.

Thus, Lieutenant Makhota's and Warrant Officer Valyavin's lack of
individual protective equipment resulted in violation of the RBZh-PL-82. Later
on, by being in the instrument enclosure, for practical purposes they sidelined
themselves from the submarine damage control efforts. Moreover, the control
room was forced to send a damage control party to free them from the instrument enclosure. The visit by Lieutenant Makhota and Warrant Officer Valyavin
to compartment three remained unnoted, which says that a line of defense had
not been organized at the aft bulkhead of compartment three, despite the order issued by the attack center at 1113. Yet another indication of the level of
the mastery of submarine damage control!

Captain Lieutenant I. S. Orlov (interrogation tape recording):

> Circulation pump No. 1 of the first loop was working at low
> speed. A fire broke out there. Compartment four commander
> Engineer Makhota made the report. He reported that the start-
> ing station of pump No. 1 was burning. I don't know how, but it
> was still working.

Designer recommendations drawn up in conjunction with compiling
the "Manual on Combat Use of Technical Resources" state that when a fire
occurs in compartment seven, the two cables (ten strands) of the control and
blocking circuits of the starting station of circulation pump No. 1 of the first
loop had to be disconnected. Because of the absence of this manual, personnel
of compartment four did not know which cables had to be disconnected, and
they did not practice this operation in damage-control training exercises. As
soon as the control circuits of the high-speed winding were damaged by the
fire in compartment seven, the semiconductor rectifier bridge of the starting
station failed, producing sparks and ejecting smoke. After this the pump continued to work at low speed. The entry regarding this in the ship's log does not

correspond to reality. Nor is the filling up of compartment four with smoke reflected accurately in it.

From the ship's log: "1122—Fifth compartment pressurized. Close shut-offs one and two. Charge the SDS in three.[1] Smoke spewing from the 'Korund' [rudder control system]. Deenergize the 'Korund.'"

The fire continued to burn in the aft compartments, and its consequences began to be felt in the control room. The submarine had already been around ten minutes without propulsion, and rudder control was gone. However, the "Korund" rudder control system was still receiving power. And it was not long before the cost of this mistake made itself known—the stand of the "Korund" console caught fire in compartment seven as a result of a short. The submarine's personnel were forced to charge the stationary breathing system and connect up to the ShDA apparatus[2], which significantly complicated further damage control aboard ship.

Here is how Vice Admiral V. V. Zaytsev, chief of the Navy's Main Directorate for Operation and Repair, evaluated the actions of the personnel during this period in his conclusion to the "Analysis of the Actions of Personnel," written by a group of specialists of the N. G. Kuznetsov Naval Academy under the leadership of Vice Admiral Y. D. Chernov:

> At 1122 the transformer block servicing the "Korund" system's rudder position indicators caught fire in the control room. Compartment three filled with gas, and so the attack center was compelled to carry out the subsequent submarine damage control actions while wearing individual protective equipment. Knowing the situation, and having made certain that the rudder control failed, the control room was obligated to give the command to deenergize the "Korund." This was not done, however.

It should be said that this was not the sole source of smoke in compartment three. Smoky gases also entered the compartment through the carbon dioxide removal line, the air line of the submarine's trim system, the high-pressure air remote control system, and the hydraulic system drain line. These lines were not closed when the damage control alarm was signaled, as is required by Articles 89, 90 and 91 of the RBZh-PL-82. Smoke gases entered compartment two from compartment seven via the carbon dioxide removal line and the oxygen feed line, which also were not closed. Thus, the personnel of compartment two were also forced to connect up to ShDA apparatus.

Warrant Officer V. S. Kadantsev (supplement to explanatory notes):

About twenty minutes later I went down into the hold and inspected it. In the region of the fore bulkheads on the right side of the air system valves of the trim system there was a strong release of air and this area was covered in black soot. I understood it was necessary to ease the air out of compartment seven through numbers three and four pressure equalizing tanks using the valves of the extracting glands for compartment three.

Warrant Officer Kadantsev did not see air coming through "the valves of the extracting glands of compartment three," in the trim system, but only from afar he "understood" it to be so. In the air of the main trim system, there were appropriate fittings designed for the conditional pressure of 100 kg/cm^2, which would practically exclude any possibility of using valves of the "extracting glands" under the pressure that was present in compartment seven at the time of the accident. Besides that, there were safety valves installed on the main valves in compartment three that were built for a pressure of 3.5 kg/cm^2. During the fire, the hermetic air seal at the main was lost and smoky gas began to enter it. When the pressure in compartment seven was higher than 3.5 kg/cm^2, the safety valves stopped working and the smoky gas began to enter compartment three. Warrant Officer Kadantsev noticed this smoky gas escaping through the safety valve. It can also be added that the emergency valves of the main air system were situated so that the main from the accident compartment was located under the plane (horizontal location) of the valve. This allows for a reliable cut-off of the main from the accident compartment even with "equalizing glands" at the valves. Furthermore, the warrant officer had no basis on which to assess the varying pressures of the equalizing trim tanks.

Addressing the inactiveness of the sergeant of the hold command: He sees the location where the smoky gas is being released and does nothing to determine the cause or to stop this release. To close the second valve to cut off the master air system from the accident compartment in the first minutes after the alarm and to do everything you can without orders; that is the objective of reporting "compartment three ready for combat."

None of this can be explained by poor knowledge of the submarine's matériel systems. The absence of any kind of organization during the damage control efforts is obvious. Everyone was running around, no one was giving concrete orders, and the crew did not know what to do in ship damage control. The absence of the "Manual on Combat Use of Technical Resources," which should have indicated the specific actions to be taken by the personnel to shut these lines, also had its effect.

In order to justify the passiveness and incompetent actions of the attack center, the Naval Institute Number One "invented" a postulate that was scientific in form but incompetent and harmful in its essence, yet was accepted by the armament leadership of the Navy. Here is how it is stated by Fleet Admiral V. N. Chernavin, the naval commander in chief, in the journal *Morskoy Sbornik* (No. 12, 1990).

> The act of the State Commission noted a peculiarity of this accident—an extremely rare simultaneous occurance of two factors that determined the high intensity and swiftness of development of the fire. These were the advent of a fire, followed by the breach of the tightness of an air line, which occurred close in time to the former. This convergence of circumstances, which required fundamentally conflicting actions by the crew—sealing off the compartments in response to the fire and unsealing them in the event of excess air pressure—significantly complicated the submarine damage control efforts.

How is this postulate incompetent and harmful?

First of all, this is not "an extremely rare simultaneous occurrence of two factors," or a "convergence of circumstances," but the logical develop-

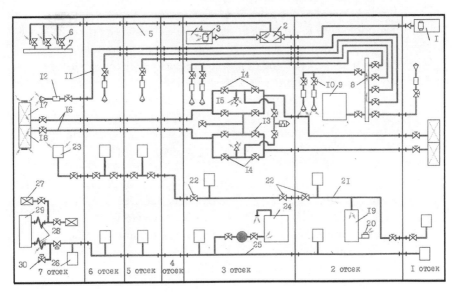

7. Sources of smoke and gas into Compartments Two and Three

ment of the accident due to the passive and incompetent actions of the submarine's leadership. Not less than fifteen minutes separate the moment that the fire broke out in compartment seven and the entry of the first injection of air into the compartment in response to the blowing of the aft group of main ballast tanks, which only to the layman can be thought of as events occurring "close in time."

Second, no "fundamentally conflicting actions" were required of the crew. Under these circumstances compartment seven should have been sealed off in order to preclude the spread of the fire and of smoke gases into other compartments. Simultaneously, there should have been controlled relief of excess pressure from the distressed compartment through one of the ship systems (preferably through the ship's pumping system) with the purpose of reducing the intensity of the fire and ensuring the strength of the bulkheads of the distressed compartment. None of this was done aboard the submarine.

Third, in concealing the truth, the authors of this postulate unwittingly introduced the harmful and mistaken idea into the consciousness of submariners that when accidents occur, there may be circumstances which create dead-end, impossible situations—that is, they demoralize and disarm submariners regarding accidents before the fact.

But let's return to the submarine *Komsomolets*.

The commands to open the first and second shut-offs of the exhaust line of the fore and aft rings of the ship's ventilation system were given simultaneously.

As soon as the "Korund" console caught fire, an announcement was transmitted through the ship: "Damage control alarm! Fire in compartment three!" There are no entries to this effect in the ship's log. However, the testimony of crew members and the logic of the development of subsequent events permit the categorical assertion that such an alarm signal was sounded after 1122.

Warrant Officer A. M. Kopeyka (explanatory report):

> A damage control alarm, a fire, was announced, the "Korund"
> control console was burning in compartment three, this was com-
> municated to us by the BCh-1 (navigation department) com-
> mander Captain Lieutenant [M. A.] Smirnov, because the loud-
> speaker communication alarm line failed, while communication
> with the navigator's console was still functioning.

Warrant Officer V. V. Gerashchenko (interrogation tape recording):

Everything happened so fast. An order was given for everyone to connect up to the ShDA. A few minutes later the navigator told me over the "Listvennitsa": "Fire in compartment three, 'Korund' [the rudder control console] burning." Ventilation and cooling were lost right away, and "temperature exceeded" warning lights appeared. I reported this to the navigator.

In response to the command "Damage control alarm! Fire in compartment three!" personnel of compartment two deenergized the distribution panel RShchN No. 7 of compartment three in accordance with requirements of Article 91 of the RBZh-PL-82.

The command apparently also reached compartment five, and complying with the requirements of Article 91 of the RBZh-PL-82, the personnel of this compartment deenergized distribution panel RShchN No. 6 in compartment three.

This forces doubt in the truthfulness of the deposition concerning the lack of a connection between compartment five and the main command post. Apparently, the telephone "twin connection" functioned with interruptions to the compartment during the course of the entire accident.

The fact that distribution panels RShchN No. 7 and 6 were disconnected is confirmed by Warrant Officer A. M. Kopeyka (explanatory report):

> . . . the second ventilation ring was working, but the temperature kept increasing, because it was not tied in [that is, not connected—D.R.] to all instrument stands. When we requested power to RShchN No. 7/1 and RShchN No. 6/1 in order to supply the main ventilation ring, no one could [act to supply the power].

Distribution panels RShchN No. 7/1 and 6/1 receive power from distribution panel RShchN No. 7 and 6, respectively.

Thus, not only the electric fan of the first (main) ring of the navigation complex's cooling system but also the electric pump of the diesel generator's cooling system, the exhaust fans of the ship's general ventilation system, and the electric fan of the cooling system of the combat data-processing and control system were left without electric power. This was one of the reasons why an order to stop the diesel generator was given at 1145. Because of this, it was impossible to begin venting compartment three in time, and for a long time the control room personnel were forced to wear ShDA apparatus, which made submarine damage control difficult. Nor could venting of the aft compartments be started in time.

Concluding our examination of this issue, we should say that after the fire in the "Korund" console was extinguished, the attack center did not transmit the command "All clear from the damage control alarm 'Fire in compartment three!,'" and it did not order delivery of power to distribution panels RShchN No. 7 and 6, which was another mistake by the submarine's leadership.

Testimony by Warrant Officer Kopeyka regarding the work of the second cooling ring of the navigation system needs to be clarified. The electric fan of the second cooling ring is supplied from sections of the disconnectable load of the main distribution panels; it was deenergized immediately after the reactor's emergency shielding was activated. Considering that instruments of the navigation system connected to the second ring were cooled by means of an open ventilation cycle, the temperature conditions of these instruments were "milder" during the accident because of natural air circulation than the temperature experienced by instruments that were connected to the first ring, which were cooled by means of a closed ventilation cycle. This apparently created the illusion to the warrant officer that the second ring of the navigation system instrument cooling system was working.

Pressure began to rise in compartment five.

Lieutenant A. V. Zaytsev (supplement to explanatory report):

Monitoring air pressure in the submarine's compartments, at the moment the fire began at the "Korund" control console I noticed an insignificant rise in pressure in compartment five, on the order of 0.5 kg/cm^2.

Captain Lieutenant S. A. Dvorov (interrogation tape recording):

I was in constant communication, and I gave the command for all of the men to stay in the central passage. It was very steamy in the vicinity of the turbopump circulating units, and my glasses were fogging over. The temperature grew. All of the men were connected up to IPs.[3] The pressure began increasing to 2.5 kilograms. We switched over to IDA-59 equipment. The pressure continued to rise.

A clarification is needed here. In his explanatory report Captain Lieutenant Dvorov made reference to pressure in compartment five equal not to

2.5 kg/cm^2 but only 0.5, and this was apparently the case. In addition, according to the RBZh-PL-82, IP-6 self-contained breathing protective masks may be used only to an excess pressure of not more than 0.2 kg/cm^2 in compartments. When the personnel put on the face masks of the IDA-59 self-contained breathing apparatus, two of them were torn, which is why Seaman V. Y. Kulapin and Warrant Officer S. S. Bondar were forced to hook up to ShDA apparatus, which predetermined their subsequent fate.

Who Discharged the Air-Foam Fire Extinguisher System?

From the ship's log: "1123—'Bukhta' operating ten minutes without cooling. Deenergize 'Sinus.' Deenergize 'Korund.'"

The "Bukhta" radar station was working without cooling. In a little while it would be disconnected as well. From this moment on, the submarine would be left without electronic observation resources.

The command was given to deenergize the "Sinus"—the power supply system of the submarine's automatic equipment control system. There was no need to deenergize the entire power supply system of the automatic equipment control system in order to put out the fire in the "Korund" console. For this, it would have been enough to deenergize the "Korund" system. When the "Sinus" system is deenergized, remote control and monitoring of all of the submarine's technical resources are lost, with the exception of the reactor's emergency shielding and certain especially important ship systems supporting ship damage-control efforts (such as the emergency main ballast tank blowing system). It is not known if this command was carried out. The entry "Deenergize 'Korund'" should be understood, due to the illegibly written suffix, as "'Korund' deenergized." The command to deenergize the "Korund" system had been given at 1122.

The State Commission Working Group, on the basis of experimental work already conducted, considered that at that time (around 1124) the blow-control valve spontaneously opened and the supply of air entered into compartment seven due to the melting of the polyamide stopper on the impulse

group plates. All the remaining air from the bulkhead VVD was contaminated
in the compartment and in main ballast tanks No. 8, 9, and 10 after two to three
minutes. However, the assertion of the working group was neither confirmed
by notes in the ship's log nor by witnesses from members of the crew; it is hard
to imagine that the spontaneous blowing of the main ballast tank would go
unnoticed. Besides that, this assumption is contradicted by the notes in the
ship's log concerning the blowing of the aft main ballast tanks at 1134.

From the ship's log:

> 1127—VPL[1] delivered to "Korund." Shut-offs one and two
> opened. Fire extinguisher brought to TsP (Control Room). Open
> flames have appeared on the "Korund." Gas concentration and
> visibility in TsP rising [sic]. VPL recharging in first. Out of the
> TsVK.[2] Burning in vicinity of seventh.

Lieutenant A. V. Tretyakov (supplement to explanatory report):

> The fire in compartment three was put out as follows: Captain
> 1st Rank Burkulakov noticed smoke coming from the "Korund."
> Then came the command "Everyone connect up to personal pro-
> tective equipment! Begin fighting the fire with the VPL!" Taking
> a socket wrench Captain Lieutenant [Y. V.] Naumenko unfastened
> the lid from the console, where he saw flames licking out. The
> VPL dispenser and hose were carried over.

They were unable to put out the console fire. It turns out that the VPL
system was discharged.

Lieutenant A. V. Zaytsev (interrogation tape recording): "We tried to
use fire extinguishers. The first produced a little foam, and then went dead. If it
had produced normal foam, the fire would have been put out completely."

We don't know if other fire extinguishers were used as well, but one
thing is clear—it cannot be said that the quality of the submarine crew's preparation for the cruise was high. Because there turned out to be nothing with
which to put out the "Korund" console fire, a command was given to recharge
the VPL station in compartment one.

According to Article 91 of RBZh-PL-82, in case of fire the personnel
must monitor the status of the VPL station and recharge it promptly without
orders from the attack center. However, personnel of compartment one did
not monitor the status of the VPL station and did not recharge it promptly,

which made it impossible to immediately put out the fire in the console of the "Korund" rudder control system.

Warrant Officer S. R. Grigoryan (supplement to explanatory report):

> VPL was recharged in compartment one in response to a command from the TsP. During recharging I noticed that the VPL pressure was 15 kg/cm², while before the regulator it was 150 kg/cm². And the pressure steadily decreased."

The fire in compartment seven continued. Air from the medium-pressure air line, and possibly from the outboard air line, continued to feed it. No one took any steps to stop the bleeding of air into the distressed compartment. At this time a report of steam buildup in the vicinity of compartment seven was transmitted from the bridge—this is the only possible interpretation of the ship's log entry presented above. Lining plates (tiles) began separating away from the starboard side of the submarine's outer hull in the vicinity of main ballast tank No. 10, which was noted by Captain Lieutenant Verezgov. It may be supposed that entry of smoke from the digital computer complex also was discovered at this time.

And while they are recharging the VPL system in compartment one, let's analyze why the system was uncharged. There was no unanimous opinion in this regard in the State Commission Working Group. Industrial representatives believed that the VPL system had been discharged by the watchstander for compartment seven as he fought the fire. Naval representatives asserted that the VPL system was discharged in compartment five after combustible gases ignited within it. The ship's log has no entry regarding such a deflagration in compartment five. Nor was the time of this deflagration noted in Captain Lieutenant Dvorov's testimony. When questioned by the State Commission, he reported that the deflagration occurred ten to fifteen minutes before normalization of pressure in compartment five; that is, in the period from 1151 to 1156, since according to the ship's log, pressure was cut off from compartments four and five from 1206 to 1218. It is stated in an explanatory report written later on that the deflagration occurred ten to fifteen minutes after the alarm, that is, in the period from 1116 to 1121.

Warrant Officer V. S. Kadantsev (explanatory report):

> While the temperature of the bulkhead between compartments five and six was being measured, the VPL reel was unwound in the central passage of compartment five. There was a puddle of

brown water beside the bell mouth, and air was hissing out from it. It was the same with the reel in the enclosure of the turbocirculation pump unit. I shut the valves.

It follows from Warrant Officer Kadantsev's report that the VPL line was leaking in compartment seven, and that air was passing from it into compartment five. Moreover, the last time the VPL system was used was in compartment five; otherwise foam would have streamed out of the open hoses after the VPL system was recharged, and personnel in compartment five would have noticed this, and shut the valves. The fire in the "Korund" control console was extinguished at 1137. Consequently, the VPL system in compartment five had already been used prior to this time. We should add to this that because of high pressure in compartment seven (around 10-12 kg/cm^2, practically no foam was expended in that compartment during this period.

Captain Lieutenant S. A. Dvorov (supplement to explanatory report): "When the fire started in the compartment, I personally reported the fire in the compartment to the TsP on the damage control telephone, but I got no answer from the GKP."

Lieutenant A. V. Zaytsev (explanatory report):

Immediately after surfacing, the "Korund" console began smoking in the control room. Captain Lieutenant Naumenko and I started putting it out. It was reported from compartment five that there was a fire in compartment five. After VPL station No. 1 was recharged, the fire in the "Korund" control console was put out.

Lieutenant A. V. Zaytsev (supplement to explanatory report):

Fires were reported from compartments four and five almost simultaneously with putting out the fire in the "Korund" console. The report from compartment four indicated the specific place of the fire. Information regarding the fire in compartment five was provided by the executive officer and the BCh-5 commander.

Captain 1st Rank B. G. Kolyada (interrogation tape recording):

There was no communication with compartment five, and we did not learn of the fire in it until the compartment was opened.

The commander of compartment five reported that they had a fully involved fire.

How do we reconcile the contradictory reports by Lieutenant Zaytsev and Captain 1st Rank Kolyada? Especially if we consider that in the supplement to his explanatory report, Lieutenant Zaytsev clearly "tried harder" to please the naval leadership. During the time that the fire in the "Korund" console was being put out, it could not have been that "fires were reported from compartments four and five almost simultaneously," since the report of fire in the starting station of the first loop pump in compartment four was received by the attack center before the fire started in the "Korund" console, which is documented in the ship's log. This fact casts doubt upon Zaytsev's testimony regarding a fire in compartment five. Still, the submarine command did apparently receive the report of a deflagration in compartment five.

Was information on the fire in compartment five reflected in the actions of the submarine command? Let's look at the ship's log:

> 1146—Report temperature in compartment five.
> 1147—Lines of defense in compartment four—fore and aft bulkheads, in three—the aft bulkhead.

These entries in the ship's log are nothing other than a reaction by the submarine command to the report they received of a deflagration in compartment five. Simultaneously, this is documented confirmation concerning the functioning of the telephone "twin connection" between the fifth compartment and the main command post. We can categorically assume from these entries that the deflagration occurred in compartment five at around 1146. Thus, Senior Seaman N. O. Bukhnikashvili, the watchstander for compartment seven, not only reported the fire but also fought it using the VPL system, as a result of which the system was discharged. Pay attention reader! Captain Lieutenant Dvorov writes about the use of the VPL system in compartment five only in supplements to the explanatory notes.

Captain Lieutenant S. A. Dvorov (supplement to explanatory notes):

> The VPL system was used to extinguish the fire in compartment five. When the valve to the reel and the valve to the disperator were opened, air came first, then condensed fluid, and only then steady foam. VPL was used to extinguish the clothes of the personnel and the flames in the compartment which were igniting

the paint on the electrical panels and the bilge of the compartment.

The captain lieutenant's information requires a thorough look at the discrepancies of the possible capabilities of the VPL. Yet this is what Dvorov said during his interrogation by the State Commission.

Captain Lieutenant S. A. Dvorov (interrogation tape recording): "There was a sheet of flames, clothes and hair caught fire, and after a minute it was gone. People extinguished their clothes."

Warrant Officer V. S. Kadantsev also wrote about the unwinding of the VPL reel only in the supplements to the explanatory notes.

So far as the versions concerning the use of the VPL, the watchstander of compartment seven refutes the statements of the Navy concerning the extent of the fire in compartment seven, not excluding that these supplements to the explanatory notes from Dvorov and Kadantsev do not correspond with the actions and analysis of the leaders of the divisions and the Flotilla of the Northern Fleet.

It is necessary to go on at such length about all of this simply because the naval members of the State Commission Working Group, who ignored the facts, insisted upon the legend of a "fully involved fire" from the very beginning of the accident, and asserted that the VPL system had been discharged by personnel of compartment five.

10

List Control

RBZh-PL-82, Article 84:

> When the main ballast tanks are damaged but water does not enter the pressure hull of a surfaced submarine, one can right the submarine in accordance with documents on keeping a damaged submarine afloat and the RBITS. Then one must monitor the submarine's attitude more closely, blowing as necessary as the undamaged main ballast tanks, not equipped with Kingston valves, fill from wave action.

As was mentioned earlier, the "Manual on Combat Use of Technical Resources" (RBITS) had not been written for the submarine *Komsomolets* by Naval Institute Number One. The submarine's attitude (fore and aft trim) was not monitored during the entire accident.

From the ship's log: "1134—List to port increasing. Main ballast tank blown, list eight."

Another mistake by the attack center. Pressure in compartment seven was growing due to entry of air into it from the medium-pressure air (VSD), outboard air (VZY), and 200 kg/cm² high-pressure air (VVD-200) lines. Hot air, together with combustion products, entered the starboard main ballast tank No. 10 through the damaged emergency blow line and purged the tank. This caused the list to port to grow. The submarine command did not even try to determine the reason for the increasing list. No one checked the status of the ballast tanks. Instead of this, they repeatedly blew the end groups of the main ballast tanks. They uselessly expended the high-pressure air reserve and added fresh air to compartment seven, which intensified the fire. There are no grounds for asserting that, even after this repeated blowing, the valves of the emergency blow system of the aft group of main ballast tanks, located on air cofferdam No. 4 in compartment seven, opened spontaneously, because the watch officer at the bridge did not note spontaneous blowing of these tanks.

From the ship's log:

> 1136—VPL delivered a second time to "Korund."
>
> 1137—Transmit damage control signal. "Korund" fire put out. Damage control signal transmitted. Open supply line's clack valve.

The VPL system was recharged, and the fire in the "Korund" console was put out with it. The damage control signal was prepared for transmission nineteen minutes previously, but it was not until this time that it was first transmitted. The consequences of this delay have already been discussed. There was a great deal of smoke in the attack center and all of compartment three. It was impossible to start up the exhaust fan of the forward ring of the ship ventilation system because of the absence of power at distribution panel RShchN No. 7. Because of the lack of cooling, the diesel generator was operating at low rpm, and it was unable to remove smoke gases from compartment three. Under these conditions the submarine's leadership apparently decided to start up the electric supply fan of the forward ring of the ship ventilation system, and gave the command to open the outer clack valve on the ventilation supply line.

Lieutenant A. V. Zaytsev (explanatory note): "It was impossible to start up the supply fans."

The electric supply fans of the ship ventilation system received electric power from disconnectable load sections of the main distribution panels; they were deenergized after the reactor's emergency shielding was activated. The command to open the clack valves was apparently not carried out.

From the ship's log:

> 1141—List increasing.
>
> 1142—No communication with six. Command to open clack valve transmitted from three to four by tapping on wall.
>
> 1143—Clack valve opened on exhaust. . . . Four and five. List correcting itself.

The attack center is still unaware of the fire in compartment six. This is the only way that the entry regarding absence of communication with it can be interpreted. It is unclear in this case how Captain Lieutenant Dvorov could be so certain that he reported the fire in compartment six to the command.

At the same time the command to open the clack valve of the exhaust ventilation system between compartments four and five was transmitted to compartment four by tapping on the wall; opening the valve would reduce pressure from compartment five through the exhaust line of the forward ring of the ship ventilation system. But there was no one to carry out this command, because Lieutenant Makhota and Warrant Officer Valyavin were helpless in the instrument enclosure.

How do we interpret the two conflicting entries differing by two minutes: "List increasing" and "List correcting itself"? What was done by the personnel to correct the list? The ship's log is silent about this. Lieutenant Zaytsev, the operator of the "Molybden" console, is also silent. And what do the other participants of the tragedy have to say? Here are two explanatory reports:

Captain Lieutenant I. S. Orlov:

> There was a report "No. 1 TsNPK station is burning" from compartment four, after which there was no more communication. My subsequent actions were as follows: While monitoring the cooling process, in response to a command from BCh-5 commander Captain Lieutenant [S. A.] Nezhutin and I, the commander of the remote control division, opened and closed the vent valves of the starboard main ballast tank No. 5 to correct the list manually.

Warrant Officer V. S. Kadantsev: "When the submarine surfaced, it was listing to port, the starboard main ballast tank No. 5 and the starboard main ballast tank No. 7 were filled."

Flooding of the starboard main ballast tank No. 7 will be discussed later on; now let's analyze the matter of the starboard main ballast tank No. 5. The hydraulic drives of the vent valves of this tank (shut-offs one and two) are located practically beneath the chair of the operator of the main propulsion unit console; quite naturally, therefore, console operator Captain Lieutenant Orlov should have helped to open the tank vent valves. At the end of the tragedy Warrant Officer Kadantsev personally blew the starboard main ballast tank No. 5 on orders from the BCh-5 commander. In this connection there are no grounds for believing the testimony of Orlov and Kadantsev.

And so, in order to correct the list to port the decision to flood the starboard main ballast tank No. 5 was made in the attack center. What can be said about this decision? First of all, a list of even 8 degrees is not dangerous from the standpoint of maintaining the submarine's transverse equilibrium, and sacrificing buoyancy reserve to reduce it is highly inappropriate. Second, before the submarine's list was corrected, the reason for it should have been clarified, which was not done. Third, neither the instructions nor the training manual recommend correcting list by flooding the ballast tank in the middle group. In this case, if the decision had been made to correct the ship's list, the ballast tank of the forward group should have been flooded. This would have made it possible not only to correct the list but also to trim the submarine. The main danger to a submarine is the loss not of transverse but of longitudinal equilibrium (stability). Hence, on the whole, the decision of the submarine command to flood the starboard main ballast tank No. 5 was incompetent.

Nonetheless, the starboard main ballast tank No. 5 was flooded, but the list was not corrected—on the contrary, it increased somewhat. This must be the interpretation of the entries in the ship's log for the period from 1141 to 1143.

Why did this happen? Prior to the accident the submarine was at a depth of 386 meters. At this depth, main ballast tank No. 5 should have been connected for blowing by powder gas generators. During the emergency surfacing, and in all probability, "Molybden" console operator Lieutenant Zaytsev did not connect the tank to the high-pressure air blowing line, and the submarine surfaced with main ballast tank No. 5 unblown. When the vent valves were opened, water from the tanks on the starboard side drained off down to the water line, which resulted in a certain increase in list to port. This was apparently so much of a surprise to the attack center that it tempered its eagerness to fight listing for a long time. In addition, the carelessness in blowing the tank is, in all probability, the main reason why Lieutenant Zaytsev concealed the fact of flooding of starboard main ballast tank No. 5.

11.

Fire in Compartment Five

What happened in compartment five after pressure in it increased to 0.5 kg/cm² and continued to increase? Let's listen to tape recordings of the interrogation.

Captain Lieutenant S. A. Dvorov:

At this moment a major explosion or fully developed fire—I don't know what to call it—arose in compartment five. Blue flames shot along the entire passage from the fore to the aft bulkhead as from a flamethrower from a height of one meter above the deck all the way up to the overhead. As the sheaf of flame passed by, clothing and hair caught fire, and a minute later it was gone. The people put out the burning clothing. Serious burns were suffered by Volkov [his hands] and others. The fire traveled from bow to stern along the central passage. I believe that this was oil vapor, possibly from oil tanks of the TTsNA [not further identified] turbopump units. That's what I think.

Question: Where did the oil vapor come from?

Answer: I think through the oil tank venting system. Nothing was switched.

Question: What do you estimate the temperature to have been prior to that major explosion?

Answer: At first it was not very high, not less than 50 degrees

Celsius, but after the deflagration Kolya Volkov's mask melted. There was no smoldering or fire below. After the explosion we were in the central passage. I believe that the explosion occurred when I switched off the turbopump unit's oil pump. . . . Pressure dropped after the explosion, coming to normal ten to fifteen minutes after the explosion. Visibility in the smoke was 1 to 1.5 meters.

Seaman Y. V. Kozlov:

There was no fire. There was no intense flame. It was like a deflagration. I can't explain this. Lying on my right side, I could see from the corner of my eye that something passed by, there was a bluish deflagration. It took about a second. It burned my hand.

What was the cause of the deflagration in compartment five? There are two versions regarding this question. In one, oil vapor caught fire. This is possible only if hot gases entered one of the oil tanks of the TTsNA turbopump units from compartment seven through the oil separation line, which may not have been reset to its initial position after operation (before the accident). These gases may have heated the oil, and its vapor may have been carried through ventilation pipes into the central passage of compartment five. According to the other version, ignition of incomplete combustion products passing from compartment six to compartment five occurred. Naval representatives in the State Commission Working Group believe in this case that incomplete combustion products entered through the suction system's line and through seals in the TTsNA turbopump units, and lay responsibility for this ignition upon the designer, because this line cannot be shut off from the direction of compartment five (this design error was discussed earlier).

It is true that this pipeline, which has a diameter of 50 millimeters, cannot be shut from the direction of compartment five. It can be shut only from the direction of compartment six. This is an obvious design error. This issue also has another side: had the first and second crew of the submarine practiced the task of damage control, this design error would have been revealed right away and then corrected. However, the 300-millimeter diameter lines carrying spent steam from the TTsNA turbopump units could have been shut both from the direction of compartment six and from the direction of compartment five, but this was not done. Most (1,300 times as much) of the incomplete combustion products would have traveled from compartment six through a system of seals into compartment five via the spent steam line, and not the suction system line. In addition, calculations showed that it would have been impossible for the pressure in compartment five to increase to 0.5 kg/cm^2 as a result of entry of gases through the system of seals on the TTsNA turbopump units in the time from 1118 (the moment supply of steam to the units stopped due to activation of the reactor's emergency shielding) to 1122. This would have required not less than thirty minutes. Consequently, if we accept this version, then we would have to agree that incomplete combustion products entered compartment five chiefly through another system, specifically the pressure equalizing line between compartments five and six. The valve of this line is always open under normal operating conditions, and it may have been closed after some delay during the accident. The deflagration itself passed through the central passage of compartment five—that is, near the location of the outlet of the pressure equalizing line, and not along the sides where the turbopump units were located.

Which of these versions is plausible?

To establish this, we need to return to Captain Lieutenant Dvorov's testimony. From the explanatory report: "Compartment five was sealed off. Considerable steaming was observed in the vicinity of TTsNA units No. 1 and 2. They were stopped, which was checked by tachometers."

Interrogation tape recording: "The compartment was sealed off, the TTsNA turbopump units were already idle at this moment. I think that the reactor's emergency shielding had activated."

It follows from this that the personnel had not stopped the TTsNA units themselves. Nor were they stopped by the main propulsion unit console operator, because they could be stopped only after the main turbogear unit and the turbo-generators went off line. Nor could the TTsNA units have been stopped after activation of the reactor's emergency shielding, as Captain Lieutenant Dvorov proposes, because after cessation of steam delivery, the units would be driven by an electric drive supplied from distribution panels RShchN No. 8 and RShchN No. 9 of the nondisconnectable load sections of the main distribution panels.

The units can be stopped only by their own safety system (being shut down as a result of closing of the circulating line's clack valves is not an issue, because closure of the clack valves did not occur). Of the factors to which the response of the safety system of TTsNA units can be expected (excessive rpm, temperature of the electric drive, and oil system pressure), only a pressure drop in the oil system could have led to a complete shutdown of the units. Establishment of this fact permits the assertion that the oil separation system was not set in its initial position, and gases passing through the oil tanks of the TTsNA from compartment seven caused foaming of the oil, which resulted in a pressure drop in the oil system's pressure line and activation of the emergency safety system of the units. Simultaneously, smoke gases carried oil vapor into the central passage of compartment five, which was the cause of the deflagration in the compartment.

But the leaders of the Navy do not agree with this analysis. Captain Lieutenant Dvorov did not agree with this analysis.

Lieutenant S. A. Dvorov (interrogation tape recording):

> The [oil] separation occurred from four to six in the morning. After the separation process, the separator was unplugged and the valve had to be closed. For the entire time of my service, there was never a case when the valves were [left] opened. I am sure. Especially as Seaman Kulapin and Warrant Officer Valyavin are exceptionally honest people.

So Captain Lieutenant Dvorov convinced the State Commission that the deflagration in compartment five did not occur because of the violation of instructions concerning the operations of the oil separation system. During the commission's investigating, he brought forth the version that the deflagration in compartment five occurred due to a natural evaporation of oil during the rise of temperature in the compartment. (The falseness of this version was addressed in paragraph one of Appendix II "Design Peculiarities of the Submarine *Komsomolets.*") In 1993, S. A. Dvorov had to recognize that when he went down into the hold of compartment five, he discovered that turbine oil filled the "hold," that the hot pipe was leaking oil from the separator, and that the valve shutting off the pipe from compartment seven was open. He closed the valve. Thus, by not fulfilling the elementary instructions concerning the operations of the oil separation system, it led to the deflagration of compartment five and to the burning of the people found in the compartment. This further reflects on their damage-control ability. It can be added to this that the oil systems of both TTsNA units, in violation of operating instructions, apparently were united by the piping lineup as well as by the pumping of oil. Only one TTsNA unit, not both, would spontaneously remain on line when the lineup was in accordance with the operating instructions.

Analyzing the fire in compartment five, we can make the following conclusions.

1. The color of the deflagration was bluish, which is a sign of an elevated oxygen concentration in the compartment.

2. The deflagration did not start a fire in the compartment, which says something about the rather high fire resistance of the *Komsomolets* submarine.

3. After their use, the hose values of the air-foam fire extinguishing system were left open, which, in the absence of people in compartment five, for practical purposes led to this system's failure.

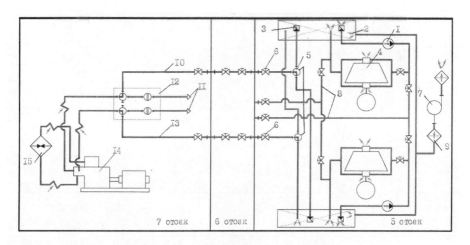

8. Entry of steam turbine oil into Compartment Five

"Shut High-Pressure Air Subgroup Valves!"

The fire in compartment seven, which was fed by air from high-pressure air cofferdams No. 1, 3, and 4, continued. The quantity of air entering compartment seven exceeded the quantity of air bled overboard, and pressure in compartments six and seven continued to grow. The leaking of hydraulic pipes in compartment seven led to the loss of fluid from the ship hydraulic system.

From the ship's log:

> 1145—Three distress signals transmitted. No acknowledgement.[1] Diesel cooling system not working. Shut off diesel. Establish communication with chemical service chief.
>
> 1146—Report temperature in compartment five.
>
> 1147—Diesel stopped. Lines of defense in compartment four—fore, aft bulkheads. In three—fore bulkhead.

As was said previously, Captain Lieutenant Dvorov's report of the deflagration in compartment five was received. The submarine command designated new lines of defense. In this case an order was apparently given from the attack center to compartment five personnel to move to compartment four. This can be the only explanation for designating the lines of defense in compartment four and for the next entry in the ship's log: "1158—No communication with four. Approximately nine men in four."

This order to personnel in compartment five was not received, and it could not be carried out because the airlock door was jammed.

From the ship's log:

> 1150—Find what's wrong with the diesel's cooling system! Order from the commander: Summon the ship's surgeon to the control room, and calculate the time of relief of pressure from compartment six. Thirteen atmospheres in compartment six.
>
> 1153—Markov to find out what's wrong with the diesel's cooling pump power supply.

At 1150 the pressure in compartments six and seven was equal to 13 kg/cm^2, compared to a 10 kg/cm^2 design strength of the bulkheads. This was the first and last entry concerning pressure in the compartments in which specific values were indicated. The pressure probably continued to grow for some time more in the compartments. The decision to calculate the time of relief of pressure in the distressed compartments sounds very strange. The process of change in pressure in the distressed compartments was proceeding out of the control of the attack center. The attack center did nothing to contain and stop this process, but it did perform calculations having no practical value. In addition, it would have been naive to suppose that the watchstander for compartment six might still have been alive at this time.

Lieutenant A. V. Zaytsev (explanatory note):

> The BCh-5 commander suggested relieving pressure through the salvage line. But it was already too late for me to do this, because the systems controlling and monitoring the positions of fittings in compartments six and seven were out.

One could have tried to relieve pressure from compartments six and seven (with regard to the possible loss of airtightness of the rubber-coated metal branch nozzle in compartment seven) through the pipeline with successive work of the main bilge pumps. This could be accomplished by opening the valve and Kingston valve in compartment three manually. But in order to make this decision, one had to have a good knowledge of the ship's pumping and salvage systems. However, in this particular situation of inaction, a successful effort to force reduction of pressure in compartments six and seven would have led to the earlier loss of the submarine.

The command to prepare the diesel generator for start-up was given at 1117. Thirty-six minutes went by, and the personnel were unable to start the diesel generator's cooling pump. The reason is simple: The diesel generator's distribution panel receives power from distribution panel RShchN No. 7, which was deenergized by personnel of compartment two in response to the command "Damage control alarm! Fire in compartment three!" Under these conditions it would have been sufficient to awaken (start) the generator, and the cooling pump would have been started off of the diesel generator itself. The crew's poor knowledge of the equipment was the reason why the diesel generator was not started.

From the ship's log:

> 1156—Pressure concentration in compartment six being relieved. VII. [sic—D.R.] No information on pressure, temperature in seven, no communication.
>
> 1157—Seaman Filippov feeling poorly. Sent up.
>
> 1158—All who have communication, contact the control room. Air bleeding in compartment three. The reason, oh boy, not yet determined [sic—D.R.] Shut down cofferdam high-pressure air valves, close subgroup valves in one. No communication with four. Approximately nine men in four.

Thus, the start of the decline in pressure in compartments six and seven was recorded at 1156. The maximum pressure they experienced is unknown.

Captain Lieutenant A.G. Verezgov (interrogation tape recording): "Dvorov told me as he was going up that the pressure in compartment six was fifteen kilograms."

It is fully possible that the pressure in the distressed compartments attained 15 kg/cm². As a result of the inaction of the attack center, according to tentative calculations, around 6,500 kilograms of air entered compartment seven from the high-pressure air system during the time from 1106 to 1158—that is, in fifty-two minutes. This was twenty times greater than the volume of the compartment. A kind of "blast furnace" was created in the compartment—thirty to forty times more powerful than the maximum possible fire under ordinary conditions. Tentative calculations show that the average temperature within the volume of compartment seven may have been around 800-900 degrees Celsius. This means that in the upper part of compartment seven, where the cable lead-ins are located, the temperature was high enough to melt aluminum and copper alloys, while in certain places the pressure hull's metal may have heated to the recrystalization point. Hot gases from the starboard main ballast tank No. 10 and from the fire in compartment seven caused leaking through the cable conduits of the starboard reserve propulsion system.

Where did the pressure from compartment six and seven go? As was said earlier, the pressure was bled into other compartments of the submarine through the oxygen dispensing and carbon dioxide removing lines of the air regenerating system, through the air line of the trim system, through the high-pressure air remote control pipeline, through the drain line of the hydraulic system, and through the system of seals on the TTsNA turbopump unit. In addition, hot gases escaped through the emergency blow pipe into the star-board MBT No. 10. At this time new pathways for gas to escape from compartment seven appeared. The operator of the main propulsion unit console had not closed the Kingston valve of the cooling system of the stern-tube gland (when reactor power is limited to 30 percent, the cooling system does not influence the submarine's power, and in accordance with Article 91 of the RBZh-PL-82 it should have been inactivated without orders). The fire caused the leaking and burning of the rubberized metal nozzle of the stern-tube gland's cooling system. Gases began passing from compartment seven into the heated nozzle and escaped overboard through the open Kingston valve and the coil of the stern-tube gland's cooling system. The hot gases "eroded" the gasket on the cable lead-ins of the starboard reserve propulsion system, and began escaping into the starboard main ballast tank No. 10. The port cable lead-ins did not lose their airtightness, because the port ballast tank No. 10 was filled with water, which provided for intensive cooling of the gaskets.

At this moment another incompetent decision was made in the attack center. Rather than shutting the 200 kg/cm² air pressure line, the outboard air line and the medium-pressure air line passing into the aft compartments (three valves had to be shut in compartment three!), the command was given to close the subgroup valves at high-pressure air cofferdam No. 1, located in compartment one, and at high-pressure air cofferdam No. 3, located in compartment three. This is the only interpretation that can be given to the entry in the ship's log: "Shut down cofferdam high-pressure air valves, close subgroup valves in one."

In this case they apparently wanted to write the amount of air remaining in these cofferdams in the ship's log, but for some reason they were unable to do so. From the explanatory reports:

Warrant Officer V. S. Kadantsev: "I shut the subgroup valves of cofferdam three on orders from the BCh-5 commander."

Warrant Officer Y. N. Anisimov: "The sound of high-pressure air bleeding could be heard during the alarm, the subgroup valves of cofferdams one, two, and three were shut on orders from the TsP."

And once again, Warrant Officer V. S. Kadantsev (interrogation tape recording):

In closing the valves to cofferdam three, I discovered that the pipelines from high-pressure air to medium-pressure air and from the VZY regulator were frosted over. Air was bleeding into the stern from the VVD-400 system through the regulator. I shut the subgroup valves at cofferdam three, and pressure in it remained at 80 kilograms.

After fulfilling the command of the attack center to close the high-pressure air subgroup valves, the submarine was left without air, and for practical purposes without damage control resources.

Warrant Officer A. P. Kozhanov (explanatory report):

You could hear the ballast being blown, and we realized that the submarine had surfaced (we understood this from the depth gauge and from the rocking); after that the whistling of air could be heard for some time longer, after which we could see from the pressure gauges that high-pressure air cofferdams one, three, and four were completely discharged. In response to a command from the TsP we attempted to recharge the fore VPL station, but we were unable to do this because of the absence of air in the system.

And that's not all. Personnel of compartments two and three as well as two persons in compartment five were connected up to ShDA apparatus of the stationary breathing system. The attack center had to know this, and when it gave the order to shut the high-pressure air subgroup valves, the submarine's leadership was cutting off, in the direct meaning of this word, oxygen to people connected to ShDA apparatus. And it was not long before this mistake was paid for.

13.

Reconnaissance by the Division Commander

From the ship's log: "1206—Captain 3rd Rank Yudin and Lieutenant Tretyakov are in compartment four. Yudin connected up to an IP-6 at 1200. Lieutenant Tretyakov connected up to an IP-6 at 1206."

Forty-five minutes had passed after the last message was received from compartment four, and twenty minutes or more after the report from compartment five on the deflagration, but a group of scouts was not sent to compartment four until 1206. An unforgivable delay! After all, the command to prepare the damage control party was given fifty-six minutes earlier at 1110. Apparently, the fight to correct the listing devoured the time and all of the crew's efforts. However, the damage control division commander went on reconnaissance, as if he had no other duties. Departing his post would indicate that the cause of the submarine's listing to port seemed completely clear, there were no problems with MBT No. 5, the sources of smoke entering compartments two and three were identified and shut, steps were taken to replenish the high-pressure air reserves, the cause of the pressure drop in the distressed compartments had been clarified, the draft, trim and longitudinal stability of the submarine had been determined, the damage-control plan was ready, and all tasks facing the damage control division commander regarding the accident, as prescribed to him by Article 45 of the RBZh-PL-82, had been carried out.

RBZh-PL-82, Article 45:

"The Commander of a damage control division must:
■ control changes of stability and buoyancy of the submarine

■ carry out the necessary calculations and report to the commander of the BCh-5 data for making decisions in the process of damage control for the submarine (according to methods of straightening the submarine, maintaining depth, or surfacing by means of damage control and others)

■ control the expenditure of the VVD and the means of extinguishing the fire, to report to the Commander BCh-5 their supply

■ control the pressure in the accident area and the adjacent compartments

But a contradictory order had been received, and had to be carried out. Therefore, Captain 3rd Rank Yudin went on reconnaissance. Obviously, this was the sole person in the crew who knew the submarine well.

From the ship's log: "1207—Communication established with compartment two. Six gm/liter in two—fourteen men. Connected to SIZ (ShDA),[1] feeling satisfactory.

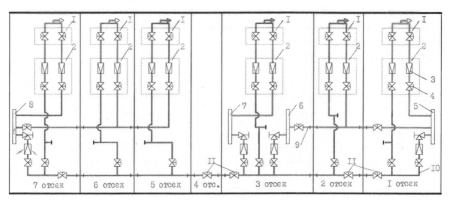

9. Diagram of ShDA breathing system contamination by gas
and smoke from Compartment Seven

The carbon monoxide concentration in compartment two was 6 gm/m^3 (there is an error in the ship's log). The personnel were connected up to ShDA apparatus. And although they were feeling satisfactory for the moment, they were already breathing poisoned air from compartment seven. In the control room they knew that people in compartment two were connected up to the system, to which no air was being supplied, but they didn't give the order to switch to other individual protective equipment. The same thing was also happening with the people in compartment three, who were wearing the ShDA apparatus.

From the ship's log: "1210—Eight distress signals transmitted, no acknowledgements."

With what words can we comment on this entry, so full of tragedy? The situation was desperate. The raging firestorm had engulfed four of seven compartments. There had been no communication with those compartments for as much as an hour, and what was going on in the compartments was unknown. The level of smoke in two of the three remaining compartments was at its maximum. It was impossible to start the electric exhaust fan and vent compartments two and three. The diesel generator still had not been started, and it had not taken on a load, thus, the load was borne by the batteries. The electric capacity of the batteries is not infinite. It would not be long before the submarine would find itself without electric power, and consequently without communication with the outside world. Practically the entire reserve of high-pressure air—the principal means of damage control and of maintaining the submarine's stability—was gone. Because of the absence of high-pressure air, the air-foam fire-extinguishing system was inactive. It was time to transmit an SOS signal. Had it been transmitted at this time, the tender *Aleksey Khlobystov* could have reached the site of the accident before the submarine's loss, and most of the crew would have been saved.

But the submarine's leadership apparently did not have enough courage to adopt an untraditional decision, so the radio distress signal was sent only in encoded text. And this is understandable—we fear our leadership more than any accident. For such initiative, the submarine command would have received harsh treatment, despite the fact that there's no official prohibition on transmitting an "SOS."

From the ship's log: "1210—Oil slicks on starboard side in vicinity of seven, air being bled [from bridge]."

Pressure was dropping in compartments six and seven. Air escaped from them together with combustion products through the starboard MBT No. 10 and the cooling Kingston valve of the stern-tube gland, which was confirmed by the report from the fore bridge.

Captain Lieutenant A. G. Verezgov (interrogation tape recording):

> And then air started coming out, as if they were blowing No. 10 on the starboard side. A large bubble came up from starboard.
>
> Question: At what time?
>
> Answer: It's hard to say. My impression is that this was happening the whole time. A bubble would escape periodically over the course of two to three hours.

From the ship's log:

> 1211—Situation normal in one. Hydrogen, oxygen and carbon dioxide normal, condition of personnel good.
> 1212—[S. P.] Golovchenko, [S. Y.] Krasnov lost consciousness in compartment two. Switch them to IDA,[2] turn on oxygen bottle (order from TsP). Open intake in three.
> 1215—Move unconscious personnel of compartment two up. VSK[3] [rescue chamber] ready to take on four men."

The inaction of the crew to contain the poisoned air in compartment seven was having a deleterious effect: People connected up to the ShDA apparatus began losing consciousness. A general command to use other breathing equipment in place of the ShDA apparatus was not forthcoming. An attempt was made to prepare compartment two for venting, in support of which an order was given to shut the check valves controlling intake ventilation between compartments two and three. A command to prepare the rescue chamber for oxygen decompression treatment was given during this same period.

Warrant Officer V. S. Kadantsev: "Before leaving for compartment four, as ordered by the attack center, I prepared the rescue chamber for oxygen decompression treatment" (explanatory report).

"The two bottles in the rescue chamber are not enough for oxygen decompression treatment. To do this, we connect a rubberized metal hose from the 200-kilogram pressure air line through the shaft nozzle. After I did this, I was in the TsP" (interrogation tape recording).

The submarine had just a single free exit up through the hatch of the rescue chamber. Under these conditions the decision to prepare the rescue chamber for oxygen decompression treatment within it was absolutely wrong. Things did not go farther than the preparations. Apparently, the submarine's leadership itself came to understand the absurdity of this undertaking. But preparation of the chamber for oxygen decompression treatment in it had further consequences.

A report came in from compartment one. How sharply it contrasts with the situation in the other compartments!

Warrant Officer Y. N. Anisimov (explanatory report):

> I heard the damage control alarm while in the washroom in

compartment two. In an instant I was in compartment one, as per the emergency bill. I closed the starboard valve supplying oxygen to the compartment, and the carbon dioxide valve, sealed off the carbon dioxide absorption apparatus, and stopped the fans of the battery venting system. Captain Lieutenant [I. L.] Speranskiy used a hydroelectric manipulator to close the bulkhead clack valves, and Warrant Officer Kozhanov began preparing the ShDA apparatus and deenergized electrical equipment not affecting the submarine's power and control.

No more need be said.
From the ship's log:

> 1218—Personnel in instrument enclosure of compartment four kor. R. [transliteration] Personnel can't get out of instrument enclosure. Yudin, Tretyakov got out. Men in airlock in compartment five can't open doors. Krasnov, Golovchenko raised to VSK. Grundul came up on his own. Measure gas composition in two, three. Pressure measured in four, five, get personnel out. Warrant Officer Kadantsev . . . connected to IDA twenty minutes. Open hatches of compartments four and five. Udovl [transliteration].

Lieutenant A. V. Tretyakov (interrogation tape recording):

> Went with Yudin to scout compartment four. The status of compartment four: high level of smoke and gas, moved around by touch. Pressure was high in the instrument enclosure of compartment four and in compartment five, and the doors would not open.

Apparently, compartment four was under some pressure, which was relieved as the scouts entered. This can be the only explanation for the higher pressure in the instrument enclosure as compared to atmospheric pressure, and for the high gas level in the compartment. After pressure was relieved from the compartment, the instrument enclosure evacuating compressor turned on automatically, and it was impossible to enter the enclosure until this pressure was relieved. The scouts also relieved pressure from compartment five. The bulkhead door into compartment five was closed, but the door to the airlock of this compartment could not be opened because it was stuck as a result of the deflagration that occurred in the compartment.

The three men who had been poisoned by carbon monoxide in compartment two were delivered to the rescue chamber.

Pressure was relieved from compartments four and five, and Yudin, Tretyakov and Kadantsev were ordered to get the people out of them. The abbreviation "kor. R." apparently means "on the reactor shell," and "Udovl." refers to the satisfactory condition of the members of the damage control party.

From the ship's log: "1225—Acknowledgement to distress signal received. Get thermal underwear topside."

A message that the distress signal had been received and decoded was finally received. Sixty-seven minutes had passed after the distress signal was ready for transmission and forty-eight minutes after it was transmitted the first time.

Such is the efficiency of the work of the Navy's communication structures.

Poisoned crewmembers were taken to the conning tower superstructure, and thermal underwear was brought up for them.

Secret Documents—To the Rescue Chamber!

From the ship's log: "1230—Seaman Filippov connected up to IDA-59. Check out compartment three."

Warrant Officer V. F. Slyusarenko (explanatory report):

Then I saw Seaman Filippov, who ran over carrying an IDA-59. He was connected up to a PDU[1] and he tried to switch over to the IDA-59, but his hands were shaking, and he didn't know what to do to put it on. I helped him switch over from the PDU to the IDA-59. After this he hurried over to prepare the diesel generator for starting in the hold of compartment three.

Such was Seaman R. K. Filippov's effort in putting on the IDA-59. Who was supposed to be responsible for such crew training?

From the ship's log: "1233—Two men transferred from compartment four: Makhota, Valyavin. Went topside."

Warrant Officer V. S. Kadantsev (explanatory report):

After the fire in compartment four, the personnel of this compartment took shelter in the instrument enclosure. A damage control party consisting of damage control division commander Captain 3rd Rank Yudin, me, and Lieutenant Tretyakov was created for their evacuation. We put on our IP-6s and left for compartment four. The compartment was extremely smoky. The damage control division commander opened the air lock to the instrument enclosure and went in, closing the door behind him. At this time I checked the compartment's readiness for venting into the atmosphere. Rapping could be heard from compartment five. Opening the bulkhead door leading to compartment five, I entered the compartment five airlock, but I couldn't open the airlock door. I couldn't do it together with the damage control division commander either.

Lieutenant A. V. Makhota (interrogation tape recording):

The first party of scouts couldn't open us up. The second party did, obviously because the evacuating compressors were working [they were relieving pressure]. We donned our PDUs and left compartment three, and we were led up to the superstructure.

Due to the aggressive actions taken by Captain 3rd Rank Yudin, it was possible to lead the personnel of compartment four out of the radio room. At this time the readiness of the fourth compartment for venting into the atmosphere was checked. But another two hours and twenty-four minutes passed before venting of the compartment was started. There is no justification for the delay.

From the ship's log:

1235—Smoky in VTsK. Filippov. Report gas composition of two. Take SPS[2] documents up to VSK (commander's order). Entry of smoke into compartment three stopped. 3 gm/m^3 in compartment two (initially through the ShDA). Compartment three inspected. High smoke content in TsVK, no open flames.

By this time the fire in compartments six and seven had apparently gone out. The pressure in them continued to fall, and by 1235 it decreased to 3 kg/cm^2. The safety valves of the trim system's air line stopped bleeding air and combustion products from compartment seven into compartment three. Entry of smoke into compartment three diminished abruptly, which is noted in the ship's log. Still, air continued to enter compartment three through other unclosed pipelines, albeit in small quantities. Poisoned air was entering from the air console of the high-pressure air fitting control system, located in the TsVK compartment.

Warrant Officer V. S. Kadantsev (interrogation tape recording):

> The smoke level in the aft section was very high, and a large amount of air was being bled from the main air console (from the far left manipulator). The entire interior of the air console, where all of the pipes connect to 45 kg/cm^2, and all of the pipes were sprayed with dirty soot.

Considering the way the pneumatic fittings of the high air pressure system were configured, why would smoky gas go through the system in compartment three, and what could have been done to stop its introduction? A control valve was located on the air control panel. It is subject to the average air pressure. These valves are connected to pneumatic piping with high-pressure fittings. When the valves controlling the piping are closed, the control valve is vented to the atmosphere in compartment three. When the control valve is open, its piping is disconnected from the atmosphere of the compartment and medium pressure air is directed into the openings of the corresponding fittings of high pressured air. When the control valves are closed simultaneously, stopping the supply of medium air pressure, the pneumatic piping control valve is connected to the atmosphere of compartment three, the pressure from the piping is compromised, and the high air pressure fitting closes. At the time of the accident, the air console controlling the high air pressure fitting was located in the initial position; that is, the control valves were closed, but the pneumatic piping was connected to the atmosphere of compartment three. During the fire, the pneumatic piping fittings for blowing the stern group of the MBTs became frozen ("blind effect" due to condensation of moisture in the air) and smoky gas from compartment seven began to enter compartment three unimpeded, as Warrant Officer Kadantsev discovered during his visit to the location of the TsVK. And again, his inaction is incomprehensible. The warrant officer saw the location from where the smoking gas was leaking and did nothing to stop it. In order to stop the introduction of the smoky gas, the supply of the medium air pressure had to be released at the air console and the fitting control valve for blowing the stern group of the MBTs had to be opened. By doing this, the pneumatic piping going to compartment seven would be separated from compartment three and the introduction of the smoky gas into compartment three would have been stopped. But apparently, a poor understanding of the ship's systems and the unsatisfactory execution of the damage control tasks, due in part to the absence of the RBITS, did not afford the warrant officer the ability to stop the introduction of gas through this piping.

Lieutenant A. V. Tretyakov (explanatory report): "In compartment three, the executive officer gave orders to inspect the hold, and to find seamen [A. V.] Mikhalev and Filippov. We checked the hold, and reported through Lieutenant Fedotko that neither was there."

At this moment Seaman Filippov, who had donned his IDA-59, returned to the hold of compartment three and was helping to start the diesel generator.

The attack center's supposition that fires were burning in compartment three was not confirmed. Venting of compartments two and three had not yet been started because of the absence of power at distribution panel RShchN No. 7, which is why the amount of smoke in the compartments remained high. The carbon monoxide concentration in the air of compartment two exceeded the maximum permissible concentration by over 600 times. However, the concentration of carbon monoxide in compartment three could not be measured because of the absence of measuring equipment.

Warrant Officer V. F. Slyusarenko (explanatory report):

> The submarine commander gave orders to measure the CO concentration in the compartment. I took the measurements with a PGA-VPM[3] for low concentrations, because I couldn't find any indicator tubes for high concentrations; the limit for low concentrations was 50 mg/m^3, and the tube showed much more. I reported this.

What was the estimate of the accident situation during this period by the submarine's leadership?

Captain 1st Rank B. G. Kolyada (interrogation tape recording):

> According to the BCh-5 commander's calculations, in the worst case scenario—flooding of the aft compartments—the submarine would lose stability by 1500. The command "Prepare for evacuation to approaching vessels" was given.

Nothing was known about how things stood with the evacuation of people, but at this time the submarine commander gave orders to evacuate secret business documents, which was documented in the ship's log.

Warrant Officer E. D. Kononov (explanatory report): "In response to the command from the control room I went to the control room, and then took the documents up into the rescue chamber on the commander's orders."

Later on Captain 1st Rank Kolyada talked long and often about the submarine's loss being a surprise to the crew, which is why the personnel were unable to make full use of rescue resources. The ship's loss was, in fact, a surprise to most of the crew. On the other hand, the leadership was well aware of the impending danger, and it was only its indecision that led to numerous sacrifices.

Such are the facts.

15

The First Victims

From the ship's log:

> 1241—Yudin, Kadantsev, Tretyakov came out. High smoke level in compartment four.
> 1245—Exhaust system clack valves opened between compartments two and three. Ventilation clack valves of intake system between compartments two and three opened.

Warrant Officer V. F. Slyusarenko (interrogation tape recording): "I handed the wrench to the executive officer to open the vent between compartments two and three. The executive officer opened them himself, and I was ordered to open the intake ventilation system. I opened it."

Thirty minutes had passed from the moment the command to open the clack valves was given.

From the ship's log:

> 1246—In one: hydrogen—0.4, oxygen—23 percent. Situation normal. Radio room inspected. No remarks. VVD-200 disconnect closed in one. No information from five.
> 1253—VVD-200 disconnected at stern and at bow.
> 1255—Makhota connected up to IP-6. Valyavin in IDA-59, going to four, five. Warrant Officer Gerashchenko feels poorly in VSK [rescue chamber]. Airlock window broken to equalize pres-

sure with compartment five.

1300—Count all men. VVD-200 regulator charged. Diesel ready for starting.

Everything was in order in compartment one. The concentration of hydrogen and oxygen was within normal. Prior to loading, the 200 kg/cm² air main was cut off at the stern to avoid bleeding of air into compartment seven, and at the same time it was cut off at the bow as well. A necessary measure, but a little too late.

Warrant Officer V. S. Kadantsev (explanatory report):

> On order from the BCh-5 commander, I cut off the subgroup valves of cofferdam three and closed the disconnect valves for the VVD-200 system in compartment three and in compartment two. After this I charged the regulator for the VVD-200 system from cofferdam two, and supplied air to the VVD-200 system. The diesel generator started right away.

This is the explanation given by Warrant Officer Kadantsev, the chief of mechanics, for all of the manipulations with the 200 kg/cm² air main. And we could have agreed with this, if this main were used to start the diesel generator. But actually the diesel is started by ship's 400 kg/cm² main pressure or the automation system. The automation system provides no less than three consecutive start-ups of the diesel on a cold engine and no less than six consecutive start-ups on a warm engine. And as we can see, all of the entries in the ship's log regarding VVD-200 confirm in writing the submarine personnel's poor knowledge of the submarine's systems.

Lieutenant A. V. Makhota (explanatory report):

> Then the two of us were summoned to the control room, and we were ordered to connect up to IP-6s, leave for compartment four and help the personnel in compartment five. On reaching compartment four we entered the airlock between compartments four and five. The airlock door would not open, it was stuck. Then we kicked it open and helped six men get out.

Warrant Officer V. S. Kadantsev (interrogation tape recording):

> The BCh-5 commander sent two new scouts there and told them to break the glass in the airlock door to compartment five

in any way possible. When they broke the glass, this didn't do anything to make it easier to open the door, that is, there was no pressure in compartment five. The door was kicked in.

Because the power supply to the fan of the main ventilation ring was switched off, the navigation system instruments began failing due to overheating. Warrant Officer A. M. Kopeyka (interrogation tape recording):

> There was no smoke in the gyro-compass room. Everything was working normally. I checked all of the units and went to report to the team chief that we were not going to have any problems with the power supply. The second ventilation ring was working poorly. We requested power several times from compartment two, but the BCh-5 commander said that they couldn't deal with this now, and to do everything we could. It was after I dragged the team chief up when he started feeling poorly that the command to measure CO in the compartments was transmitted.

The electrical navigation group tried to do everything possible to prolong the work of the navigation system with the ventilation system not working. In order to improve cooling the panels were removed from their pedestals, but it was all in vain. It would have been much easier to supply power to the electric fan of the cooling system, or to shut off the system right away.
Warrant Officer V. V. Gerashchenko (interrogation tape recording):

> I disconnected the "magistral" system. I was feeling bad. I began to see brown spots before my eyes, my vision began to go dark, and I had an intense headache. Warrant Officer Kopeyka noted this, tore the ShDA mask off of me, and helped me topside. . . . I began to feel better after forty to fifty minutes, and I asked to be allowed to go back down. . . . I looked over the gyro-compass room and concluded that we had to shut everything down, because the instruments and the internal cabling could catch fire.

The navigation system was soon shut down.
After Warrant Officer Gerashchenko was poisoned, a command was given to personnel in compartment three to switch from the ShDA to other individual protective equipment.

It is hard to understand the entry in the ship's log that there was no information from compartment five. The control room knew that people were in there, and that they could not open the airlock door. To get the door open, a command to break the glass in the airlock to equalize pressure in compartment five was given, despite the fact that there was "No information from compartment five." Lieutenant Makhota and Warrant Officer Valyavin were sent to compartment five without spare individual protective equipment.

From the ship's log:

> 1305—Diesel water drain working. Taken out of compartment five: Volkov—1, Tkachev—2, Kozlov—3, Dvorov—4, Zamogilniy—5, Shostak—6. Kulapin in five connected up to ShDA. He has no IDA. Alive.
>
> 1308—Connected up to ShDA in compartment five—Bondar on port side. Six men from five—topside. Forward of the sail.
>
> 1307—Dvorov, Makhota—to five after Kulapin and Bondar. Connected up to IP-6's. Valyavin arrived from five, carried Bondar and Kulapin to airlock. Moderate smoke level in compartment five. Valydvin went topside.

Six men were taken out of compartment five; the numbers after their names indicate the order in which the people were taken out of the compartment. It is not entirely clear why the entry in the ship's log for 1308 was ahead of the entry for 1307.

Warrant Officer Bondar and Seaman Kulapin, who were connected up to ShDA equipment, remained in compartment five.

There is an inaccuracy in the ship's log: Warrant Officer Valyavin only tried to carry Kulapin over, but he was unable to do this.

Lieutenant A. V. Tretyakov (explanatory report): "Warrant Officer Valyavin reported that he had tried to drag Seaman Kulapin out of the compartment, but he was so heavy and Valyavin was feeling so poorly that he was unable to do this alone."

Captain Lieutenant S. A. Dvorov (explanatory report):

> About 1.5 hours later the airlock door was opened from compartment four, and we were taken into compartment three. I put on a new IP-6 and once again left for compartment five with two IP-6s to evacuate Seaman Kulapin and Warrant Officer Bondar, who were connected to the ShDA. They were found unconscious

in compartment five. Warrant Officer Valyavin and I carried them into compartment three.

The impression is created that in his position as compartment commander, during his presence in compartment five Captain Lieutenant Dvorov had not monitored the condition of people connected to ShDA apparatus. It is unclear from his explanations whether attempts were made to put IP-6 face masks on Warrant Officer Bondar and Seaman Kulapin. In addition, not only Captain Lieutenant Dvorov and Warrant Officer Valyavin but also Captain 3rd Rank Yudin, lieutenants Tretyakov, Makhota and Fedotko, Warrant Officer Slyusarenko and Senior Seaman Y. E. Vershilo helped to evacuate these people. It should be noted in this case that the submarine command, which knew that there were still two people connected up to ShDA apparatus in compartment five, was unable to organize a larger damage control party for simultaneous evacuation of the victims. The two persons sent to compartment five were unable to carry out two of the victims right away.

RBZh-PL-82 Article 11: "Damage control of the submarine is to be carried out by the entire crew, including the supernumerary, regardless of specialties."

Electric power to the diesel generator's cooling pump was sorted out over an hour after the order was given. Power was supplied to distribution panel RShchN No. 7 from the unconnectable load section of the main distribution panel No. 1, located in compartment two, and the electric cooling pump was started. Venting of compartment three with the exhaust fan of the forward ring of the general ship ventilation system was started simultaneously, although there are no entries to this effect in the ship's log.

Lieutenant A. V. Zaytsev (interrogation tape recording): "Then we turned on the diesel engine and exhaust fans; air began flowing into the submarine."

How long were the personnel of the main command post located in the ShDA apparatus?

Ensign Y. P. Podgornov (explanatory report): "In the third compartment, where I was located, there was a thick screen of white smoke, you could only see your hand 10 to 15 centimeters in front of you. When the party exited with the victims, I reported to the main command post. I was in the ShDA one hour and twenty minutes."

Captain Lieutenant I.S. Orlov (interrogation tape recording):

Question: How long were you in the ShDA?
Answer: Periodically. When the fire began, I got a mask. My

glasses misted up. The fire was extinguished in literally a minute.
We discarded the hot pulley. At about 1300, the mechanic took
the ShDA away. They had already ventilated the compartment
and I took off my mask.

Agreeing with the ship's log, the flare-up at the "Korund" post console occurred at 1122. Thus, personnel of the main command post were in the
ShDA nearly one and a half hours. This is confirmed by the notes in the ship's
log at 0100. The entry in the log at that time noted that the diesel generators
were ready to start and this means that the RShchN No. 7 switchboard was
providing electrical feed. At that time they already could have started ventilat-
ing the forward ventilation rings with the ship's ventilation system.

    From the ship's log:

> 1319—RDO[1] No. 12 transmitted.
>
> 1325—Definite acknowledgement to RDO No. 12 received.
> No information on Kolotilin, Bukhnikashvili, tentatively in com-
> partment six.
>
> 1327—Kulapin led out [sic—D. R.] of five. Communication
> session initiated. Personally addressed to us. No pulse felt on
> Kulapin, raised topside.
>
> 1333—Slyusarenko, Fedotko, Dvorov, Valyavin gone to stern.
> Load picked up by DG [diesel generator].
>
> 1339—Status of GEU: reactor stopped with all absorbers, AZ,
> KR, at lower limit switches. Loop one temperature 75 degrees
> Celsius, loop one pressure 105 kg/cm^2, level in KO 3—19 per-
> cent, cooling proceeding through BBR system, two TsNPK work-
> ing. GEU control totally absent. Kulapin has no pulse.
>
> 1340—Dvorov lost consciousness in compartment three.
> Bondar in compartment three in airlock.
>
> 1341—No people in compartment five. Compartment five in-
> spected. Valyavin, Slyusarenko, Fedotko, Vershilo came out. In
> compartment one: Grigoryan, Anisimov, Kozhanov, Speranskiy.
> In compartment two: Markov, Gregulev, Bondar came up [sic—
> D. R.] (unconscious)

The diesel generator (DG) picked up the load two hours and sixteen
minutes after the command was given. The reactor had been stopped with all
absorbers (safety rods AZ and shim rods KR), which were resting on the lower

limit switches, since 1123; however, an entry to this effect was not made in the ship's log until 1339. According to the control log, control of the main propulsion unit (GEU) was lost at 1119, with the exception of control over mechanisms and units of the reactor compartment. The "Shtil" system, which supported the reactor's emergency shielding, was working. The entry to this effect in the ship's log is imprecise. Accelerated cooling of the submarine's nuclear reactor by way of the batteryless cooling system (the BBR system) was proceeding with forced circulation of water in loop one by the loop one circulating pumps (TsNPK). The ship's log entries regarding the loop one temperature and the water level in the volume compensator (KO), equal to 9 percent, indicate a high degree of reactor cooling.

The automatic system and equipment of the reactor compartment activated the emergency shielding, managed the reactor's steady cooling, and monitored all of its parameters until the submarine went down. Evacuation of personnel from compartment five was completed. It took thirty-six minutes to evacuate the two persons from compartment five. Seaman Kulapin was raised topside in twenty minutes. It took a larger damage control party only eight minutes to evacuate Warrant Officer Bondar. There are full grounds for believing that the submarine command was unable to man large damage control parties. They were made up of only eleven men out of a crew of sixty-nine; in this case damage control division commander Captain 3rd Rank Yudin was forced to go to the aft compartments eight times as a member of damage control parties.

Despite all of the efforts by the senior lieutenant of medical service, L. A. Zayats, Seaman Kulapin and Warrant Officer Bondar could not be saved. The possibility is not excluded that the mistakes made by the commander of compartment five and the delay of evacuation led to the tragic outcome.

16

The Fight Against Listing Continues

From the ship's log: "1344—Open valve to equalize pressure between five and six."

It should be noted that the term "open valve" could also be read as "valve opened." Analysis of preceding and subsequent events permits us to assume that this was a command, but its execution was not documented.

Captain Lieutenant S. A. Dvorov (interrogation tape recording):

Then I went back to compartment five and took another man with me—Warrant Officer Valyavin. The BCh-5 commander gave the command to open the bulkhead clack valves between compartments five and four, and to seal off compartment five in order to relieve pressure from compartment six. I was unable to open the bulkhead clack valves, because the bulkhead was very hot, and the high level of smoke was a hindrance. We found Bondar in a dead-end corridor on the left side at the bow. He was connected up to the ShDA and unconscious.

This was in the period between 1333 and 1340. Then the command to open the pressure-equalizing valve was given. The command remained unexecuted. What was happening at this time in the submarine? Pressure was falling in compartments six and seven. Because of leaks in the pipelines, when the pressure dropped below 2 kg/cm^2, water began leaking from the air conditioning and cooling systems of the ship-power consumers. Apparently, at around 1330 the operator of the "Molybden" console was forced to stop the pumps of the cooling system that supported ship-power consumers (Lieutenant Zaytsev gives a time of 1230 in his explanatory report, which is not very probable).

A decision was made to relieve pressure from the distressed compartments through the aft ventilation ring exhaust main. This is the only interpretation that can be given to the command received by Captain Lieutenant Dvorov. How do we evaluate this decision? Pressure was falling in the distressed compartments. There was a report from the bridge that bleeding of air was observed from the right side in the vicinity of compartment seven. It may be concluded with certainty that the pressure hull of compartment seven was no longer airtight. Consequently, as soon as the pressure fell below a certain value, water would rush into the distressed compartment. And rather than implementing all measures to seal the bulkhead between compartments five and six (or between four and five) and prepare to pressurize the distressed compartments, an attempt was undertaken to relieve pressure in them—a decision equivalent to suicide. Luckily, it was impossible to carry it out; otherwise, the submarine may have sunk an hour earlier, and no one would have been saved.

By 1200 the entire reserve of high-pressure air was exhausted, with the exception of the reserve in the commander's tank group, but no actions were taken to replenish it, and no attempts were made to find out what was happening in the aft part of the submarine, or what sort of change was occurring in draft and trim.

Senior Watch Officer Captain Lieutenant A. G. Verezgov (interrogation tape recording): Question: "And couldn't you have gone aft?" Answer: "I thought about it, but no one went there."

RBZh-PL-82, Article 42: "In case of accident the submarine senior watch officer is obligated: . . . to directly lead the personnel's damage control efforts on the upper deck and in the superstructure when the submarine is on the surface."

More interrogation tape recordings:

Electrical navigation group engineer Lieutenant K. A. Fedotko: Question: "Was listing documented?" Answer: "We had bigger problems—the ship had trim."

Damage control division engineer Lieutenant A. V. Zaytsev:

> According to the pressure gauges the pressure in compartments six and seven reached zero. I reported this to the commander. It took a long time to relieve the pressure. I don't remember when

pressure was bled from compartments six and seven, but I do remember that our trim was 1 degree aft at around 1300.

A correction needs to be made in Lieutenant Zaytsev's statement. The submarine had a zero trim by the stern as of 1300. The trim appeared later. See table 16-1 for how the fourth and seventh sections of the State Commission Working Group evaluated change in the submarine's draft and trim over time, on the basis of an analysis of photographs taken from an aircraft.

table 16.1

Time	Draft in Meters	Trim by Stern in Degrees
1500	7.5–8.5	1.5–2.0
1600	8.5–9.0	2.0–2.5
1630	9.0–9.5	2.5–3.0
1645	9.5–10.0	3.0–3.5

We can see that change in draft and trim occurred gradually, and it could have been predicted beforehand. Therefore, all of the assertions that appeared later in the press regarding an alleged unexpected loss of the submarine that hindered preparation of rescue equipment are inconsistent with reality. Such assertions serve to cover up the inaction of the ship's leadership in ensuring the rescue of the crew.

At this time events developed ashore in the following way. At 1219 (and possibly even at 1141) the distress signal was decoded. At 1239 an IL-38 aircraft was dispatched to the accident location, but for some reason, without a submarine specialist aboard. As a result, the headquarters of the Northern Fleet was deprived of an offboard source of objective information up until the end of the tragedy, while the submarine crew was perhaps deprived of good aerial information and specialist recommendations that might have dramatically altered the subsequent progress of accident recovery efforts.

At 1250 the headquarters of the Northern Fleet transmitted a radio message to the *Komsomolets* forbidding the ship's submergence and suggesting it remain adrift. It was also communicated that an airplane was en route to the submarine with an estimated time of arrival of 1400.

Unfortunately, the headquarters of the Northern Fleet did not furnish documents to the State Commission Working Group regarding communication exchanges between the distressed submarine and the fleet command post. The message cited above and subsequent ones are from a document of the fourth section of the State Commission Working Group, signed by Vice Admiral Zaytsev, the naval deputy commander in chief and the chairman of this section.

It may be concluded from the radio messages that the submarine command concealed the true scale of the accident from the headquarters of the Northern Fleet from the very beginning. For practical purposes there was no reserve of high-pressure air aboard the ship (except for the commander's tank group), it was dead in the water, and pressure in the distressed compartments was close to 13 kg/cm². How could there be any talk of submerging the submarine in a disaster of such a scale? Apparently, the command of the *Komsomolets* lacked not only the ability to organize ship damage-control efforts but also the courage to report the status of the submarine objectively and promptly.

Twenty-three minutes (and possibly even sixty-one) had passed after the distress signal was decoded, and it was not until then that the headquarters of the Northern Fleet thought to ask the Sevryba Association to report the location of its vessels. The time was 1242. A reply was received in the same minute. Another eight minutes went by, and finally at 1250 the headquarters of the Northern Fleet made the decision to send the tender *Aleksey Khlobystov* to the place of the accident. As a result, the tender was unable to begin traveling to the coordinates indicated by the Northern Fleet headquarters until 1320.

The list to port was a constant concern to the submarine command. And as soon as rescue of people from compartments four and five was completed, it set to correcting the list.

From the ship's log: "1354—Kadantsev—open vent valve of MBT No. 7."

The side on which the vent valve had to be opened and the tank had to be filled was not indicated in the ship's log. But the reference is to the starboard MBT No. 7.

Lieutenant A. V. Zaytsev (explanatory report): "On orders from the BCh-5 commander Warrant Officer Kadantsev bled air out of the starboard MBT No. 7. After this the list became 0 degrees."

Warrant Officer V. S. Kadantsev (interrogation tape recording):

The BCh-5 commander ordered me to open the vent valve of

number seven on the starboard side in order to correct the list. I donned an IDA-59 and went to the aft ventilation enclosure of compartment three, where I delivered [Kadantsev meant to say "bled."—D. R.] batches of air. The list was corrected. The smoke level in the aft section was very high, and a great deal of air was bleeding out of the main air console, out of the far left manipulator.

Two and a half hours had gone by after the submarine surfaced. During this time the attack center could have ascertained that a list of 6 to 8 degrees is not dangerous to a submarine, and that it would make no sense to waste time and resources correcting it. Contrary to this, the submarine command stubbornly tried to correct the list, and in doing so, it used the most irrational method. Rather than filling one of the starboard bow tanks, a stern tank was filled. This diminished the buoyancy reserve, and did not improve the parameters of the ship's longitudinal stability.

The impression is created that the principle followed in flooding the MBTs (first starboard No. 5 and then No. 7 on the same side) was not that of the greatest expediency but that of having the possibility to subsequently blow them with air reserves remaining in high-pressure air cofferdam three.

Bleeding of smoke gases from distressed compartments into compartments two, three, and five continued, and nothing was done to stop it. Despite the fact that ventilation was working in compartments two and three, the carbon monoxide concentration in those compartments exceeded the maximum permissible concentration by several times.

From the ship's log:

> 1355—Yudin, [I. O.] Apanasyevich, Tretyakov, Slyusarenko connected up to IP-6s.
> 1356—Slyusarenko, Tretyakov—safeties, Yudin, Apanasyevich—damage control party in compartment six. RDO No. 13 transmitted.

A damage-control party was sent to compartment six. The goal of the patrol, as was said earlier, was to deliver a fire extinguisher into compartment seven. But the reference is to something else. Sending the damage-control party to compartment six meant that in the opinion of the submarine command the fire had gone out in it, and pressure in the distressed compartments had fallen to a value close to zero. If we consider that pressure was measured with a pressure gauge having a scale reading from 0 to 16 kg/cm^2 with a precision class of 2.5, then at 1355 the pressure in the distressed compartments was close to 0.5 kg/cm². A qualitatively new stage had started. Bleeding of air out of the starboard MBT No. 10 was coming to an end. By this time, taking the actual draft of the submarine into account, the scupper grates of this tank were at a depth of 4.5 to 5 meters—that is, pressure in the distressed compartments was equal to the pressure in the MBT. Soon air would begin passing from the starboard tank No. 10 through the burnt-out cable lead-ins into compartment seven, and then from it into compartments two, three, and five, and partially overboard through the cooling Kingston valve and pipeline of the stern-tube gland.

The fire in the distressed compartment had gone out by this time. As was said earlier, around 6,500 kg of air had passed into the distressed compartments out of the high-pressure air system. Not more than 700 kg of fuel, expressed in units of carbon, could have burned in this quantity of air. Three hours would have been more than sufficient to burn this quantity of fuel in two fully involved compartments.

The organizational side of the preparation of the damage control party for its mission is astounding. The pressure in the distressed compartments was around 0.5 kg/cm², and it was pressing against the bulkhead door of compartment six with a force of over 2,000 kilograms. The door opens into compartment five. Had the damage-control party been able to turn the rack-and-pinion and release the latch, this damage-control party and its safeties would also have been killed by the door or by the air flow in fractions of a second. And it is difficult to say what other misfortunes would have come upon the submarine and its crew. But this is just one aspect of the issue.

Now let's imagine the compartment in which a fire of great intensity had just gone out. Everything was red hot. Nothing in it could be handled. Total darkness. A poisoned atmosphere. Each step is dangerous—the flooring could collapse, if it's still there. And here was the damage-control party, without heat-resistant overalls, wearing only IP-6 gas masks, making ready to enter this hell. Had the ship's leadership considered that by sending people into compartment six it was sending them to certain death? Quite clearly, compartment five should have been sealed off and pressure in it should have been increased to the pressure level in the distressed compartments first. Only after this should the bulkhead door between compartments five and six been opened, and then people, dressed in heat-resistant overalls and IDA-59s, been sent into the distressed compartment. And four men were clearly not enough for this work. Moreover, whatever the case, there were no guarantees that the damage-control party could fulfill its task. At this moment only one goal could have justified the risk of sending a damage-control party into the distressed compartments: closing the cooling Kingston valve of the stern-tube gland and opening the emergency pumping valve in compartment six or seven. It would have been much simpler and easier to seal off the aft compartments and maintain excess pressure in them. Unfortunately, no one thought of this throughout the entire accident.

From the ship's log:

> 1357—Warrant Officer Kadantsev filled MBT No. 7, closed vent valve.
> 1402—Kulapin and Bondar dead, doctor's conclusion.
> 1407—RDO No. 13 transmitted repeatedly. From moment of RDO No. 13 from first time. CO in hold of two [is] 5.6 gm/m^3. Smoke to starboard, at location of reversible VPR [400 Hz converter], visibility better to port. CO on middle deck [is] 2–3 gm/m^3.

The starboard MBT No. 7 was flooded. The list was corrected, although this was not reflected in the ship's log. There is an oxygen dispenser near the location of the 400-Hz converter (VPR) and the reversible converter. Smoke gases were passing from it into compartment two. This entry in the ship's log is nothing other than written confirmation of the oxygen version of the cause of the fire. The oxygen delivery line in compartment seven was open before the accident and, during the fire, smoke gases entered through the line into the oxygen header of the electrolytic unit, and then through the manually opened oxygen delivery line into compartment two. In the meantime, it is asserted in the explanatory reports, submitted by Captain Lieutenant V. A. Gregulev five days after the interrogation, that the oxygen delivery valves were closed at the header in compartment two, and that the carbon dioxide main was shut. This is clearly inconsistent with reality. The region where smoke gases were bleeding was known, and, still, nothing was done to stop the leaks. Hence, the concentration of carbon monoxide in compartment two was extremely high, despite continuing ventilation. What was meant by the unfinished phrase in the ship's log "From the moment of RDO No. 13 from first time" is unclear.

17

"No Flooding!"

1412—Yudin, Fedotko, Slyusarenko, Apanasyevich arrived. Compartment six bulkhead temperature over 70 degrees [Celsius], entry impossible.

1415—IP-6s recharged; Yudin, Apanasyevich, Slyusarenko left for five to deliver LOKh into compartment six.

1418—UHF communication established with airplane.

1420—LOKh delivered to compartment six from five. Captain 3rd Rank Yudin, Seaman Apanasyevich arrived, Warrant Officer Slyusarenko didn't go.

Warrant Officer V. F. Slyusarenko (interrogation tape recording):

Then the executive officer ordered Yudin to deliver LOKh from compartment five into compartment six. And he ordered me to go as a safety. They couldn't find anyone else, because practically the entire crew was topside. Warrant Officer Valyavin, who knows compartment five well, went below. Valyavin couldn't go because he had breathed in a lot of CO. He was forbidden to go. While they were searching for another man, Yudin had already gone down to compartment five and returned. I don't know whether or not Yudin delivered LOKh into compartment six from compartment five.

From this statement it is clear that the manning of the damge control parties was not appropriate. Let's turn attention to the temperature of the fore bulkhead of compartment six, and the time. At 1412 the bulkhead temperature was over 70 degrees Celsius. It had to be estimated subjectively because the damage control party did not have any measuring instruments. It was said earlier that the fire was no longer burning in compartment six; hence, delivery of LOKh into it made no practical sense.

Here we must talk about the version that was produced by the working group of the State Commission. The point of discussion was the possibility of the ventilation valves of the MBTs No. 8, 9, and 10 to open spontaneously during the fire in compartment six. This is what is said about it in the joint act sections entitled, "The Damage Control Operation" and "Shipbuilding": "Examinations of the drawing of the hydraulic system and the piping to the ventilation control valves (No. 577-32-1424) drawing reveals, in principle, the possibility of opening ventilation valves during the heating and boiling of hydraulic fluid in the cavity of the hydraulic machine and control piping. In view of the complexity of the process, occurring when the hydraulic fluid boils, only a full-scale experiment can answer this question." The working group of the government did not provide an answer to this question.

When could the ventilation valves of the MBT open spontaneously? The most favorable condition for this is created during the period between the time of the highest pressure in compartment six, that is when there was a high-volume mean temperature, and the time of attaining the lowest pressure in compartment six, when enough volume of the high mean temperature was at the lowest pressure in the system's portside main hydraulics. These favorable conditions began at 1158, when the air entering into accident compartment was released, and continued until 1356, when the emergency party was organized to enter compartment six. What kind of after-effects would there be when the ventilation valves opened spontaneously and water began to fill the MBTs 8, 9, and 10? The submarine would be down by the stern with a trim near 1.5 degrees and would have a list to the port side. However, the actions of the crew at 1357 to straighten the list of the submarine to the port side and photographs taken by a plane at 1440 synonymously verify that the spontaneous opening of the ventilation valves had not occurred up to the time of 1440. The conditions for this were not right at this later time.

From the ship's log:

> 1426—On the bridge: Move away from "Ivolga" for radio transmission.

1427—RDO No. 13 transmitted third time. Six RSP-30 mm[1] handed up to bridge: two red, two green, two white.

1432—AV. stop. UKV "Komar" set at "beacon."

1440—Airplane sighted visually. Smoking, coming in from port, marking its location, four-engined.

1441— "Komar" "beacon" switched on. IL-38—classified.

The airplane arrived in the area, established communication with the submarine, and the first photographs were taken. The airplane communicated that surface ships would reach the submarine by 1800. At this time a query was relayed to the submarine from Northern Fleet headquarters via the airplane regarding entry of water into the pressure hull and regarding the fire. The attention of the submarine command was simultaneously turned to the need to: utilize all possibilities of the LOKh system to deliver freon into compartments six and seven; to seal off the aft compartments; to prevent gas contamination of the other compartments of the submarine; to monitor continuously the gas composition in the compartments; and to make economical use of individual protective equipment. Having no information about the accident's development and the course of damage-control measures, the Northern Fleet's command post was forced to transmit a set of typical recommendations known even to young seamen.

In the meantime, the submarine began listing to starboard as the starboard MBT No. 10 filled. All of the effort to correct the list to port turned out to be not only useless but also harmful. The buoyancy reserve was lost purposelessly. Water began entering compartment seven through the cooling Kingston valve of the stern-tube gland. A small patch of bubbling water on the starboard side in the vicinity of the indicated Kingston valve could be seen distinctly on a photograph taken from the craft at 1440—this was air "gurgling up" from compartment seven. There are no precise references to the time when the list began shifting to starboard and when filling of the starboard MBT No. 10 was finished. The testimony of the crew members is contradictory.

Warrant Officer V. S. Kadantsev (explanatory report):

> In order to measure the temperature of the bulkhead between compartments five and six, after compartments four and five were vented, I left for compartment five and set a thermometer, capable of reading to 100 degrees Celsius, on the aft bulkhead of compartment five. The thermometer read a temperature above 100 degrees Celsius—approximately 115 to 119 degrees Celsius.

At this time the trim was 1.5 degrees by the stern. The list began changing to starboard.

According to the ship's log the time the temperature was measured was 1539.

Lieutenant A. V. Zaytsev (explanatory report):

> On orders from the BCh-5 commander Warrant Officer Kadantsev bled air out of the starboard MBT No. 7. After this the list became 0 degrees, and then shifted over to the starboard, becoming 4 to 5 degrees to starboard. . . . At around 1400 the starboard MBT No. 7 was blown with air remaining in high-pressure air cofferdam No. 3. The list became equal to 0 degrees.

It may be surmised from Lieutenant Zaytsev's explanatory report that listing had shifted to starboard before 1400. But this could not have been, because the starboard MBT No. 7 was not flooded until 1357, and it could not have been blown at 1400. Analysis of photographs taken from the airplane permits the assertion that the starboard tank No. 10 was flooded at around 1500, and then water rushed into compartment seven through the cable conduits.

On the submarine *Komsomolets*, as on many other submarines of the Navy, the MBTs are not equipped with Kingston valves [rather they are equipped with open floodports that depend on the air pressure in the tanks to avoid flooding of the tank]. This gave the leaders of the Navy grounds to maintain that one of the main reasons the submarine sank was the absence of Kingstons on the MBTs, in particular on the MBT No. 10. To consider this charge, we can examine scenario variations of the submarine's accident if it had a Kingston on MBT No.10. As was said earlier, the submarine surfaced without blowing MBT No. 10 on the port side and with a partial blowing of MBT No. 10 on the starboard side. To blow the tanks the Kingston valve must be open. For this scenario we will allow that, after surfacing, the crew would have been able to close the Kingston valve of this tank. When the increased pressure in compartment seven was greater than 3 kg/cm^2, the hot gas would begin to be blown through the damaged pipe and enter into MBT No. 10 on the starboard side, thereby raising the pressure in it. When the excess pressure neared 0.5 kg/c^2, the Kingston valve would be displaced and water would begin to be forced out of the tank. After blowing water out of the tank ended, the hot gas would continue to exit through the Kingston and would destroy the effectiveness of the rubber seal. Thus, the seal of MBT No. 10 of the starboard side would be lost and the further development of the accident would be factually analogous to the actual events. The inevitable destruction of the effectiveness of the rubber seal of the Kingstons is confirmed by the exfoliation of the rubber [hull] covering the region of MBT No. 10 on the starboard side. That exfoliation indicates the coating was heated to 200 to 300 degrees Celsius—that is, to a temperature significantly exceeding the integrity of the rubber on a Kingston valve. Consequently, in such a scenario, the presence of the Kingstons in the MBT No. 10 would not have altered the development of the accident in the submarine *Komsomolets*. If the Kingston valve didn't fail there is one other scenario variation. An increased pressure in MBT No. 10 on the starboard side, which would prove inevitable if the valve didn't fail, would give rise to a higher pressure in the accident compartment—that is, a pressure above that actually achieved during the accident. It is possible that this increase in pressure would be enough to cause destruction of the solid bulkheads between compartments five and six with even more adverse consequences.

From the ship's log:

> 1442—Yudin, [A. M.] Ispenkov connected up to IP-6. Going to compartment five to stop reversible, check temperature of compartment six fore bulkhead.
>
> 1445—Reversible of five stopped. Airplane dropped a buoy.
>
> 1449—CO at bulkhead at aft end of compartment three to 5 gm/m^3. IP recharging station deployed. Spent PDUs, IPs tossed overboard [oxygen regenerating cartridges].

The diesel generator had now been carrying a load for over an hour. Two reversible converters were working, which was redundant to a certain degree. With the automatic controls of the electric power system working, the reversible converter could have been stopped from the control console, but when the "Sinus" system was deenergized, it could be stopped only from the local control post in compartment five. Sending a special damage-control party to compartment five for this purpose is unconvincing, because there was no urgent need to stop it; moreover, under these circumstances this would reduce the electric power system's reliability. Apparently, the main goal of the patrol was to get power to distribution panel RShchN No. 6 so that the electric exhaust fan of the aft ring of the general ship ventilation system could be started. But there is no one to check this with, because the entire BCh-5 electrical engineering division perished.

The damage-control party took no instruments, as it set off to check the temperature of the fore bulkhead of compartment six.

From the ship's log:

> 1457—Venting of compartment four with compartment four's exhaust fan started.
>
> 1502—RDO No. 14 transmitted.
>
> 1512—Exhaust clack valves of compartment four closed. Venting of compartment five through hatch of compartments three and four using exhaust fan of aft unit started.

The readiness of compartment four for venting was verified from 1218 to 1233, but because of the absence of power to distribution panel RShchN No. 6, this venting was not started until over two hours later.

RBZh-PL-82, Article 98:

> To maintain permissible concentrations of gases [toxic substances] in the atmosphere of compartments adjacent to distressed compartments, after the submarine rises to the surface these compartments must be vented into the atmosphere to the extent possible.

This procedure was not utilized for more than two hours.

From the ship's log: "1518—Transmitted to airplane: No water entering [no flooding]. Fire being put out by sealing off compartments. Air only in one VVD group."

The message received by the Northern Fleet's command post at 1535 reads: "Fire still burning in compartments six, seven. Seaman Kulapin, Senior Seaman Bukhnikashvili died, need a tow. VVD remaining only in commander's group. Can no longer use the LOKh system. Monitoring pressure and temperature."

It is hard to say what there is more of in these messages—half-truths or deliberate disinformation. The submarine's leadership had no basis for asserting that the fire was still burning in the distressed compartments. Over 30 percent of the ship's reserves of high-pressure air had been delivered into them. During the accident, gases flowed unhindered from the distressed compartments into compartments five, three, and two. How can there be any talk of putting out the fire by sealing off the compartments? The temperature of the bulkhead between compartments five and six had not yet been measured.

High-pressure air did, for a time, in fact remain only in one commander's tank group, but this was over three hours previously. Since that time there was no air in the submarine's mains, and the air-foam, fire-extinguishing system was not working. By this time, four persons had already died aboard the ship, but the deaths of only two were reported. The submarine needed a tow as of 1123, when according to the entry in the control log for the main propulsion unit, the emergency safety rods and shim rods of the reactor were rested against their lower limit switches. The assertion of the submarine command that water was not entering the pressure hull was also groundless. At the moment the message was transmitted, the ship's situation was catastrophic, which is confirmed by the photographs taken from the airplane. Listing of the submarine had shifted to starboard. Trim rose from 1.5 to 2 degrees by the stern. It was time to shout "Help, we're sinking!" Processes, which were not controlled and not thought through by the leadership, were occurring aboard the submarine: surfacing with a list, growth of pressure in the distressed compartments, dropping of this pressure, shifting of the list to the other side, and increasing trim by the stern. How can there be any talk of monitoring pressure and temperature when even simple recording of the events was not performed? On the whole, these messages did not reflect the actual state of the distressed submarine, and they disoriented the Northern Fleet's command post.

The State Commission Working Group believed that entry of water into the submarine's pressure hull began after 1400; and by 1500 the quantity of water that had entered compartment seven was twenty tons, as is reflected in the joint act of sections four and seven of this working group.

18.

"Explosions Observed!"

From the ship's log:

> 1521—Moved away from *"Ivolga."* RDO No. 14 transmitted. Repeatedly.
>
> 1527—Transfer diving clothing to compartment three.
>
> 1529—Compartment six bulkhead temperature over 100 degrees Celsius.
>
> 1532—Definite acknowledgement of RDO No. 14 received.
>
> 1537—Communication session begins.
>
> 1538—Message received! A submarine is 100 km away, moving toward us at fourteen knots.
>
> 1539—New personal RDO transmitted to us. Kadantsev, Yudin connected up to IP-6, left for compartment five to measure CO in five.

The bulkhead temperature data were entered into the ship's log on the basis of the results of Yudin's and Ispenkov's patrol, which ended forty minutes earlier. The temperature was once again estimated, without using thermometers.

A Soviet submarine was traveling toward the accident location. It was not moving fast. This is apparently the result of the *Komsomolets* leadership misinforming the Northern Fleet command [about the seriousness of the situation].

After the message was received from the submarine at 1535, the commander of the Northern Fleet gave orders to prepare freon in canisters and ten sets of air-dropped rescue containers (KAS-150) to be delivered to the accident location by an IL-38 airplane. The absence of complete information on exchanges between the distressed submarine and the Northern Fleet's command post makes it impossible to determine what the grounds were for dispatching the KAS-150. Did the *Komsomolets* ask for them, or was this the initiative of the command post? It is unclear how the freon canisters were to be transferred from the airplane to the submarine.

There are no special rescue detachments in the Navy that could have been delivered to the accident region by air, and that could have dropped together with rescue equipment to provide assistance to the crew. Had such detachments existed, in this case their help would have been invaluable.

From the ship's log: "1557—Kadantsev, Yudin returned from five. Compartment six bulkhead temperature 115 degrees Celsius. CO measured— 7 mg/m^3."

Warrant Officer V. S. Kadantsev (interrogation tape recording):

> We got a 100-degree alcohol thermometer from the gyro-compass room. I went alone. The third division commander remained behind at the aft bulkhead of compartment four. I inserted the thermometer into the cable lead-in from the direction of compartment five, and the temperature climbed instantaneously to over 100 degrees Celsius (somewhere around 115 degrees Celsius). I came out and reported

The RBZh-PL-82 requires that the temperature of a distressed compartment's bulkheads be checked; however, there are no recommendations as to how this is to be done. The standard submarine supply table lacks special instruments with which to check bulkhead temperature.

Despite the fact that the gas composition in compartment five was practically normal as a result of venting and reduction of the amount of entering gas, the personnel never did return to either compartment four or compartment five. It was clear that submarine damage-control efforts were gradually shutting down. Subsequently, only damage control division commander Captain 3rd Rank Yudin and the mechanics' crew chief Warrant Officer Kadantsev continued this struggle. The rest of the crewmembers (with the exception of compartment one, the watchstander at the diesel generator, and the signalmen) were in the conning tower superstructure or were providing "overall leadership."

From the ship's log:

> 1612—Kadantsev, Yudin connected up to IP-6. Went to compartment five to measure temperature of aft bulkhead of compartment five.
>
> 1624—Yudin, Kadantsev returned. Temperature of aft bulkhead of compartment five 111 degrees Celsius. Shocks reminiscent of explosions in vicinity of compartments six and seven observed. Believed to be regenerating cartridges.[1] Ten cans in compartment five, eleven cans in seven.
>
> 1625—In one, hydrogen—1 percent, oxygen—23.5 percent, personnel feeling satisfactory.

Warrant Officer V. S. Kadantsev (interrogation tape recording):

> Five minutes later the BCh-5 commander sent us back there again to shut the bulkhead clack valve [it was supposed that it was open, and was why the temperature was not falling and the fire continued to burn]. When we looked, the clack valve was in its normal closed position, and the pressure-equalizing valve was closed. We tried to open it—the temperature climbed instantaneously, you couldn't keep your hand on it, there was a whistling sound. We closed it. There was pressure in compartment six after all. Not much, but it was there.

In the meantime, outboard water was entering compartment seven with high intensity, compressing the air in the distressed compartments. This explains the continued presence of pressure in compartments six and seven.

Much was written in the press about "explosions," after which the submarine quickly sank. They were written by [uninformed] "armchair" captains of various ranks and other "specialists," as well as by people who were indeed qualified specialists.

For example, Vice Admiral V. V. Zaytsev stated: "Explosions were heard aboard the submarine in the aft compartments at 1624. The situation worsened dramatically at 1640. The submarine acquired a trim by the stern, which attested to entry of water into the pressure hull and a danger of flooding."[2] Here, the vice admiral draws a clear cause-and-effect relationship between the "ex-

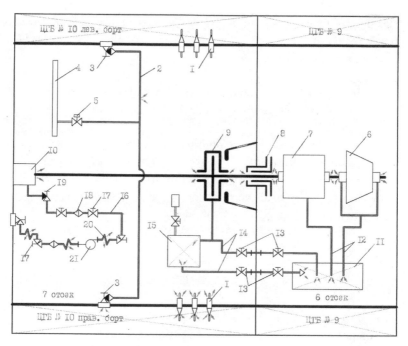

10. Sources of seawater that flooded Compartment Seven

plosions" on the one hand and abrupt worsening of the situation and the submarine's loss on the other.

Captain 1st Rank B. G. Kolyada (interrogation tape recording): "Explosions began at the stern, explosions that shook the submarine. It was decided that these were possibly the regenerating system exploding." Kolyada did, of course, make the qualification on the spot: "No, I'm not suggesting that the hull was ruptured by the explosion. The submarine was jarred, but not strongly enough to rupture the pressure hull."

Nonetheless, these "shocks reminiscent of explosions" wound up in the ship's log, and were transmitted as "explosions" in a message to the Northern Fleet's command post.

Warrant Officer V. S. Kadantsev (interrogation tape recording):

> When we entered compartment five, we heard two shocks—
> "babakh-babakh"—at the stern, before the enclosure of the turbo
> circulation pumps [The officers heard more]. We measured the
> gas composition in the compartment. This was an hour before
> the submarine sank. We had not heard shocks before this.

Captain Lieutenant S. A. Dvorov (interrogation tape recording): Question: "In what compartments are spent regenerating cartridges stored?" Answer: "We did not use them, because they were in reserve. I didn't hear any explosions."

Apparently, only Yudin and Kadantsev heard these shocks while they were in compartment five. It may be understood from Warrant Officer Kadantsev's statement that they heard them while measuring the gas composition of air in compartment five—that is, in the period from 1539 to 1557. The entry was made in the ship's log at 1624.

Thus, there is also doubt regarding the time when these shocks were heard. And more likely the "explosions" that were "heard" by Captain 1st Rank Kolyada in the conning tower superstructure and by Vice Admiral Zaytsev in Moscow have no relationship to actual events aboard the distressed submarine.

Nonetheless, Captain 1st Rank Kolyada is very reluctant to reject the desirable version of the sudden entry of water into the distressed compartments. Here is his reply to a question from the writer N. Cherkashin concerning "what served as the cause of such a powerful and unexpected rush of water into the pressure hull":

> First, the metal of the hull may have cracked due to the enormous temperature differential: It was thousands of degrees inside, and plus three outside. . . . Second, at high temperatures and high pressure, titanium can burn. The hull may have burned through at the border between compartments. Several other probable causes could be named.[3]

The writer and Kolyada firmly decided that "such a powerful and unexpected rush of water" did occur, and that all that remained to do was to find a plausible story. But such a story does not exist, and any such story would not fit with the chronology and the actual circumstances of the accident.

Several additional words should be said about the jarring of the submarine observed during the time of the accident.

Captain Lieutenant A. G. Verezgov (interrogation tape recording):

> And now, the hull shuddered violently, periodically seven or eight times. In all probability VVD was flowing somewhere, because a wave couldn't do that. . . . The episodes of shaking were long-lasting. Each about thirty to forty seconds. They began thirty minutes after surfacing, and they went on throughout the entire time the submarine was on the surface.

It is obvious from this statement that the submarine's shaking had nothing in common with "explosions," and it was associated with entry of air into the distressed compartments from the high-pressure air system, blowing and flooding of main ballast tanks, escape of gases from the distressed compartments, and entry of water into the pressure hull.

19.

"Prepare to Abandon Ship!"

What was the crew's assessment of the status of the distressed submarine at 1624, when information concerning "explosions" was entered into the ship's log? Let's see what Captain 1st Rank Kolyada, the principal author of an open letter published in the journal *Morskoy Sbornik* (No. 2, 1990), has to say.

> Yes, we were all truly certain until the last minute that we would be able to save the submarine. With the maximum possible sealing off of compartments six and seven, the delivery of fire extinguisher into these compartments and their decreasing temperature, and no change in the submarine's trim until 1620, and with no signs of water entering the pressure hull [we were truly certain].

Such was Kolyada's description of the last minutes of the tragedy in an open letter. But what was he reporting about these same minutes to the command post of the Northern Fleet? This report was received from the submarine at 1635:

> The fire is intensifying. The temperature of the aft bulkhead of compartment five grew in fifteen minutes from 70 to 110 degrees Celsius. Explosions could be heard from the regenerating system in compartments six and seven. Personnel need to be evacuated.

It would not be worth commenting on the above passage from the open letter—its falsehood is obvious. But let's do look at the message.

Clear disinformation can be discerned in this message. There were no fifteen minutes, and there was no intensification of the fire. The data (115 degrees Celsius at 1557, and 111 degrees Celsius at 1624) tell the opposite—there was no fire, and the pressure hull was cooling down. But because of the large mass of metal, it was proceeding slowly. The "explosions" fit in quite well with the message. It was apparently due to them that the personnel had to be evacuated. And although nothing is said about water entering the pressure hull, it is supposed that this was the case. Just six minutes later, at 1641, a new message was received: "The lines of defense are at the aft bulkhead of compartment five. List 6 degrees to starboard, trim three meters that corresponds to 1.5 degrees by the stern due to entry of water into the pressure hull. Personnel ready for evacuation."

The "explosions" did occur, but the description of "such a powerful and unexpected rush of water into the pressure hull" is inaccurate. Also, there is more disinformation in this message. Lines of defense had not been organized at the aft bulkhead of compartment five. The personnel were not ready for evacuation. The command to prepare for evacuation had not yet been given. The trim indicated in the message was different from the actual figure.

As was noted above, sections four and seven of the State Commission Working Group established, from an analysis of the photographs taken from the airplane, that the trim gradually increased, and that by 1630 it was 2.5 to 3 degrees by the stern. The buoyancy reserve was lost, but only gradually, and was due to filling of the ballast tanks and entry of water into the pressure hull. The loss of buoyancy reserve within the time indicated above was estimated by the working group at 760 tons; and "officially" the quantity of water that entered the pressure hull was estimated at 120 tons. However, the members of the State Commission Working Group representing industry believe that given a 760-ton loss of total buoyancy reserve, as much as over 200 tons of water had entered into the pressure hull by this time. The crew could have determined the loss of buoyancy reserve and the decrease in longitudinal stability of the submarine by measuring its draft and by performing a few simple computations. But this was not done.

In sending this message at 1635, then before the time of the message, the submarine leadership already believed that the ship was destined to sink. And even in these last minutes of the tragedy, the leadership of the *Komsomolets* lacked the courage to communicate the whole truth to the Northern Fleet's command post.

However, naval deputy commander in chief Vice Admiral V. V. Zaytsev disagrees with this conclusion. He stated the following opinion for the journal *Morskoy Sbornik* (No. 6, 1989): "Confident reports prior to 1635 indicate that ship damage-control efforts were proceeding according to plan, that the situation aboard the submarine was being monitored, and that entry of water into the pressure hull was not noted." The most important observation is that these were "confident reports."

After such statements by the vice admiral you can't help becoming confused, and you don't know whom to believe: Vice Admiral V. V. Zaytsev as the naval deputy commander in chief, or Vice Admiral V. V. Zaytsev as the chairman of section four of the State Commission Working Group, who signed the joint act of sections four and seven.

How do we explain such an abrupt change in the nature of messages from the distressed submarine? There can only be one explanation.

After returning from compartment five (at 1624), Warrant Officer Kadantsev was ordered to blow the starboard MBTs No. 5 and 7.

Warrant Officer V. S. Kadantsev (explanatory report):

> On orders from the BCh-5 commander I shut the onboard valve of the starboard MBT No. 7, and blew the starboard MBT No. 7 and the starboard MBT No. 5. Listing corrected to zero. The damage-control division engineer reported that trim was growing, and that it was already 4 degrees by the stern.

When interrogated by the State Commission, Warrant Officer Kadantsev clarified that he blew the MBTs with air remaining in high-pressure air bottles in cofferdam No. 3.

There are no entries in the ship's log regarding the blowing of the indicated tanks. Lieutenant Zaytsev also makes reference to the blowing of the starboard MBT No. 7. There is no basis for disbelieving Warrant Officer Kadantsev and Lieutenant Zaytsev.

To equalize trim, it would have been sufficient to blow one MBT. However, they decided to blow two tanks. How suitable was this decision, and how did it affect the stability and unsinkability of the submarine? MBTs No. 5 and 7 are situated forward of the submarine's center of gravity. When they are blown, in addition to an increase in buoyancy reserve, the submarine's trim by the stern will increase.

The next mistake is obvious. The attitude of the submarine worsened, and remaining high-pressure air was expanded for no purpose, even though it could have been used with great benefit to blow MBT No. 10 through the air line servicing the outboard devices.

When the two MBTs on one side were blown, the submarine was shaken severely and it abruptly trimmed down by the stern. The sternplanes disappeared beneath the water. At that time [after 1624], to my knowledge, the submarine commander, Y. A. Vanin, went topside to factually evaluate the attitude of the vessel. This abrupt change in the submarine's attitude was the cause for the change in the nature of the accident reports.

At 1630 the magnitude of the submarine's longitudinal stability reached such low values that rapid growth of the trim and the tragic outcome of the events should have been obvious to the "unaided eye" of a nonspecialist, and raised alarm to the probability that the submarine was sinking, without a single ray of hope. This is confirmed by photographs taken from the airplane as well as by crew testimony.

Lieutenant A. V. Zaytsev (interrogation tape recording): Question: "How do you correlate growth of trim with time?" Answer: "1 degree by the stern at approximately 1300, and 3 degrees until 1600. At around 1700 trim was 6.2 degrees. . . . Trim began rising abruptly from 1630 to 1700."

Senior lieutenant of medical service L. A. Zayats (explanatory report): "Somewhere around 1630 to 1640 I went up out of the submarine for the last time. The trim by the stern was already sizable, and it continued to grow quickly."

Captain 1st Rank B. G. Kolyada (interrogation tape recording): "Trim began to grow after 1600, with the rate of increase of the trim being high."

It would be pertinent to recall here the previously cited assertion by Captain 1st Rank Kolyada that the submarine's trim did not change before 1620.

From the ship's log: "1640—List 6 degrees to starboard, trim 1.5 degrees by the stern."

The trim value written in the ship's log does not correspond to the actual value, which is confirmed by the testimony cited above and by an analysis of photographs taken from the airplane at this time. The reported list value raises doubt as well.

Messages received from the submarine at 1635 and 1641 were like a bolt out of the blue to the naval command. The commander of the Northern Fleet transmitted the following order through the fleet aviation command post: "Prepare rescue chamber," and he asked the tender *Aleksey Khlobystov*: "Report the situation in compartment five, was the reactor shut down, were gas generators used, is the main bilge pump being used to drain the distressed compartments, report pressure in the distressed compartments, be ready to evacuate personnel." It is clear from this request that for practical purposes the Northern Fleet's command post had extremely scant information about the accident and the fight against it. And a cheerful report was received in response to this query (1650): "Situation in compartment five normal, gas generators were not used, damage control efforts continuing." What would you expect the Northern Fleet commander to think upon receiving such a confident report? A report, which Vice Admiral V. V. Zaytsev considers "indicates that ship damage control efforts were proceeding according to plan, that the situation aboard the submarine was being monitored, etc."

And at the same time:

From the ship's log: "1642—Prepare for evacuation. Surrender secret literature to executives. Prepare secret literature for evacuation."

Think about this phrase. It doesn't say evacuate casualties or patients to approaching vessels. It says evacuate the entire submarine crew. Thus, when it sent the message that the Northern Fleet's command post received at 1635, the submarine's leadership already believed that the ship was doomed. At 1642 an order was given to prepare the crew for evacuation from the doomed ship.

The evacuation order was given, but nothing was said about where to evacuate to. It is one thing to evacuate to approaching vessels, and another thing into the waters of the Norwegian Sea. So where did they intend to evacuate the submariners? From the interrogation tape recordings:

Lieutenant A. L. Stepanov: "After this I went below to prepare the secret literature for evacuation, because the commander said that ships would be approaching now, and only a mooring party would remain aboard the submarine."

Warrant Officer V. V. Gerashchenko: "I thought that a vessel had approached and that we were being taken off. I asked: 'But who is going to stay here?' BCh-1 commander: 'Don't worry, someone will stay. . . . Let's go topside quickly. We'll sort it out there.'"

How were the submarine personnel prepared for evacuation? And where did the "father-commanders" intend to evacuate them to?

Captain 1st Rank B. G. Kolyada: "And finally, the most important thing: We went topside not to jump into the water. There was one goal—to get some fresh air and meet the tender, which was approaching."[1]

Now there's that famous fleet hospitality for you! Over an hour would pass before the tender would arrive, and they're already going topside to meet it! And not a word about evacuation. Such was the explanation given by Kolyada to the wide masses of laborers to his egress topside from the submarine. But here is the way things really happened:

Captain 1st Rank B. G. Kolyada (report to the Northern Fleet commander):

> An IL-38 airplane arrived in the area at 1445; it reported that
> three surface ships would reach us by 1800. . . . We realized from
> the dynamics of increasing list to starboard and trim by the stern
> that the submarine would not be able to remain afloat until 1800,
> and so the personnel were given the command to "go topside"
> at 1650.

Thus, the crew of the submarine was preparing for evacuation to approaching vessels, although its leadership already knew at this time that they would have to evacuate into the water, into the Norwegian Sea. This was the first reason why the personnel wound up without rescue equipment.

How much time did the crew need to prepare for evacuation, to don thermal underwear and survival suits, or to grab life jackets and safety vests?

Warrant Officer Y. N. Anisimov: "All of the diving gear was ready in our compartment. Had we been given the command to put it on, we would have been able to dress each other in five minutes."[2]

At the same time the Northern Fleet's command post transmitted the following command to the *Komsomolets* by way of the tender *Aleksey Khlobystov*:

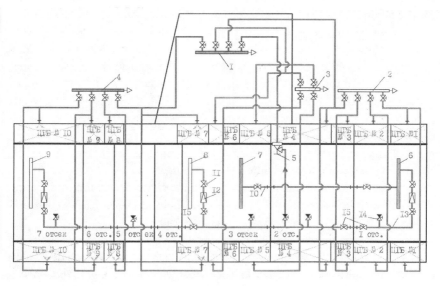

11. Diagram for emergency blow of MBT stern group with VVD No. 2
through the VZY and MBT blow piping

"Use the commander's VVD group to blow the aft group of ballast tanks. Report change in list and trim."

Use of the high-pressure air reserve in the commander's tank group for damage control would have radically altered the situation aboard the submarine even in the last stage of the accident. Given all of the conditions, this would have kept the submarine afloat until the arrival of the tender *Aleksey Khlobystov*.

However, the personnel could not use this reserve of high-pressure air because it did not know how to do this. Nor did a diagram of the high-pressure air system, which was used in an attempt to sort things out, provide any help. The absence of the RBITS again had its effect.

"We went through the entire combat training course, we prepared for several years for our independent 'great' cruise, we studied at the training center, we worked out the course problems with grades of good and excellent, and we finished our combat exercises. The training continued in full accordance with the guidelines. And, naturally, we worked on damage control problems," said Captain 1st Rank Kolyada in a letter published in the journal *Morskoy Sbornik* (No. 2, 1990).

How could the supply of VVD been used in the commander's group of airflasks for damage control in the submarine? A more rational method would be to supply air into the stern ballast tanks by the piping, which unites bulkheads VVD 1 and 2, by first isolating the main VZY from the accident compartment (by the valves located in compartment three), and then by blowing the main VZY pipes of the main ballast tanks by use of the driver. This method would have immediately provided a supply of air to the MBTs and allowed for the control of its volume and automated support of the needed pressure in the accident compartment, at the time when there was the lowest probability of a renewed fire in the compartment. However, the simplest method would have been to supply air into the distressed compartment by the master VCD or the VVD-200 directly from the bulkhead of VVD No. 2. This method have allowed for the easy regulation of the quantity of air being supplied and would have provided the optimal pressure on the accident compartment. To carry out this method, it would have been sufficient to open one valve in compartment three. However, none of these options were invoked.

And so, a command to prepare for evacuation was given at 1642. Why were the personnel unable to make adequate preparations for this?

"None of us expected such a huge inrush of water into the aft compartments, when the ship's fate was decided in a matter of minutes. This was clearly not enough time to go below into the compartments and bring up over fifty sets of individual equipment"—such was the explanation given by Captain 1st Rank Kolyada in the newspaper *Izvestiya* (January 15, 1990), and there isn't a single word of truth in this explanation.

Rather than quickly preparing rescue equipment, the personnel were occupied in the hasty evacuation of secret documents. There was enough time to go below and gather together the secret documents. These bits of paper turned out to be more precious to the submarine's leadership than the lives of the people.

Lieutenant A. L. Stepanov (explanatory report):

> Everyone in the submarine was preparing for evacuation to a vessel. The submarine commander gave orders to prepare secret documents for evacuation. The BCh-1 commander and I began gathering documents. The trim began growing abruptly. The executive officer ordered us to take our vests and go topside. We continued to gather secret documents. Lieutenant Zaytsev ran up and said that the trim was four to five [degrees], and we had to go topside quickly. We left the secrets in the submarine and raced topside.

Interrogation tape recordings:

Captain Lieutenant S. A. Dvorov: "A very great amount of time was lost evacuating secret documents."

Warrant Officer V. V. Gerashchenko: "Everyone was running topside, and we got stuck with the box of secret documents. This created a small traffic jam."

Lieutenant A. V. Zaytsev: "We exited mostly without vests, because there was no time, and it was dark."

Lieutenant Zaytsev's assertion that it was dark at this moment in the submarine is inconsistent with reality, and is not confirmed by a single participant of the tragedy.

Who can explain why boxes and bags of secret documents had to be gathered together and carried topside more than an hour before the expected arrival of vessels? Despite being so concerned about preserving state secrecy, consider the following:

Warrant Officer E. D. Kononov (explanatory report): "Carrying documents, I went topside, where I was washed overboard by a wave. I lost sight of the safe containing secret documents. One box containing documents was raised up to the tender. The second wasn't found."

Can any Navy staffer guarantee that the contents of this box, as well as of the other boxes and bags, are actually lying at the bottom of the Norwegian Sea, and not being studied in other countries?

But high-placed representatives of the Navy decided to preempt the "probable adversary" and publish most of the secret data on the submarine *Komsomolets* in the open press. The initiative in this effort belongs to the commander in chief, Fleet Admiral V. N. Chernavin, which was published in the May 13, 1989, edition of the newspaper *Krasnaya Zvezda*.

The *Wall Street Journal* cites the following statement by the U.S. director of naval intelligence, Rear Admiral Thomas Brooks: "Glasnost made it possible for us to obtain the kind of invaluable information . . . on the Soviet Union for the collection of which we would have had to spend millions of dollars and waste many long years [using traditional intelligence gathering methods]." As an example, he cited the accident aboard the submarine *Komsomolets*. Permit me, Comrade Commander in Chief, to congratulate you and your closest assistants, and offer a high evaluation of your efforts in behalf of U.S. naval intelligence!

Thus, the senseless or, more accurately, criminal order to evacuate secret documents was the second reason why the personnel were unable to prepare for evacuation. Just due to this, members of the *Komsomolets* crew failed to put on survival suits, and did not take their safety vests and life jackets. The submarine's leadership failed to give the order to prepare the LAS-5M lifeboat located in compartment one, and it did not give the command in time to prepare the rafts and rescue chamber for separation from the submarine. The one thing that the leadership of the *Komsomolets* did manage to do was to report to the Northern Fleet's command post at 1641 that the personnel were ready for evacuation.

20.

The Life Rafts

From the ship's log: "1645—Compartment one unsealed. Prepare battery tank for venting."

This was the last entry in the ship's log.

What does this note in the ship's log mean? This is how the leaders of the Navy comment upon it.

> Turning our attention to the last note in the ships log made at 1645. . . . Is it possible that it reflects the oncoming inevitability? The specialists comment on it as such: At 1644, the commander of the submarine and the crew still did not have sufficient basis for the abandonment of the vessel or the conclusion that it was just about to sink.[1]

But what were the facts?

Warrant Officer S. R. Grigoryan (explanatory report):

> By command from the main command post, I opened by hand the exhaust ventilator for the ventilation of the storage hold into the atmosphere. This occurred at the beginning of the alarm around 1700. Then the command to prepare to abandon the compartment came from the command post. We took the remaining regeneration IDA-59 CGP cartridges to the bulkhead door of

the first compartment and opened the lower entrance hatch. After that Captain Lieutenant Kalinin already had given the command verbally to leave the compartment and go above.

Warrant Officer A. P. Kozhanov (explanatory report):

> In four or five hours from the central post, the commander of the BCh-5, Captain 2nd Rank Babenko, informed us that there was a voluminous fire in compartments six and seven. Two people remained in the stern and two others were there, but whether they were alive or not was not known. Then came the order from the command post regarding the resealing of the hole in the accumulator and the abandonment of the compartment.

From the information from Warrant Officer Grigoryan and Warrant Officer Kozhanov one can come to only one conclusion. This note in the ship's log reflects preparing the compartments of the submarine for the forthcoming flooding. To avoid an explosion of the storage battery during the flooding, the storage hold was opened to the atmosphere, the first compartment sealed, and the lower cover of its entrance hatch was opened for assisting the work of the diver when the submarine is located on the bottom. The notes in the ship's log at 1645 documents the evidence about how the TKN knew of this and was preparing for the anticipated flooding of the submarine.

For practically the entire duration of the accident, Lieutenant I. A. Molchanov noted the incidents in the ship's log under the command of the senior assistant commander of the ship, Captain 2nd Rank O. G. Avanesov. We cannot silently overlook the fact that I. A. Malchanov was not only a lieutenant, he was still the commander of the mine-torpedo combat section BCh-3.

RBZh-PL-82, Article 46:

> During an emergency a commander of the combat sections (divisions, groups) and leaders of the services must lead damage control by arms and technical means in his submarine unit in accordance with special directing documents, determine the degree of damage and the possibility of further utilization [of the damage equipment], and report to the command point of the combat part (service, division) or to the command post.

And this forces the question to arise: Why on this submarine, "bulging" with torpedoes and missiles (including nuclear arms), did the commander of the BCh-3 fulfill the duties of an ordinary military clerk for the extent of the emergency? The clarification of this enigma would not only add a new perspective to the combat and professional readiness of Captain 1st Rank Y. A. Vanin's crew, but also would provide some insight to the purpose of the activities of the "combat" cruise of the submarine *Komsomolets* that ended with tragedy on April 7, 1989.

Warrant Officer V. S. Kadantsev (explanatory report):

> The engineer ordered me to close the bulkhead door between compartments four and five, close shut-off number one of the aft block's exhaust ventilation system, and shut the bulkhead door between compartments four and three. Before shutting the bulkheads between compartments four and five, I walked back toward the stern and checked the temperature of the compartment six bulkhead. It was exactly 100 degrees Celsius. I closed the bulkhead and started to close shut-off number one of the exhaust ventilation system, but I could not close it completely, because air began entering the ventilation shaft.

This is one more confirmation that there was no fire in the distressed compartments, and that the pressure hull was cooling down.

Fulfilling the incompetent order to close shut-off number one of the exhaust ventilation system, Warrant Officer Kadantsev simultaneously opened the exhaust ventilation shaft-flooding valve—that is, he unwittingly promoted faster flooding of the submarine, another indication of the personnel's poor knowledge of the ship's systems.

The rescue vessels were still far away, while the cold waters of the Norwegian Sea were right there. Now came the time to put rescue equipment to use. We have already mentioned the survival suits, the thermal underwear, the safety vests, and the life jackets. Because of the poor administrative skills of the submarine's leadership, most of the crew were without them. Also, the LAS-5M life raft was not deployed.

Immediately after the submarine surfaced, the personnel began preparing the PSN-20 life rafts for launching. This required from one (according to Lieutenant Stepanov) to two (according to Captain Lieutenant Paramonov) hours. The crew voiced complaints in this connection regarding the long time it took to prepare the rafts for use. It is hard to say how justified these complaints were. The *Komsomolets* is the only submarine in the Navy that carries rafts outside the pressure hull. It may be said without exaggeration that this location of the rafts saved the lives of most of the surviving crewmembers. And it is no accident that one of the measures for improving the survivability of submarines includes studying the possibilities of locating rafts outside the pressure hull. As for the time it takes to prepare the rafts for use, the designer placed his priority (in the absence of any requirements and standards) on the reliability [of the mechanisms] with which the raft containers were secured to [and released from] the rescue chamber.

And so, the raft containers were prepared for launching. In order for everyone to understand what has to be done to launch the rafts, a few words about the structure of the raft launcher are necessary. The rafts of the submarine *Komsomolets* were in hard containers, each with two rack-and-pinion releases. The upper release and lid were intended for extraction of the raft at a naval base for certification purposes, while the lower release was intended to be used (in an emergency) to drop the raft onto the water. When the lower rack-and-pinion is turned, the lower part of the hard container falls into the water together with the raft and sinks, while the raft remains on the water surface. The raft-inflating system is activated by two tugs on a line. Thus, one minute is enough time to deploy the rafts that are ready for launching. Instead of this, the crew began pulling the rafts out through the top of the containers, lowering them by hand to the deck of the superstructure, and activating the inflating system there. Considering the great weight of a raft (around 90 kilograms) and the position of the containers when they are moved out of their recesses, one can imagine how much effort it took for the people to launch a single raft. Using that method, not enough time was left to extract the second raft from its container.

Why did this happen? Did Captain 1st Rank Vanin's crew know how to deploy the rafts?

Submarine Senior Watch Officer Captain Lieutenant A. G. Verezgov (interrogation tape recording):

> All I had were two log books for the rafts and some brief written instructions. But I never read about or saw how to use the rafts in the rescue chamber's recesses. Twice I inspected the rafts on the rescue station, removing the upper lid and pulling the rafts out from the top by hand.

But it would be wrong to assert on the basis of this statement by Captain Lieutenant Verezgov that no one in the crew understood how to deploy the rafts. Who was the first to begin pulling the rafts out from the top, thus guiding the actions of the personnel in the wrong direction?

Warrant Officer S. R. Grigoryan (explanatory report):

> There were already many people topside. . . . Captain 1st Rank Kolyada tried to pull out the rescue raft, but he wasn't strong enough. I helped him extract the raft. Then I began pulling out the second raft.

Warrant Officer V. V. Gerashchenko (interrogation tape recording):

> We pulled out the raft on the left, and tried to open it up. Political Affairs Chief Burkulakov and Warrant Officer Grigoryan were standing on the right side. They were trying to pull the second raft out. I started helping them drag it up. The joke was on us. There's supposed to be a pedal there. You press it, and the raft falls down and opens up. But here we were dragging it up.

So there you have it. The technical ignorance of the "father-commanders" aggravated the tragedy. Much time has passed since the accident, but Captain 1st Rank Kolyada still believed that the rafts had to be pulled out through the top. For example, in the January 15, 1990, edition of the newspaper *Izvestiya*, he stated, "Using the rafts was the only correct decision in that situation. But the design of the rafts turned out to be so imperfect that it was extremely difficult to extract them from the sealed containers, and beyond that, they were very easily upset by a wave." The tragedy had not taught Kolyada anything.

How did events develop subsequently? Let's look at the explanatory reports:

Warrant Officer V. V. Gerashchenko:

> People on the port side of the upper deck were trying to deploy the raft, but they were washed over the starboard side by a wave. It was impossible to pull the raft on the right side out of its container, and the water level rose over my legs. I swam over to the raft, on which people were already gathering.

Warrant Officer S. R. Grigoryan:

> I couldn't pull the second raft out by myself; I called out to Captain Lieutenant A. G. Verezgov and he began helping me.

Suddenly I found myself pulling on the raft alone—Verezgov, it turns out, jumped overboard. I looked at the bow of the ship. It was up rather high, but people and hats were already floating near the ship. I never did realize that the submarine was sinking, and so I continued pulling at the raft. Suddenly, the water went over my head as the submarine rose to vertical and the impact of the water [*sic*—D. R.]. Even so, I was able to extract the raft, but let go of it as it pulled me down.

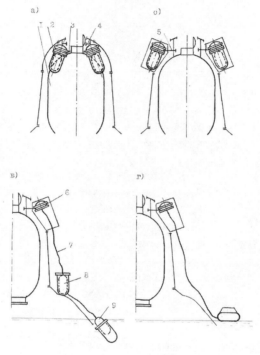

12. Rescue raft locations and launch sequence

As the submarine sank further, the positive buoyancy of the raft caused the line by which it was secured to the railing on the conning tower superstructure to break, and it rose to the surface.

What assessment did the crew members give to the raft?

Captain Lieutenant S. A. Dvorov (interrogation tape recording):

The rafts are good for nothing, and their design is a disgrace. If we had other rafts, we could have saved some people. . . .

Question: Did you practice launching the rafts in your daily life over the last five years?

Answer: Never in our lives. In the Navy we spent our time scribbling on paper, rather than practicing damage control. Never in all of my career of twelve years had anyone ever deployed the life rafts. We never practiced egress through the torpedo tubes either. We studied this at the training station, but it wasn't hands-on. We don't know how to open up the aircraft rafts. I never saw the aircraft rafts.

Such is the assessment, which is very full of emotion and very lacking in practical knowledge. But this didn't keep Captain Lieutenant Dvorov from subsequently continuing his bemoaning of the rescue equipment and talking about the crew's high combat proficiency. Journalists as "armchair-seamen" began a campaign to bemoan and deride Russian equipment and to investigate its mythical inadequacies on the basis of statements by "experts," but more about that later. For the moment, let's listen to a specialist.

Chief Designer B. S. Taubin:[2]

Inflatable life rafts (PSN) are a group rescue resource used by navies of all the world. Owing to the speed of their automatic deployment, their invulnerability to blows against the side of a vessel, and other positive qualities, rafts are commonly considered to be the most effective modern rescue craft. In coordination with competent use of rescue rafts and training of all seamen in their use, equipping vessels of the country's fishing fleet with them had completely excluded the loss of human lives in ship accidents and sinkings resulting from imperfections of rescue equipment. . . . In the accident aboard the submarine *Komsomolets*, rather than dropping the inflatable raft onto the water from its container, and then activating the gas-inflating system by tugging the inflating line, the personnel, who were not trained in the rules of using such a raft, undid the lacing and extracted the raft from its container. This defeated the raft deployment design, and the raft filled with gas while upside down, which resulted in the death of many people. The lack of training of the crews of warships and naval auxiliary vessels practically cancels out the reliability of inflatable rafts and promises bitter consequences. Nor does the Navy have stations at which inflatable rafts could undergo annual certification, which is contradictory to the technical conditions governing their use. For your information, there are around fifty such stations working in contact with the manufacturing plant within the Ministry of the Fishing Industry, the Ministry of the Maritime Fleet, and some other civilian departments of the country.

We should add to this that violation of the rules of using rafts caused the upper floats and awning supports to be underinflated, and this prevented the personnel from turning the raft over in the water, reduced its buoyancy, and sharply worsened the conditions of the people inside it. And the submariners paid for these mistakes with their lives.

It was precisely at this time that the last message was received from the submarine: "Trim increasing abruptly. All personnel are topside."

21.

The Rescue Chamber

Much was written in the press about why submarine commander Captain 1st Rank Y. A. Vanin went back down into the submarine. In the opinion of the authors of such articles, while topside the commander learned that there were still people down below, and this motivated him to go back inside the submarine. Much was said in this case about old naval traditions and about heroic deeds. It seems that all of these authors were paying a dubious service to the commander, at least because according to old naval tradition, before abandoning ship the commander must make sure that he is, in fact, the last to leave. But tradition does not foresee departure of the commander from a ship followed by his subsequent return. So why did the commander, who was topside, go back inside the submarine?

Let's backtrack a little. At 1645 the Northern Fleet commander ordered the commander of the *Komsomolets* to prepare the rescue chamber (VSK) for separation from the submarine.

Warrant Officer S. R. Grigoryan (explanatory report): ". . . after which I began pulling out the second raft. At this time the commander gave orders to prepare the VSK for release, and crawled into the VSK."

Apparently, the submarine commander went topside in order to estimate the situation and to give the order to prepare the rescue chamber for separation from the ship because at this time all the personnel were topside. This can be the only explanation why Captain 3rd Rank V. A. Yudin, Warrant Officer A. V. Krasnobayev, and S. I. Chernikov were in the chamber in addition to the commander and Warrant Officer Slyusarenko.

Warrant Officer V. F. Slyusarenko (interrogation tape recording):

I took the secret file the BCh-1 commander gave me and went over to the security officers, to whom I turned over the file, because the evacuation was to begin. There was no one in the gyro-compass room, so I grabbed two vests (I couldn't find any more) and ran to the exit. I could see the commander standing with one leg on the ladder beneath the hatch. He asked me. "Are you the last?" I replied: "Yes," because I hadn't seen anyone else. It was then that Yudin shouted from above that Captain 3rd Rank Ispenkov was still back there—he was attending to the diesel generation; he replaced Seaman Filippov when the latter became too weak. I ran back for Ispenkov, and at that moment the submarine tilted severely to the stern. I went down the ladder and shouted to Ispenkov, who dropped everything and ran topside. He was wearing ear muffs. As he was climbing up, he shouted that water entered into compartment three. A jet of water was beating against the right side from the back of compartment two.

It follows from Warrant Officer Slyusarenko's statement that Captain 3rd Rank Ispenkov had not been informed of the evacuation. It was asserted later in the press[1] that Ispenkov "probably didn't hear the often-repeated command to evacuate." Even the novice submariner knows that next to a working diesel generator the human voice cannot be heard beyond just one or two meters away, and no vocal commands can reach the action station beside the diesel generator. Captain 3rd Rank Ispenkov should have been informed of the evacuation by a special messenger, but this was not done.

In addition, Slyusarenko's statement confirms that the lighting was functioning in all the submarine's compartments until the very last moment, and Lieutenant Zaytsev's assertion of the opposite is inconsistent with reality.

How suitable was the order to prepare the rescue chamber for separation from the ship? Under certain conditions the chamber could have become a very great help in the survival of people in the frigid waters of the Norwegian Sea; therefore, the order was suitable. Unfortunately, it was given late, but even then all was not yet lost.

Much has been written about the rescue chamber. Most authors, who won't make an effort to even try to understand this device, condemn the rescue chamber, calling it the "chamber of death."[2] The impression has been created that even special technical articles devoted to rescue chambers are written by dilettantes.[3] Therefore, something needs to be said about the rescue chamber on the *Komsomolets*.

As is the case aboard other submarines, the rescue chamber of the *Komsomolets* was intended for the rescue of the entire crew when the submarine is stranded on the bottom. It should be stated that the question of the possibility of detaching the rescue chamber from the submarine when the submarine hull collapses at depth (named as damage control problem No. 4) had been examined in the planning process. Studies on that case produced a negative result.

The rescue chamber is secured at its coaming by a rack-and-pinion release to the coaming of the submarine, such that a waterproof space (the fore chamber) is created between it and the ship's hull. Detaching the rescue chamber after its occupation by the crew requires a series of specific procedures. These include closing and locking the lower conning hatch and the lower hatch of the rescue chamber; setting the catch manually; turning the rack-and-pinion ring pneumatically or by hand; filling the fore chamber with water and equalizing its pressure with the outside water pressure; and, when necessary, feeding air to the pneumatic jack for initial separation of the rescue chamber from the submarine.

That is all that needs to be told about the rescue chamber.

The submarine *Komsomolets* began sinking with a trim of around 80 degrees by the stern.

Warrant Officer A. M. Kopeyka (interrogation tape recording): "The engineer shouted: 'Close the hatch—there are people in there!' The submarine was already going down, but I managed to force the upper conning tower hatch down with my legs."

Warrant Officer V. F. Slyusarenko (explanatory report): "I ran to the exit, to the VSK, and started climbing up. but the water falling from above washed me away. I got rid of the life jackets and started climbing again, but the water swept me away again."

Warrant Officer V. S. Kadantsev (the newspaper *Podvodnik Zapolyarya*, April 20, 1989): "They were in the VSK. Kopeyka used his leg—slam! And the catch on the hatch cover engaged. Had those who remained in the chamber battened it down, everything would have been all right."

And so, the upper hatch of the rescue chamber was held in place only by its catch. Water entered the chamber. Calculations show that the water that entered the chamber reduced its positive buoyancy to the minimum, equal to around 1 to 1.5 tons.

There is no need to discuss the difficulty with which Warrant Officer Slyusarenko managed to get inside the rescue chamber. It was not until the submarine's trim equalized that Captain 3rd Rank Yudin and Warrant Officer Chernikov were able to drag Warrant Officer Slyusarenko into the chamber. A great deal of effort had to be expended to close and batten down its lower hatch.

Warrant Officer V. F. Slyusarenko (interrogation tape recording):

> I was pulled by my arms into the VSK on the commander's orders, and they began closing the hatch right away. Krasnobayev and I held onto the lower hatch of the VSK by a rope tied to the handle. . . . Then water started coming in from above, completely flooding the fore chamber—dirty liquid. [He is referring to the coaming of the lower hatch of the VSK, and not the fore chamber.—D. R.] The commander gave the order to batten down the hatch in the fore chamber. Using a monkey wrench, Yudin and Chernikov managed to close the hatch. Before the hatch was closed we heard noise reminiscent of boiling water—obviously air was escaping from the sinking submarine.

As we can see from this, air entered the chamber from the moment the lower hatch of the rescue chamber was being battened down, creating an elevated pressure within it. Unfortunately, no one who remained in the chamber attached the proper significance to this, because toxic gases entered the chamber together with the air. It is hard to estimate the depth at which the lower hatch of the rescue chamber was closed, and how high the pressure was within it. We can assume that the depth was 300 to 400 meters, and the pressure was 1 to 2 kg/cm^2.

And what about the lower conning tower hatch, which should have been used first?

Warrant Officer V. S. Kadantsev (interrogation tape recording): Question: "Had the fore chamber hatch been battened down? [The reference is to the lower conning tower hatch.—D. R.]" Answer: "No. Because the ladder had to be dropped. There wasn't enough time."

But the ladder was not the only thing that prevented closure of the lower conning tower hatch. The air hose that had been installed for oxygen decompression treatment would also have been an obstacle to closing it. In addition, the rescue chamber was "tethered" by this hose to the submarine's pressure hull. This meant that the rescue chamber could surface only after the submarine compartments were completely flooded and the pressure within it was equalized with outside pressure, on the condition that the chamber's buoyancy would be sufficient to break the air hose. But the men who remained in the chamber didn't think of this.

Warrant Officer V. F. Slyusarenko (explanatory report): "At this moment we heard a rapping from below. In all probability this was Ispenkov. The commander began shouting: 'Come on, open the hatch, they might still be alive there!' He obviously didn't know that Ispenkov was alone."

But it was already too late. Soon after, there were several shocks—the transverse bulkheads were obviously breaking. Then the noise stopped.

Warrant Officer Slyusarenko (interrogation tape recording)

> The commander said: "Hurry and release the VSK." You could hear the bulkheads cracking. I asked: "How deep is the sea?" They told me: "1500. Hurry, or we'll be crushed." The depth gauge read 400 meters, and the pointer was no longer moving— it had gone off the scale. Yudin started releasing the valves. One was used to flood the fore chamber, and the other used for emergency release of the VSK. Yudin opened the VSK release valve, but nothing happened. The commander said: "What's this, have you forgotten how to release the VSK? Come on, remember!" Chernikov began reading the instructions on releasing the VSK. Following the instructions, Yudin began turning the VSK's rack-and-pinion. The three of us started turning the rack-and-pinion with a wrench, but we were unsuccessful. The commander said that if we reach bottom, the VSK would collapse, when suddenly there was a shock beneath us, like a bomb exploding, followed by intense vibration.

The sequence of the personnel's actions following separation of the rescue chamber from the submarine was presented somewhat differently in Warrant Officer Slyusarenko's explanatory report. In particular, it may be surmised from the report that first they tried to turn the rack-and-pinion by hand, using a wrench, and only after that did they try to do it by opening the valves. But that's not the point. We cannot be fully certain that the personnel had carried out all of the operation necessary to separate the rescue chamber from the submarine correctly, even with the help of the posted instructions. This is despite the fact that the crew is supposed to know how to do this even in the absence of light. The ignorance of the personnel of the *Komsomolets* of the physical laws and principles of action of the rescue chamber releasing devices can be clearly recognized in this episode. With the lower conning tower hatch open, the crew could not have done anything to separate the rescue chamber from the submarine until pressure within the submarine equalized with the outside water pressure.

Nor was Captain 1st Rank Kolyada able to sort this out. With the aplomb of that "scholar who lived next door" in the Chekhov novel, he discusses the "reasons" why they were unable to disconnect the rescue chamber in time, and he believes that it separated by chance.[4]

What actually happened? Apparently, after the latch securing the rescue chamber (figure 13) was released, the pneumatic system was used to turn the rack-and-pinion to the position permitting separation of the chamber. An attempt to once again turn the rack-and-pinion manually with a wrench was unsuccessful under these conditions. Opening of the fore chamber flooding valve produced no results because the lower conning tower hatch was open, and outside pressure continued to press the rescue chamber against the coaming of the submarine's pressure hull with great force since it had not yet completely flooded.

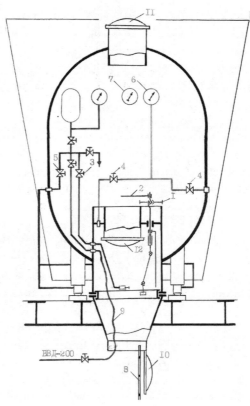

13. Rescue chamber diagram

14. Torn-off coaming and forward hatch of *Komsomolets*

At what depth was the ship when that shock, reminiscent of an explosion, occurred, and how many shocks of this kind were there? Captain 1st Rank Kolyada and warrant officers Slyusarenko, Kopeyka, and Grigoryan heard one shock. Captain Lieutenant Orlov believes that there were two shocks. What could have caused the explosion-like shocks?

A review of videotapes and photographs of the submarine *Komsomolets* lying on the bottom revealed damage to the upper cover of compartment one's entry hatch (the lower cover of the entry hatch was opened by the personnel during evacuation). The nature of the damage and the positions of the damaged structures clearly indicate that this damage occurred after the submarine struck bottom. Of all the possible causes of damage to the upper cover of the entry hatch (explosion of ammunition, explosion of gases released from the storage battery or torpedoes, a shock wave caused by elastic deformations of the pressure hull as the submarine struck bottom, and hydraulic shock occurring with rupture of the pressure tanks), hydraulic shock is the most probable cause. When the submarine struck bottom, the pressure tanks in compartments two and three ruptured, producing a hydraulic shock. It damaged the upper cover of the entry hatch of compartment one, and helped the rescue chamber to separate from the submarine. This shock, which resembled an explosion, should have sounded like a double shock, and it was detected by the people in the rescue chamber and aboard the life raft.

This discussion of hydraulic shock is based on the practical experience of designing the submarine *Komsomolets*. In 1975, during strength trials on an experimental compartment of this submarine, the testing chamber was ruptured by a hydraulic shock. Many of the parameter conditions causing the shock during the strength trials were repeated during the submarine tragedy.

Warrant Officer V. F. Slyusarenko (explanatory report):

> . . . but suddenly an explosion of terrible force occurred beneath us, and vibrations passed through the entire hull. I thought the VSK had been crushed, but no water came in. The commander asked: "So tell me, has the VSK been released or not?" Yudin said that we didn't know. Then someone shouted for everyone to connect up to their IDAs. Chernikov and I connected up, but Yudin and the others didn't. Yudin lost consciousness, he went into convulsions, and was snoring. . . . From the upper tier the commander began giving orders to connect Yudin up to an IDA, which Chernikov and I did with great difficulty, because the mask was tight, and it was very hard to put it on. After we connected Yudin up and placed him comfortably on a bench, he began taking infrequent but deep breaths; wondering how the commander was doing because I was no longer hearing any orders from him, I crawled up. The commander was sitting on a bench with his head lowered. He was snoring, and an IDA was lying near his legs. Krasnobayev was lying on his side, showing no signs of life. He never did manage to pull his IDA from its storage compartment.

In figure 15 the details of the destruction of the forward exit hatch, the infringement of the overhead rack-and pinion ring, and, in the background, the coaming of the exit hatch can be seen.

The attempts by Slyusarenko and Chernikov to place the mask of the breathing apparatus over the submarine commander's head were unsuccessful.

This brings to mind the article in the newspaper *Krasnaya Zvezda* (October 7, 1989) in which Captain Lieutenant Verezgov discusses the political

15. *Komsomolets'* superstructure over Compartment One

16. *Komsomolets'* ship clock

department chief, Captain 1st Rank T. A. Burkulakov: "He was the one who came up with the contest for the best beard of the cruise." The degree to which this "contest" is associated in this case with difficulties in donning IDA masks is unknown. Previously, submariners had been prohibited from growing beards because of the need to use individual protective equipment.

In the words of Warrant Officer Slyusarenko, immediately after the "explosion" the air in the rescue chamber became filled with a dense mist, and it became much harder to hear.

The rest of the crew of the submarine *Komsomolets* was continuing its fight for its life during this time.

Warrant Officer A. M. Kopeyka (interrogation tape recording): "People were floundering all around in the water, because they didn't know how to swim. . . . We were all without life jackets, no one had expected the submarine to disappear so quickly."

Captain 1st Rank B. G. Kolyada (report to the Northern Fleet commander): "On finding themselves in the water, the personnel were forced to use just the one PSN-20 raft; the second had been swept about 100 meters away, and there was no swimming up to it."

And in the newspaper *Podvodnik Zapolyarya* (April 20, 1989) the participants of the event shared their memories:

Captain Lieutenant V. A. Gregulev: "And some didn't know how to swim. Seaman Mikhalev for example, a mechanic. A good seaman, conscientious. He went down so quietly, silently. Only because he didn't know how to swim."

Captain Lieutenant Y. N. Paramonov: "I was fully conscious the entire time, and I knew that it would be hard to make it on a single raft. But the second had drifted about fifty meters away. I could see that this was a desperate situation, that we might all die, and so I decided to swim over to the second raft."

Unfortunately, Captain Lieutenant Paramonov was unable to follow through with his intentions.

Warrant Officer V. V. Gerashchenko (interrogation tape recording):

> The raft was in the water. Waves broke over us head-high washing people off. Nothing could be done.
>
> The rescued submariners said that fewer would have died, had the submariners had individual inflatable life rafts, such as the kind naval pilots have. They would have been so useful to those jumping overboard into the frigid sea.[5]

There was an LAS-5M aircraft emergency inflatable life raft of this kind, with a capacity for five men, in compartment one. But the crew was so "well" trained that apparently it didn't even know of its existence. This life raft could have changed the situation in the most fundamental way: it could have provided the possibility to reach and make use of the second PSN-20 raft and the rafts dropped from airplanes. And then all of the submariners could have been accommodated on the rafts, and even those who couldn't swim would have been saved.

Warrant Officer V. F. Slyusarenko (explanatory report):

> Simultaneously with calling out to Chernikov for help I heard the noise of rushing water—this was the sound of the VSK rising to the surface, and the pointer of the depth gauge jerked and began dropping down abruptly from the 400 mark; the pointer on the pressure gauge also began crawling down. In one to two minutes the VSK surfaced. Chernikov had managed to come only half-way up. At this moment the pressure inside the VSK blew the catches on the upper hatch of the VSK, and Chernikov was ejected out like a cork. The force took me only half-way out, because I was a slight distance away from the hatch, beside the commander. . . . I saw Chernikov twenty meters away from the VSK, water rushed in through the open hatch from all directions, and in five to seven seconds the VSK took on water and went down to the bottom like a rock. I stayed on the surface.

Given that the pressure in the rescue chamber was over 2 kg/cm^2, the cover of the upper hatch may have been torn off from its catch, and the rush of air could have ejected Warrant Officer Chernikov out of the chamber. The possibility is not excluded that Chernikov himself released the catch on the hatch cover. Regardless of this, the carelessness of the submariners who remained in the rescue chamber (they hadn't battened down the chamber's upper hatch with its rack-and-pinion) resulted in its sinking and the loss of the people inside it.

The reactive force of the air jet emerging from the upper hatch forced the chamber below the surface, and "swallowing" water, it sank. Tentative calculations show that an initial chamber pressure of only 0.5 kg/cm^2 would have been sufficient for this to occur.

How do we explain and tie together the "explosion," the mist, and the worsening of audibility, coupled with the almost simultaneous loss of consciousness by three persons who had not put on the masks of their breathing apparatus?

There are no sufficiently persuasive explanations for this. But all of this could be explained if we assume that the "explosion" and the vibration were separate in time from the rest of the events. Apparently, right after the "explosion" the rescue chamber began surfacing; and as it approached the water surface, the pressure inside the chamber unseated the upper cover of the chamber somewhat (this cover was held by a catch). The air in the chamber began bleeding overboard, and the pressure within it started falling swiftly. This caused the ears of the people to "plug up," and worsened their hearing. The drop in pressure caused cooling of the air remaining in the chamber, and when the "dew point" was reached, a mist formed. Because the chamber was filled with air having a high concentration of carbon dioxide and carbon monoxide, and consequently a reduced oxygen concentration, the drop in pressure reduced the partial pressure of oxygen in it below permissible limits. As a result of this, three of the crewmembers who had not put on their IDA-59 self-contained breathing apparatus lost consciousness due to oxygen starvation, and were poisoned by carbon dioxide and carbon monoxide. All of the subsequent actions by Warrant Officers Slyusarenko and Chernikov to put the IDA-59 masks over the faces of Yudin and submarine commander Vanin occurred while the rescue chamber was on the surface. It follows from this version that the cover of the upper hatch had not been torn from its catch by the inside pressure. Rather, the hatch had been released from its catch by Warrant Officer Chernikov.

17. Remains of *Komsomolets'* rescue chamber

Looking at the videotapes and photographs taken from submersibles in the summer of 1989, one significant detail can be noted, one that would have been wrong to hide or discard as unimportant. On an image of the visible part of the rack-and-pinion ring securing the rescue chamber to the submarine hull, one section of this ring may be classified as a section with a broken tooth (see figure 17). In the meantime, the neighboring teeth show no visible damage. However, the absence of imagery of the matching paint on the release on the submarine's pressure hull does not permit any definite conclusion. This question could be clarified fully only by raising the rescue chamber or submarine. But it would be very important to clarify and it would help reduce the following conflicting statements by the tragedy's participants to a common denominator. Interrogation tape recordings:

Warrant Officer V. F. Slyusarenko: "We never were able to release the rack-and-pinion of the VSK. I feel that we were torn away from it, that we hadn't released it, because it was said that there was an additional fastening bolt."

Warrant Officer V. S. Kadantsev: Question: "What kept the rack-and-pinion of the VSK from turning?" Answer: "A locking device. There was no additional bolt."

In August–September 1991 a deep-sea submersible inspected the matching part of the rack-and-pinion release on the submarine's pressure hull. All of the teeth on the rack-and-pinion ring on the ship's pressure hull are undamaged, which clearly indicates that the system for separating the rescue chamber had worked "by the book," and confirms the absence of any additional fastening bolt that supposedly hindered turning of the rack-and-pinion.

The rescuers pulled thirty living crew members out of the water. Three submariners died onboard the tender. How did this happen?

Captain Lieutenant V. A. Gregulev (newspaper *Podvodnik Zapolyarya*, April 20, 1989): "The doctors were not guilty for the deaths of Molchanov, Nezhutin, and Grundul. But an irreversible process had already begun in their organs. We have already determined this here in the hospital, the post-mortem examination showed this." Such is the official position of the Navy concerning the reasons for these deaths of the three seamen. And in *Morskoy Sbornik* No. 4 from 1994, there appeared an article by Captain 1st Rank V. Y. Krapivin, "Tragedy of the Ship and the Honor of the Crew," where it is said

> I. A. Molchanov maintained the ship's log, which was located in the main command post, from the first minute to the last minute. Only one time did he come up to breathe fresh air. He was raised from the water onboard the tender. He was one of the

first to feel good and went to smoke. . . . Then the doctors stated that an irreversible change had already taken place in his organs which was the cause of his death.

As far as I know, this is the only publication where the details are contradictory with the official position of the Navy concerning the effects of smoking. The question about the cause of submariners' deaths on the tender was discussed during the interrogation of a member of the crew by the State Commission.

Lieutenant K.A. Fedotko (interrogation recording): Question: "What did the two people onboard the tender die from and how did they feel up to that time?" Answer: "I didn't see that, I can't tell you. . . . Then they said to me that they smoked, ate, and then smoked."

As a matter of fact, three people died, and each after he had smoked. In connection with this, the official position of the Navy about some irreversible process sounds somewhat unconvincing. The submariners at the time of the accident to the end were breathing carbon monoxide. They were weakened by a prolonged stay in the cold water. They were found on the brink of life and death. Smoking the cigarette added the next portion of carbon monoxide, which in their state was a most violent-acting poison. That portion of carbon monoxide cut their lives short. One thing is not understandable, why it is necessary to hide the circumstances of this additional tragedy.

Concluding our discussion of the rescue chamber, we can say the following. It sank together with the commander of the submarine, Captain 1st Rank Y. A. Vanin, Captain 3rd Rank V. A. Yudin, and Warrant Officer A. V. Krasnobayev, and it is now lying on the bottom of the Norwegian Sea with the upper hatch open, in ideal conditions for raising. The technical resources available to the Navy can accomplish this raising in a short time without significant expense. But the commander in chief of the Navy has nothing to say, his numerous admirals have nothing to say, and captains of all ranks have nothing to say. They have obviously exhausted the limit of their concern for the crew of the submarine *Komsomolets*, such that there was not enough left for giving three submariners a decent human burial in the ground. It might be said that raising the rescue chamber from a depth of around 1,600 meters is a complex engineering problem, and failure would be possible. I agree. But he who does nothing, gets nothing. Yes, we might even fail, but we still need to make the attempt to raise the chamber.

In coordination with an order of the president of the Russian Federation, there was an undertaking to attempt to raise the rescue chamber from

August 17–30, 1993. The TsKB of the sea techniques "Rubin" fulfilled the function of the principal organization in preparing and coordinating the work in connection with raising the chamber. The technical guidance for the task of raising the chamber was carried out by the search and rescue service of the Navy. Taking part in the work under agreement with the TsKB of the sea techniques were the science-research vessel *Mstislav Keldish* with the deep underwater apparatus *Mir*, the collector *KIL-164* of the Northern Fleet, NPO *Khimvolokno*, and a number of business ventures.

18. Open upper hatch of the rescue chamber

Figure 18 shows the details of the retrieval apparatus and the securing and launching line of the rescue raft.

The attempt to raise the chamber began on August 27, 1993, at 0741. During the raising, according to accounts, "the stern part of the collector shifted vertically with an amplitude of 2 to 3 meters. As far as raising the chamber, the maximum load on the line continuously increased from 30 tons when it was broken loose from the bottom to 58.5 tons when the chamber was located at a depth of 250 meters. At 1230 "the stern part of the *KIL-164* was raised unexpectedly by large irregular [ocean] waves resulting from superpositioning [wave on wave interaction] and having a height near 3.5 to 4.0 meters, abruptly raising it [the stern of KIL-164] to approximately that height." During this, "at the moment the stern rose, the line shook away from the pulley roller by 15 centimeters, forming a knot and when it was lowered to the pulley, it ripped off at this place." At that moment the chamber was located at a depth of 190 meters, and the maximum load on the line was equal to 65.4 tons. It can be added that this unsuccessful operation was preceded by the haste in conducting experimental construction and work preparation, which predetermined their [lesser] quality. In addition, during the periods of preparation and conduct of the operation to raise the rescue chamber, a series of solutions were adopted that were very risky and reflect a fair portion of unprofessionalism.

A year later, at the time of the science-research vessel *Mstislav Keldish*'s expedition in 1994, the rescue chamber was repeatedly located and investigated. It was hopeful that in 1995, the chamber would be raised successfully. Unfortunately, much time has passed since the day of the tragedy and, even during efforts to raise the chamber, there have been no signs of the remains of submariners.

Concluding my narration of the actions of the crew of the submarine *Komsomolets* during the accident, it would be wrong not to mention the heroic and self-sacrificing actions of certain members of the crew. Among them, Captain 3rd Rank Anatoliy Matveyevich Ispenkov, who carried out his military duty to the end, should be named first. Nor can we forget Senior Seaman Nadari Otariyevich Bukhnikashvili and Warrant Officer Vladimir Vasilievich Kolotilin, the first to meet the challenge of the situation; Captain 3rd Rank Vyacheslav Alexandrovich Yudin, who did much to save the crew; Captain 3rd Rank Aleksandr Vasilyevich Volodin, Lieutenant Vadim Vladimirovich Zimin, and Warrant Officer Gennadiy Vyacheslavovich Kovalev, who maintained communication until the last minutes of the tragedy; and Warrant Officer Yuri Fedorovich Kapusta, who shared his rescue equipment with comrades.

22

The Results of this Analysis

And so, we can make the following observations on the basis of the foregoing examination of the circumstances of the accident:

1. Analysis of the crew's actions during the accident revealed its total inability to fight for the submarine's survival. Weak combat and occupational training of the crew, specifically their unfamiliarity with ship systems, emergency procedures, and life-saving equipment, led to the tragic outcome of the accident aboard the submarine *Komsomolets*.

2. Until the very last moment of the tragedy there was a possibility for radically changing the situation in the fight for the submarine's survival through active and competent actions, and, in all cases, to keep the submarine afloat until rescue vessels could arrive. The submarine sank with 25 percent of its reserve of high-pressure air unused, with the diesel generator operating, with an operating electric power system, with working damage control equipment, and with functioning electric lighting. The absence of a RBITS (a manual for the proper operation of the ship's systems under patrol conditions) negatively affected both the crew's training in submarine damage control problems and its actions during the accident.

3. The delay of the submarine's attack center in transmitting the distress signal, the irresponsibility of the Northern Fleet's command post in organizing rescue operations, the lack of any leadership by the ship's command in evacuating the crew from the sinking submarine, and the

personnel's poor knowledge of the rules of using rescue equipment were the causes of the loss of the greater part of the crew.

4. There is no evidence that the submarine *Komsomolets* went to sea with a serviceable oxygen gas analyzer and with a serviceable television monitoring system. The faulty oxygen gas analyzer in compartment seven and the grossest violations of the rules of operating the technical resources were the most probable causes of the fire in compartment seven. Absence of a technical crew aboard the submarine *Komsomolets* and, as a consequence of this, poor quality preparation of the ship for the cruise, were the preconditions for the accident.

5. Real or imaginary imperfections in equipment, systems, or the submarine itself were neither the cause of the accident and the fire in compartment seven, nor did they influence the tragedy's outcome.

6. During the accident all equipment of the main propulsion unit operated trouble-free, blocking and safety systems foreseen by the design worked normally and ensured timely deenergizing and accident-free inactivation of all equipment in distressed compartments. The reactor control system and emergency shielding reliably inactivated the reactor and cooled it down without mishap.

7. The conclusion reached by the State Commission in the investigation of the circumstances and causes of the loss of the submarine *Komsomolets* is unobjective as regards establishing the probable cause of the accident, and as regards the evaluation given to the events that led to the accident's development and to its tragic outcome. As a consequence, the State Commission's assessment of the accident itself and the causes that brought it about are not objective. By looking at the accident of the submarine *Komsomolets* as an isolated case, and because the members of the commission belonged to the integral military-industrial complex, the State Commission was incapable of objectively and faithfully identifying the real causes of the high accident rate in the Navy, and of giving this tragedy a proper assessment.

At the end of this analysis of the tragedy's development and of the actions of personnel of the submarine *Komsomolets*, it should be said that the author does not claim to have available the absolute truth in interpreting particular events and facts. He may err in some things, and he may understand other things the wrong way. But he is convinced of one thing: the tragedy of the submarine *Komsomolets* was as the result of poor preparation for the cruise, which was a consequence of the low combat and occupational training of the crew.

The responsibility for this must be borne by the Navy's Main Directorate for Combat Training and the Main Directorate for Operation and Repair. There are still numerous unanswered questions, which arose during the investigation of the circumstances surrounding the accident of the submarine *Komsomolets*. The author believes there wouldn't be any remaining questions, if the naval leadership hadn't done everything it could to hinder this investigation.

23.

The Assault of the Pundits

As the State Commission's work proceeded, and as the causes of the accident and the real circumstances that led to the loss of the submarine *Komsomolets* became ever more clear, an extensive campaign to identify possible deficiencies in the design of the ship that could be alleged to as having led to the tragedy was undertaken in the press with the encouragement and complicity of certain representatives of the Navy. Let's examine the ten major assaults.

Assault #1: Captain 1st Rank Kolyada

In the January 15, 1990, edition of the newspaper *Izvestiya* and in the No. 2, 1990 edition of the journal *Morskoy Sbornik*, Captain 1st Rank Kolyada used the *Soviet Military Encyclopedia* in an attempt to persuade everyone that the submarine *Komsomolets* was simply "a vessel intended for experimentation, specially equipped and fitted out for various tests on new armament and hull structural units, and for experimental research on propulsion units, engines and other technical resources at sea." And that this submarine had supposedly been classified as "nominally" in the first line, that is, on the fighting team, with the "grace" of the Navy.

The reader is supposed to make his own conclusion from this—that the demands put upon the submarine were too great, that there could be little talk of quality when what the designer created was not a submarine, but something incomprehensible. No, this is not so. The *Komsomolets* was not "a vessel intended for experimentation," but an "experimental ship," that is, an experimental model of armament. And thus, they are "two very different situations." The *Soviet Military Encyclopedia* states that experimental models of weapons (armament) are created "for the purposes of testing new design (technological) ideas and solutions."

It was for the purpose of testing new design ideas and solutions that the submarine *Komsomolets* was created. But not only for them. This was a fighting submarine, and it was designed, built, and transferred to the Navy on the basis of standards and requirements imposed on a fighting submarine. High specifications and performance characteristics in the reliability of the technical resources, confirmed by experimental operation, made it possible for the first time in naval practice to adopt this submarine in 1988, to promote it up from the experimental category, and to award it the status of a fighting submarine. The government decree on adoption of the submarine *Komsomolets* by the Navy was coordinated with many military leaders, including the naval commander in chief and the USSR minister of defense. In this respect, contrary to Captain 1st Rank Kolyada's opinion, the submarine *Komsomolets* did not require any additional certification. And the simple truth that submarines that are "nominally adopted into the first line" do not go on patrol duty with a complete outfit of ammunition aboard, including nuclear devices, should have been explained to Kolyada. All of these elementary truths should have been known to the deputy commander of the division to which the *Komsomolets* belonged, and people should not have been misled with fables about "a vessel intended for experimentation."

Unfortunately, this has not ended the discussion of the experimental submarine.

Assault #2: Captain 1st Rank Bystrov

The newspaper *Krasnaya Zvezda* (March 15, 1990) carried an article by Captain 1st Rank S. I. Bystrov citing the following pronouncement by Naval Commander in Chief V. N. Chernavin in his interview with academician A. P. Aleksandrov: "Evidently, Anatoliy Petrovich, you've introduced this term, 'into experimental operation,' with good advantage. Such transfer of ships is still going on. This is the way the worst ships get accepted. When builders begin to feel the pressure of a deadline, they all return to this term." I don't know if the naval commander in chief really made such a statement, but a lie remains a lie, no matter who speaks it. The complaint made by the naval commander in chief against those who transfer "the worst ships" sounds strange, particularly when he says nothing about those who accept these "worst ships." But that's not the point.

From the very beginning, with assignment of the preliminary specifications in 1966, the submarine *Komsomolets* was designed as an experimental ship as regards problems associated with diving depth, and as a fighting ship in all other parameters. Its experimental operation was foreseen from the very beginning as well. Moreover, for what sort of other operation can an experimental submarine be transferred besides experimental?

I will dare to assert that all experimental models of equipment (including experimental submarines) are distinguished as a rule by high quality of manufacture, and the new technological concepts employed in these models are worked out meticulously in the testing process. And in order to be persuaded of this, it would be sufficient to compare experimental models of Russian articles at exhibitions with the series-manufactured models of these same articles sold in stores.

But this lie was not born in a vacuum. It has its own history, one which has no relationship to the submarine *Komsomolets*.

In 1980–1981, adoption of third-generation prototype submarines was threatened by failure. For various reasons these submarines had not undergone their basic trials. And then someone came up with the idea of transferring the prototype submarines into "intensive operation," during which the trials could be completed. So appeared a new term in shipbuilding—"intensive operation." This is when the "conspiracy of the century" occurred. But this was not a conspiracy between "wolves from industry" and "naive and liberal sheep" from the Navy. The conspiracy was "between equals," because the Navy was the main culprit. The torpedoes they had adopted couldn't be fired and the missiles wouldn't fly because of the absence of these submarines. The USSR Council of Ministers and the CPSU Central Committee also participated in this conspiracy. A political behind-the-scenes contribution was made as well: The great marshal of "Malaya Zemlya" had already announced to all the world the USSR's creation of the "Tayfun" strategic sea-based system to spite the "infamous" American "Trident" system. Something had to be done to save the day. The prototype submarines were transferred to "intensive operation," and the participants of the deal were generously decorated with orders, medals, the titles of Lenin, and state prize laureates. I don't know how things are going at the Mint, but the Committee on Lenin and State Prizes in Science and Engineering had exhausted its appropriations for several years into the future.

And so this unseemly history culminated with slander directed at the submarine *Komsomolets*. We need not dwell on the numerous publications referring to many unspecified mistakes or imperfections of various kinds, because they were written by people who did not have adequate information or who were far from knowledgeable about the essence of the issue. But there is one article that needs to be discussed.

Assault #3: Vice Admiral Kalashnikov

The newspaper *Na Strazhe Zapolyarya* (November 30, 1990) carried an article entitled "Assigning Responsibility for the Tragedy" by Vice Admiral V. S. Kalashnikov, the Naval Academy's deputy chief for training and scientific work. It reads: "The *Komsomolets* was a unique submarine, and its design deficiencies were also unique in their own way. Professionals know that their presence in a submarine directly influences its survivability." And that's all that the vice admiral, a professional, and the Navy's highest specialist in "training and scientific work" could say about "deficiencies." The vice admiral's logic is astounding: If it is a unique submarine, then it must have unique design deficiencies. The vice admiral is not troubled by the fact that his article does not cite any specific "unique design deficiencies," or that it contains no analysis of their influence upon the accident's development. He fouled someone else's doorstep and now feels his work is done.

On the other hand, there is more than enough specific misrepresentation and slander in this article. One can see right away that the author is in his element. To prove my point, let me cite a few examples. Vice Admiral Kalashnikov asserts: "And the conclusion of the commission, which contained representatives of the Navy, the designer, and industry, is categorical: 'In the situation as it was, it was impossible to save the ship.'" This assertion by the vice admiral is a misrepresentation. The statement by the State Commission, published in the press on September 6, 1990,[1] reads: "In the fight to save the submarine, the crew displayed self-sacrifice and courage, but in the situation as it was, the submarine could not be saved." This wording differs fundamentally from Vice Admiral Kalashnikov's assertions.

Nor are there any assertions in the commission's conclusions that in the fight for survival, "the crew did even more than it could have in that situation." Kalashnikov lifted these "conclusions of the commission" out of the conclusions of the Navy's Main Directorate for Operation and Repair on the "Analysis" made by Vice Admiral Y. D. Chernov. Moreover, the thoughts of the admirals in the "Combat Training" section of the State Commission Working Group concerning the high proficiency of Captain 1st Rank Vanin's crew are claimed to be the opinion of the State Commission, which is also a misrepresentation. Also, clearly slanderous is Vice Admiral Kalashnikov's assertion that "Vice Admiral Chernov is principally at fault for the poor training of Vanin's crew," that "a tendency to keep the second crew off of the ship could be seen distinctly in its training schedule during the time that the flotilla was under Comrade Chernov's command. It was not until after his departure in summer

1987 that the attitude toward this crew, its training, and time at sea changed abruptly for the better."

Let's look at the facts. Vice Admiral Chernov commanded the submarine flotilla until June 1986, and not until summer 1987, as Kalashnikov asserts. For only ten months of the four years and nine months' existence of Captain 1st Rank Vanin's crew was it directly subordinated to Vice Admiral Chernov. Given these facts, only dishonorable people can discern any kind of trend and accuse Vice Admiral Chernov of training this crew poorly. There were another two years and eight months after Vice Admiral Chernov's departure from the flotilla for Captain 1st Rank Vanin's crew to prepare for its first independent cruise. This would have been fully enough time to form and train a new crew for any submarine. Many more examples of this sort could be presented, because Vice Admiral Kalashnikov's article is full of lies, beginning with the accusations against the commander of the first crew, Captain 1st Rank Y. A. Zelenskiy, and ending with the dirty insinuations addressed toward Vice Admiral Chernov regarding a "set of Japanese video recording equipment" he supposedly received as a gift. Unfortunately, it is still very difficult in our country to prosecute slanderers, especially when they slander "in the performance of official duty."

Assault #4: Captain 1st Rank (Reserve) Gorbachev

Considerable attention needs to be devoted to an article by Captain 1st Rank (Reserve) A. N. Gorbachev, a former submarine commander, printed in the newspaper *Komsomolskaya Pravda* (April 29, 1989), and to his interview with this paper on December 17, 1989. In both publications Gorbachev blames the loss of the submariners and the submarine itself on the designer on the basis of rumors and discussions with "yardkeeper acquaintances" of his. But it is not among designers, it is not in the shipbuilding industry, it is not in the military acceptance system, and, finally, it is not in the Navy's Main Directorate of Shipbuilding that we must seek those "who sank this ship as well," as Gorbachev does.

To put it briefly, the tragedy occurred due to a catastrophic gap between the level of the equipment installed in modern submarines, the level of occupational training of submariners, and the quality of routine maintenance and repairs carried out during preparation of submarines for cruises. High personnel turnover brought about by the lack of social safeguards for submariners doesn't play an insignificant role either. As for the culprits, they must be sought among those who permitted this situation to develop. As for "ensuring this nuclear-powered submarine against accidents," the high fire and explosion safety of the submarine *Komsomolets* was confirmed by an expert commission appointed by the Navy after a hands-on inspection of its condition during the period from October 11 to October 20, 1983.

The fact that a fire didn't start in compartment five, even after a deflagration occurred in the compartment, attests to the fire safety of compartments of the submarine *Komsomolets*. And it was not from a random electric spark or flash that the fire started in compartment seven, as Gorbachev asserts. The fire was predestined by the poor preparation of the ship for the cruise and the grossest violations of the rules of operating the submarine's equipment.

Nor was the compartment fully involved aboard the submarine in the initial period of the accident. It was not until fifteen to twenty minutes after the fire started, and as a result of the incompetent actions of the ship's command, that the compartment became fully involved.

Praising or, on the other hand, cursing the LOKh fire-extinguishing system using freon as the fire extinguisher wouldn't change anything. There are no alternatives today, and there were none before 1995. And, in the meantime, the existing LOKh system is the most effective firefighting system. That the fire aboard the submarine *Komsomolets* had not been extinguished by this system does not put this system at fault: the fact is that the freon extinguisher was not delivered to the distressed compartment.

The rescue chamber was discussed earlier. There are full grounds for believing that the devices of the rescue chamber were designed "by the book." The built-in electric lighting functioned in the chamber until the very last moment. Unfortunately, the mistakes and vexing lapses of the personnel resulted in the fact that only one of five men survived. I am compelled to report, with Comrade Gorbachev in mind specifically, that the rescue chamber had been tested by the first crew of the *Komsomolets* during the period of experimental operation with the direct participation of representatives of the designer, the shipbuilding plant, and the Navy's search and rescue service; and that the testing involved actual separation of the rescue chamber from the submarine and its surfacing. Thus, the references by Gorbachev to a "chamber of death" and his rhetoric —"who designed this chamber, and at what level of mind and heart?"—are groundless, and may be qualified as slander against the designer. I dare to assert that the chamber was designed by competent specialists with the highest "level of mind and heart."

The former commander of a submarine asked some questions that sound very strange coming from him: "Who taught the submariners to use the life rafts and prepare them for use? And who taught the lads to find their individual protective equipment in total darkness and never lose contact with them?" Is this really something that must be done by nannies from Moscow, or by governesses enlisted from abroad? Isn't this the responsibility of the command of each submarine and the fleet formations? Or does Gorbachev believe that the command responsibility is confined only to telling a seaman who doesn't know how to swim: "Jump, jump, my boy, swim out from the side. Our ship will soon go beneath the water."

Concluding, let's consider Gorbachev's question ". . . is he [Gorbachev] capable of meanness?" What other word can you use to describe the attempt to blame the designer for the submarine's loss without any proof or justifications? How do we qualify his unsubstantiated accusation of the Sevryba Association in the death of the submariners? It would appear that Captain 1st Rank (Reserve) Gorbachev found a suitable descriptor for his own action.

Assault #5: *Khimiya Izhizn*

The journal *Khimiya Izhizn* (No. 11, 1990) printed an article entitled, "Did the *Komsomolets* Sink Accidentally?" by doctor of physicomathematical sciences V. N. Mineyev, candidate of technical sciences V. V. Korenkov, and candidate of physicomathematical sciences Y. N. Tyunyayev. The authors assert that "as in Chernobyl, the disaster aboard the *Komsomolets* was embodied in its design." Their main argument that this is the case is the absence of obvious words, such as "reliable," "unsinkable," and "safe" from the supposedly official name of the submarine *Komsomolets*—"experimental torpedo nuclear-powered submarine." Relax, comrade scientists, everything is in order with the official name of the submarine *Komsomolets*. It was named as is required by the warship classification established in the Navy. Moreover, there were no sudden fires in electrical equipment aboard the submarine *Komsomolets*, the fuel and oil pipelines didn't crack, oxygen didn't flow into the zone of fire, fossil fuel didn't catch fire, and neither titanium nor the powder of gas generators or torpedo detonators burned. There were no explosions, and, equally so, there was no iron scale or chlorate plugs. And the titanium hull did not heat to a temperature of 900 to 1,100 degrees Celsius.

According to calculations of specialists, during the entire time of the accident around 700 kilograms of flammable materials (expressed in units of fossil fuel) burned in compartments six and seven. In light of this, dear scientists, all of your "calculations" are far afield of both chemistry and reality.

As for flammable materials, unfortunately our science has not yet created non-flammable paints and varnishes for submarines, nonflammable thermal insulation for the pressure hull, nonflammable insulation for ship electric cabling, and nonflammable oils and supplies, or introduced them into production. When it comes to food products, it is true that there has been some forward progress: They are still flammable, but consuming them as food is dangerous.

Nor are Gosstandart (State Committee for Standards) or the ship minister at fault.

And, of course, it is forgivable for you, dear scientists, not to know that Kingston valves are not installed aboard submarines for the purpose of flooding compartments, or that all Soviet submarines were equipped with standardized rescue hatches and coamings for attachment of rescue craft long before 1971. Nor could you have known that the American submarine *Thresher* sank not due to "inadequate underwater unsinkability" but for an entirely different reason. None of this information is contained in the adventure novels on the basis of which you probably developed your ideas about submarine building. And don't recall Admiral S. O. Makarov and academician A. N. Krylov in vain, believe me that submarine designers also understand unsinkability and the procedure for designing specific systems and entire submarines. By the way, let me make note that the term "underwater unsinkability" has not yet been introduced into shipbuilding theory and practice.

And so, comrade scientists, return to your "hockey arenas" and play quietly with your little "pucks." All the more so because not all of your scientific works and dissertations begin with the words "original," "distinctive," or "highly scientific." And in your free time, it wouldn't be wrong to think about why our country, which is first in the world in the number of scientists per capita, is in the backwaters of world science. To reassure you, let me give you the full official name of the submarine *Komsomolets*: "deep-sea large nuclear-powered torpedo submarine." As you can see, this name does not contain the ominous term "intended for experimentation" that troubled you so.

Assault #6: N. A. Cherkashin

Something has to be said about the articles written by the writer N. A. Cherkashin, a former submarine deputy commander for political affairs. While I do not believe it necessary to fully analyze the author's version of the crew's actions during the accident, we do need to examine some of the questions associated with the submarine's design, and dwell on certain aspects of this version.

Cherkashin writes: "The fire aboard the *Komsomolets* was altogether unprecedented. It was unique, because the nuclear-powered submarine was itself unique: a special hull, navigation at very great depth. . . ."[2] It seems that a fire depends on the structure and material of the hull, as well as on the depth at which a submarine travels. There can be only small fires on submarines that do not travel deep, while fires aboard submarines with a unique depth of navigation can only be unique. How far must we go in the effort to somehow find fault with the submarine *Komsomolets*?! And that's not the only assertion of this sort by the writer: "First about the ship. It was noteworthy only in its ability to reach depths beyond those of all modern submarines. But at least because it was the first of its kind, as is true with all prototype ships, initially the *Komsomolets* needed further design improvements, that is, it was not perfect. Even American experts say this."[3] There's logic for you: If it's first, then it must be poor. All the more so because some mythical "American experts" say this.

Still, we should be thankful to the writer for his high assessment of the deep-sea qualities of the submarine *Komsomolets*. As for design concepts not associated with deep-sea navigation, they are all standard, tested by many years of practical Soviet submarine shipbuilding, and they correspond to the requirements of the Navy, the sector's standards, and state standards. Five years of accident-free operation confirmed the high operating reliability of the submarine, and this time was fully sufficient to reveal any deficiencies, if there were any.

There is one other statement by Cherkashin that cannot be ignored: "The positions of the sides were extremely polarized. The builders: The ship was good, and the crew was poorly trained. The Navy: The ship had flaws, and the crew was sufficiently trained."[4] The author goes on to say: "In discussing the causes of the disaster, even the most frantic revilers of the unfortunate crew are forced to kick the ball through their own goalposts: 'Accident prevention aboard this nuclear-powered submarine remained at the level of previous years. There is nothing new in it to protect against electric sparks. A single spark can create an inferno. No, when it comes to protection from accidents, Soviet designers have not gone very far.'" The writer shouldn't have juggled the facts in this way, even to prove his dubious version of a conflict between industry and the Navy. The cited statement of a "frantic reviler" belongs to Captain 1st Rank (Reserve) A. N. Gorbachev, and it was printed in the newspaper *Komsomolskaya Pravda* (December 17, 1990). As everyone knows, Captain 1st Rank (Reserve) Gorbachev is not a submarine builder, and if he is trying to "score a goal," he is not doing it through his own goalposts. He knows quite well that such a polarity between the sides—the builders versus the Navy—does not exist. Following the laws of nature as it should, the watershed extends vertically, and not horizontally as the top brass of the Navy and their protégés try to persuade everyone.

Vice Admiral Y. D. Chernov, Captain 1st Rank Y. A. Zelenskiy, Captain 2nd Rank V. V. Stefanovskiy, and many other submariners are not builders of submarines, but this doesn't keep them from making a realistic assessment of the level of occupational training of submarine crews. None of the builders or submariners named above intended to revile Captain 1st Rank Vanin's crew. The crew did everything it could. And this was not so much its fault as its misfortune, because there were many things that it had not been taught, and many things for which it was unprepared. Their reference is to those responsible for the weak combat and occupational training of all submarine crews, to those who, rather than engaging in honest, open, and principled dialogue, are hiding behind the backs of the deceased members of Captain 1st Rank Vanin's crew, and who are dealing with dissidents out of public view.

The writer Cherkashin also has specific complaints against the design of the submarine *Komsomolets*: "Before 'the red-hot walls of the pipelines ruptured,' their plastic gaskets melted out, causing the release of high-pressure air into the compartment. Previously, these gaskets were made of fire-refined copper (with a far higher melting point than plastic). Pursuing the noble goal of economizing the people's money, they substituted this nonferrous metal by polyamide, omitting the possibility of fire from their calculations. . . . The conditions under which the fire burned aboard the *Komsomolets* had never been encountered before, and I believe they wouldn't be encountered if the polyamide gaskets were to be substituted by fire-refined copper."[5]

Allow me to inform you, my respected writer, that the sorry specialists from the 1st Submarine Flotilla misled you. No one ever substituted polyamide gaskets for fire-refined copper gaskets in high-pressure air pipelines. And despite this, the conditions under which the fire burned aboard the submarine *Komsomolets* may recur, especially if the wearers of "unsoiled uniforms" and their defenders continue to close their eyes to the bad state of combat and occupational training of submarine crews.

It would be pertinent here to cite the following statement by Division Deputy Commander Captain 1st Rank Kolyada, as represented by N. A. Cherkashin: "The submarine behaved normally. A mechanical engineer told me that after the two aft compartments (the sixth and the seventh) were flooded, according to the stability diagram the ship would have remained afloat."[6]

When compartments six and seven are flooded at the same time that main ballast tank No. 10 is flooded, the submarine loses 50 percent of its buoyancy reserve at the stern. This is not counting the unblown tank No. 5 and the flooded starboard tank No. 7. Elementary logic tells us that no submarine can remain afloat with such loss of buoyancy and with such an upsetting longitudinal moment. It is hard to say how poorly trained you must be not to understand this simple truth. It was because of this professional incompetency that the crew found itself in the frigid waters of the Norwegian Sea without rescue equipment, and was forced to pay for that incompetency with great loss of life.

In his effort to show the crew's actions as heroic, Cherkashin loses his sense of proportion, and steps beyond all permissible limits: "Not knowing yet whether the submarine was sinking or surfacing, the 'keeper of the reactor,' remote-control group commander Captain Lieutenant Igor Orlov, began shutting down the menacing heart of the nuclear-powered submarine. He lowered the shim rods to the lower limit switch and quenched the fire of the 'nuclear boiler.'"[7] I read this, and I am astonished. Is this a military crew welded together by military discipline, or is this an unruly mob in which each person can do whatever he likes? It is shameful for the former submarine deputy commander for political affairs not to know that any action associated with changing a submarine's propulsion parameters is made only on the basis of orders from the attack center, and not on one's own initiative. As far as the specific circumstances are concerned, the reactor was stopped by the emergency shielding system when the ship was already on the surface. The main task of the operator of the main propulsion unit under these conditions is to not "get under foot" when the automatic system goes into action. We could continue with such examples, but what more can one say about an author who expands the abbreviation "RB" (radiation safety) as "radioactive underclothing?"

Assault #7: Captain 1st Rank (Retired) Boyko

The newspaper *Smena* (15 April 1990) carried an article by Captain 1st Rank (Retired) V. A. Boyko entitled "No Culprits as Usual?" Everything the author says is as clear and as simple as it can be. Submarines must have the "tenacity" "not to sink as a result of any kind of fire," and fire-extinguishing equipment must put fires out "with maximum possible force." The matter of designing such submarines, Boyko believes, is simple; it is something "that is taught in basic courses at shipbuilding VUZes."

Further, he believes that, rather than designing such submarines, designers, builders, testers, recipients, and operating executives "administer justice over crews, laying emphasis not on saving people but on their own prestige and well-being." And as for mistakes made by personnel, "certain mistakes have always been made and will continue to be made in such difficult, stressful, life-threatening situations." Such is his position. And one unwittingly thinks that perhaps the designing of submarines needs to be assigned to students dropped for poor performance, and their operation should be given over to cadets who have not undergone the full course of training, to whom it was explained in the first year that it is harmful and dangerous to make mistakes.

Fortunately, however, V. A. Boyko himself leads us out of this dead end. As it turns out, in order to create submarines with "tenacity," we need to first "improve the concept of and requirements on submarine survivability," and not until this should we "realize them in design and construction, and test them out in trials and during certification—thus designing submarines with tenacity." Then it would be up to the "specialist on survivability," as Boyko refers to himself. He is in a better position to know how imperfect the concepts of and requirements on submarine design are in relation to survivability. Captain 1st Rank (Retired) Boyko served most of his career behind the walls of Naval Institute No. 1, which develops such "imperfect concepts of and requirements" for survivability.

As for specific complaints regarding the design of the submarine *Komsomolets*, there is nothing to say—Boyko simply didn't have any. Obviously, it is easier to complain in general—this approach requires neither substantiation nor even existence of specific complaints.

Assault #8: An Open Letter from Captain 1st Rank Kolyada

An open letter written by Captain 1st Rank B. G. Kolyada and his associates[8] cites the following specific "deficiencies" of the submarine, which, in the opinion of the authors, influenced the tragedy's outcome.

"The absence of an integrated system aboard the ship for estimating the situation in the distressed compartment on the basis of objective data, especially in the absence or incapacitation of personnel, made it impossible to estimate the situation in the distressed compartment in the first minute," Kolyada announces. Could the authors of the remark explain to me what this "integrated system for estimating the situation in the distressed compartment" is? What is it that it must estimate integrally, on the basis of what objective data, and in what units of measurement?

Fire detection equipment was installed aboard the submarine *Komsomolets*. The fire was reported by the watchstander for compartment seven, and there were objective warning signals indicating both an increase in temperature in compartment seven and a low insulation resistance in the electrical system. Objective information on the fire in compartment seven could have been obtained with the installed television camera, had the television system been working. Is this really not enough to be able to classify the fire in compartment seven? If it isn't, then what do we make of the command issued at 1103 to deliver a fire extinguisher into compartment seven?

Analysis of the personnel's actions shows that throughout the entire time of the accident, the attack center of the *Komsomolets* was unable to really estimate the situation in the distressed compartments, to really monitor the submarine's buoyancy and stability, and to take real steps to fight for its survival. All of this affected the accident's outcome. The absence of "an integrated system for estimating the situation" has no relevance to this.

All of this does not exclude the need for improving existing equipment for detecting fires in compartments. As for an integrated system for estimating the situation, no ship of the Navy has such a system. Not even the concept of such a system has been developed, and exploratory research in support of its creation has not been conducted. Thus, any talk today about such a system is pointless.

The authors of the letter have other complaints against the structures of the submarine: "The situation was aggravated by 'design deficiencies,' to wit: The LOKh system; a standard system for relieving excess pressure in distressed compartments; an integrated system that would help the personnel to forecast the possible development of events in extreme situations on the basis of objective data; the impossibility of controlling the airtightness of compartments from the control room." Let's examine these "design deficiencies."

The detailed design of the submarine *Komsomolets* was developed to include a LOKh firefighting system equipped with remote control from the control room. However, because of the supposedly insufficient reliability of remotely controlled electromagnetic valves, a joint decision of the USSR Ministry of Shipbuilding Industry and the Navy in 1975 prescribed a transition to manual control of the LOKh aboard all submarines. After the new valves were developed, in 1987 the Navy ordered an assignment to study installation of a remote-controlled LOKh system in submarines, but for some unknown reasons a decision was made not to introduce a remote-controlled LOKh system into the *Komsomolets*. Such are the facts.

Remote control of the LOKh firefighting system is not included on all submarines today, and this must be considered in the operation of the ship. All submarines also lack a special system for relieving pressure from distressed compartments. Such a system does not exist in the Navy's requirements on submarine design. Thus, it would be wrong to refer to something that was never ordered as a design deficiency. In the best case, this may be viewed as a proposal for study.

In addition, Article 275 of the RBZh-PL-82 foresees development of recommendations on relieving pressure from distressed compartments. The leadership of submarine formations is responsible for such development. As the division deputy commander, Captain 1st Rank Kolyada bears a certain amount of responsibility for the fact that such recommendations were not drawn up for the submarine *Komsomolets*.

There is no need to bring up the fact that not a single submarine of the Navy has an integrated system for forecasting possible development of events in extreme situations on the basis of objective data. The concept has not been developed, and exploratory research in support of creating such a system has not been conducted. During the accident the leadership of the submarine *Komsomolets* did not undertake any action to measure the parameters of the ship's attitude or determine the elements of its buoyancy and stability, which would have made it possible to forecast the accident's development. Given such a passive attitude toward ship damage control, no integrated systems of any kind can help.

No submarines of the Navy have a system for controlling the airtightness of compartments from the control room (with the exception of a certain class of submarine with a limited number of personnel). Development of such systems for compartments intended to be manned is not foreseen in the Navy's requirements on submarine design. Thus, even this "design deficiency" can be treated only as a proposal for development. Introduction of such a system into a submarine would be equivalent to complicating the design, increasing the weight and size characteristics of the equipment, and reducing its reliability. In addition, the system may turn out to be unserviceable in emergency situations due to failure of control circuits. As for the degree to which these negative indicators could be compensated by the anticipated increase in submarine survivability, the answer to this question can be provided only through meticulous design development.

At the same time, remote control of the airtightness of compartments cannot solve the problem completely. Analysis of the actions taken by personnel of the submarine *Komsomolets* during the accident showed that the submarine's leadership had not given the order promptly to take the main turbogear unit (GTZA) off line, and then to seal off the bulkhead of compartment seven. The operator at the console of the main propulsion unit did not shut the Kingston valve of the stern-tube gland's cooling system, which is equipped with remote control. The mains were not closed throughout the entire time of the accident, even though closing them manually did not present any difficulty. Hence, the same simple conclusion follows: No technical tricks will help in the absence of the needed combat and occupational training of the crew.

Summarizing all of the "design deficiencies" of the submarine *Komsomolets* stated by Captain 1st Rank Kolyada and his associates, we can make the following conclusions: Not one of the indicated "deficiencies" could have resulted in special circumstances that led to this tragedy; and these "deficiencies" are inherent to all or most submarines of the Navy.

Assault #9: Captain 1st Rank Krapivin

In the magazine *Morskoy Sbornik* (No. 4, 1994), an article was published, which was devoted to the first edition of my book, "Tragedy of a Ship and Honor of a Crew" by Captain 1st Rank and candidate of technical science, V. Y. Krapivin.

With what aim was this article written? To defend the honor of Y. A. Vanin's crew? To provide the author a headline article with the first lines of the text? How much does this title correspond to the facts? In the article there is nothing that defends the honor of the crew or its actions during the period of the accident. It appears that this article is an attempt to show that the crew was well trained and prepared in the field of the ship's damage control, that only special circumstances during an accident, including those called "emergency machine scenario" (situations of disabled equipment) that do not allow the crew to do anything (to avert a tragedy). This direction is clear and motivated by personal bias. Captain 1st Rank V. Y. Krapivin was, at the time, the head of the damage control department of the First Institute of the Navy. The same institute which did not prepare for the submarine *Komsomolets* "Guide to Combat use of Technical Resources (RBITS)," the very document that is intended to prove the theoretical basis for working out problems of a ship's damage control, and for which the crew of Y. A. Vanin was deprived. The basic aim of this article appears to be to convince the readers of *Morskoy Sbornik* that the absence of the "Manual" by no means influenced the degree of combat and professional readiness of the second crew, and, consequently, the First Institute of the Navy did not contribute to the tragedy on the April 7, 1989. To satisfy this, Captain 1st Rank Krapivin even worked out his own "scenario" of the accident and gave a "scientific basis" of the influence of psychomotor characteristics on the behavior of a person in extreme conditions, for which "it would have been good not to be prepared."

The article is accompanied by accusations of the author's book as being nonobjective and slanderous. During this, V. Y. Krapivin does not offer concrete evidence but rather slips into lies and smears. Not considering a need to provide answers to these attacks, it follows to look at the technical aspects of the article by Captain 1st Rank Krapivin. On the basis of his scenario of the accident, V. Y. Krapivin supplies the version concerning the spontaneous opening of the valves supplying air into compartment seven at the beginning of the accident period. Captain 1st Rank Krapivin does not know "the cause and source of the flare up," but suggests it is sufficient to know the exact place of the center of the fire—the region near the valve supplying the air in compartment seven. Concerning the fire center, its obvious influence was exerted on this valve only, and did not affect the analogous valves to blow the stern ballast tanks, which are arranged next to that valve. Captain 1st Rank Krapivin does not trouble to point out that in that region of all the valves, nothing else was burned.

The article is noteworthy in that in it V. Y. Krapivin speaks about the center [locational] character of the fire in compartment seven but not about the volume. This is contradictory to the official version of the Navy. Captain 1st Rank Krapivin "chops the branch" on which "sits" the legend stating that at 1103 the intensity of the fire was great due to the seal of the high air pressure system. Thus, during the period when the submarine was in the depth interval of 150 to 50 meters, as Krapivin maintains, a spontaneous opening of the valve supplying air to compartment seven occurred. This period corresponds with the time from 1112 to 1114 when the command was given to raise the radio location station "Bukhta" and the periscope and to blow the aft group of the main ballast tanks. The main post knew about the fire at 1103, so at that time the command was given for the supply of LOKh into compartment seven.

Thus, according to the "version" of V. Y. Krapivin, the time between receiving the information about the fire in compartment seven and the spontaneous opening of the valve supplying air into the compartment has an interval of no less than nine minutes. Why couldn't a "well trained crew" in that time go into compartment six, supply LOKh to compartment seven, and extinguish the center of the fire? The time to fulfill this was sufficient. But Krapivin was quiet about this because he was told no facts.

And further in the article there is something inconceivable. In the misrepresentation of Lieutenant A.V. Zaytsev's testimony, V. Y. Krapivin maintains that at a depth of 50 meters, "The air control systems of compartments six and seven opened." However, for some reason, it did not prevent Lieutenant Zaytsev from blowing MBT No. 8 and No. 9. For some reason blowing MBT No. 10 was not successful, although the valves for blowing and the controls of all of the main ballast tanks are located in compartment seven in one location. But, apparently, Krapivin does not know about this and that is why he writes it so. Later, he maintains the valves blowing the main ballast tank opened spontaneously, but during this, only the starboard tanks were blown. The port tanks were not blown due to the destruction of the high-pressure blow pipe. The blowing of the MBT No. 10, supposedly, was observed by Captain Lieutenant Verezogov, and this was after 1120. (At 1120, which agrees with the ship's log, the hatch to the rescue chamber was opened. After that, Verezgov could exit onto the fairwater fin and could observe the blowing of the main ballast tanks.)

Supposedly, Captain 1st Rank Krapivin does not know that the MBT No. 10 of both sides is blown from a common valve, and not from different valves. Looking at everything, not looking just at the mistakes of Captain 1st Rank Krapivin indicated above, this is the primary discrepancy of the "scenario." The calculations show that, had the valves supplying air to compartment seven opened spontaneously at 1112, the entire supply of air from bulkhead VVD No. 4 would have bled into compartment seven in no less than eight minutes. Consequently, for the blowing of the MBT No. 10, according to the version of V. Y. Krapivin, there would already be no air in the VVD No. 4 bulkhead. And further, there would be no air for the repeated blowing of the aft group of the MBT, which according to the ship's log was carried out at 1134. Experimental work, carried out by the State Commission Working Group, shows that the spontaneous opening of the valves supplying air to the compartment (and blowing valves being analogous to it) may occur after being subject to a temperature range of 200 to 250 degrees Celsius for more than thirty minutes. This also disproves V. Y. Krapivin's version. This version does not agree with the testimony of Lieutenant Zaytsev, who says that after the blowing of the aft groups of the main ballast tanks, the pressure of the first, third, and fourth bulkheads VVD was near 150 to 200 kg/cm^2.

From that point onward, all the flimsiness is obvious in Captain 1st Rank V. Y. Krapivin's version concerning the spontaneous opening of the valve supplying air into compartment seven. Together with this version, the "machine scenario" of a developing emergency, when supposedly "all basic physical processes and changes in the positioning of fittings were no longer dependent on the will of the people," is shown to be unsubstantiated. To this it can be added that the approximate calculations, fulfilled by the working group of the State Commission, show that the total amount of air going into compartment seven during the accident was equal to 6400 kg with nearly 3700 kg coming from the bulkhead VVD No. 1 and No. 3 at the locations in compartments one and three, respectively. In other words, a large part of the air entering into the accident compartment was not subject to the "machine scenario" when those conditions existed. Notwithstanding, the tragedy would not have occurred if three valves of the main air system in compartment three had been shut. For practically the entire duration of the accident, basic actions could have been undertaken from the main command post that would have changed the course of the accident and, in any case, would have provided support to keep the submarine afloat until the arrival of rescuers. If this was not done, it is only due to the weak combat and professional readiness of Y. A. Vanin's crew. A significant portion of the blame lies on the First Institute of the Navy for not providing the "Manual on Combat Use of Technical Resources."

There is no sense in looking any further at V. Y. Krapivin's "scenario." It will be enough to just recount the basic absurdities in which the article abounds. Inspections of the submarine on the bottom show that the rubber covering [coating] remained in the region of the MBT No. 10 on the starboard side only; therefore, the assertions by Captain 1st Rank about the high temperature in MBT No. 8 and MBT No. 9 are unfounded. Estimated calculations show that in the region of compartment six the pressure hull could not have heated up to a temperature of 100 degrees Celsius, and the air in the main command center did not reach 80 degrees Celsius. There is no basis to address, as he has, the sealing of tanks. Captain 1st Rank Krapivin maintains that the course of the events could only be influenced from compartments six and seven, that it was impossible to go to the stern to control the operations of the vessel, and that near 0200 the MBT No. 10 of the port side blew. These, and many other statements, do not correspond with the facts.

What conclusions did Captain 1st Rank V. Y. Krapivin make from the tragedy of the submarine *Komsomolets*? In his own words: "A critique of the *Komsomolets* tragedy shows that among the important starting premises that shape views on the problem of survivability, one has to single out the possibility of an emergency situation arising." Glory to be, gentlemen! At last they are now enlightened! The sinking of nearly ten of our submarines during peace time was needed "to single out the possibility of an emergency situation arising." It appears that Captain 1st Rank Krapivin had considered earlier that the accident began spontaneously without an emergency situation arising. Here V. Y. Krapivin "misses" a terrific possibility to address the preconditions that stipulate "the possibility of an emergency situation arising" on the submarine *Komsomolets*, starting with the absence of technical crew and ending with the poor quality preparation of the submarine for the combat cruise and the weak combat and professional preparation of Y. A. Vanin's crew. He takes this "opportunity" toward another direction: "there must be a means of diagnosing a pre-emergency state of the complex objects, and this is already a state-wide task." It is not clear which kind of "means of diagnosing" V. Y. Krapivin means, or where they must be placed, either on the ships or in the offices of the leaders of the Navy. By reading the article, only an uninformed person would get the impression that on the submarine there was no system to control the temperature, no electro-insulation resistance, no means to monitor gas composition in the air of the compartments, and no available parameters on the working of the equipment or other means of information that would allow an emergency situation to be exposed and the necessary measures taken. This obvious availability of these systems, of course, does not signify that there is no need to engage in the modernization of these means and to the addition of new capabilities. Besides, in order to engage these questions, V. Y. Krapivin appears detached and transfers the problem to a series of "state-wide tasks."

In the article Captain 1st Rank V. Y. Krapivin relays a "conception" of damage control for submarines. "An emergency situation may develop beginning with some type of momentum, and proceed like a complex derivative of simultaneous or successive actions with two or more fire factors, during the process of which one may identify definite termination points and stages." For this part of his writing there is no objection. But based on that statement, the following doubtful conclusion is drawn: "Therefore, defensive measures are foreseen only for the initial phase, and even with regard to their active implementation by the crew, these may turn out to be insufficient."

Proceeding from these false premises, Captain 1st Rank Krapivin suggests that during the design phase the designers "analyze all the stages of the development of an emergency," "right up to the hardest stage," and "for every stage" "to develop measures for the counteraction of all fire factors." In order to further muddle the question, V. Y. Krapivin considers that "looking at the scenario of the development of an emergency must, of course, be supplemented with the possible actions of the crew, but with a sobering estimation as to what measure one may use to calculate their active and decisive actions."

How the head of the damage control department of the First Institute of the Navy understands the words, "to what measure one may calculate the active and decisive actions of the crew" is clear from the following declaration "establishing a now highly organized investigation of the psychomotor characteristics of a man under extreme conditions without presupposing logic in his concrete actions, but rather to consider that it would be good to be an unprepared man, and that every emergency situation is always unexpected for him and that is why his actions may be improper." And again from indisputable stated facts about the unexpected rise of an emergency situation, Krapivin draws an incorrect conclusion about the possibilities of mistaken actions "of a prepared person." Such "science" is the basis of the notorious "right to a mistake" which is expected to eliminate an emergency in the Navy.

V. Y. Krapivin ends his "conception" with the following indeterminable conclusion. "It turns out to be much easier to foresee a few regimes of combat and daily action, rather than to forecast all variations of a rising and developing emergency situation. And without this it is impossible to determine the sufficient collection of defensive capabilities and provide detailed instruction for the personnel." Such is the summary of the "concept." [Editor's note: This was an accepted perspective at the First Institute in the 1990s and was based on the "realization" that the submarine's crews had proven their limitations; hence, automatic should be implemented to the fullest to keep the crew out of the decision process during an emergency.]

Contrariwise, and in the opinion of the author of this book, science and technology must be developed to embrace the following principles to improve the damage control potential of ships:

First: The foreseen means and measures at the initial period of an emergency must take into account the possible paths of its development and be sufficient to guarantee localization and suppression given the timely, competent, and active actions of the crew. Attempts to carry out damage control during an emergency only at the time of a figurative avalanche of accumulation of fire factors, as is the rule, will result in doom by the fire, as in the appearance of a new front for combat against the emergency [during which] means for this combat will be compromised and the planned measures will not be implementable. During this, often it will be impossible to anticipate the paths by which the emergency can spread.

Second: The equipment and the systems of the submarine must inhibit the fire factors of the emergency and not aggravate them over the course of time; they must be sufficient to reveal the accident and to take measures to localize and suppress it. During this process it is necessary to set conditional parameters from the initial stages of the emergency, with regards to analyzing the actual emergencies on submarines over the past years.

Third: The crew does not have the "right" to make mistakes by breaching the procedure directed in the ship's regulations (RBZh-PL), the directions and instructions for the operation of combat and technical means, or other guides. This required ability provides a possible guidance for professional selection, which should also include psychological stability in extreme conditions in combination with combat and professional preparedness.

Embracing these principles, in the opinion of the author, allows one to carry out work in reducing emergencies in the Navy. This course of action is practicable and does not depend on the creation of an artificial and indeterminable concept [regarding the psychological and intellectual limitations of submariners] as has been proposed in V. Y. Krapivin's article.

Assault #10: Captain 1st Rank Kolton

In the newspapers *Komsomolskaya Pravda*, (June 30, 1989), *Literaturnaya Gazeta*, (September 2, 1992), and *Moskovsky Komsomolets* (October 25, 1994), an article was published in which great significance was given to the rescue chamber and its role in the tragedy of the submarine *Komsomolets*. In all of these articles "by leading specialists" to certain degrees, retired Captain 1st Rank I. B. Kolton, a former representative of Permanent State Acceptance Commission of the Navy Ships came forward "as judge." What gave him the right to enter into this role? It turns out that in 1982 the industry supposedly appeared to agree with Kolton to establish a government testing program for the submarine *Komsomolets*. Not seeing a separate requirement for testing the rescue chamber in this program, Captain 1st Rank Kolton tried to develop a separate method for testing the rescue chamber, and he insisted that it be included in the program for these tests. "Naturally, the test should be conducted at a depth of 1,000 meters with a list, as it was positioned, and under a load of special ballast according to the weight of the personnel." He justified his request by the fact that "there were no similar tests conducted in the previous stages of the rescue chamber construction, even on the model." However, "on the spot, in two weeks" after the presentation of the program of the government's tests to the chairman of the State Acceptance Commission and the head of the Commission of the Navy, and, as Kolton claimed, behind his back, the industry formed a "collective decision not to fulfill this point in the period of government testing. After an examination of the submarine, it was transferred to experimental operation." As a result of the industry's maneuvers with the government's testing program, when the submarine went to the sea, an unsanctioned separation of the rescue chamber occurred, and the chamber sunk. "We found the chamber, we found a defect in the construction, and again tested it, but not by the method that I [I. B. Kolton—D. R.] wanted, but a simplified test, at 30 meters, on an even keel." It was as a result of insufficient tests, Kolton maintains, that during the accident of the submarine *Komsomolets*, the chamber killed people. Further, that "the study of criminal actions concerning the disaster of the *Komsomolets* shows that the possible reason for the deaths of the seamen was the faulty construction of the rescue chamber." Such is the position of the former representative of the Permanent State Acceptance Commission as to the question of the rescue chamber.

How, in fact, could the government testing program of the submarine *Komsomolets* have been agreed upon? I, as assistant chief designer of the *Komsomolets*, personally took part in the agreement and approval of the government testing program. The program was developed, agreed upon, and consolidated not in 1982 as Kolton maintains, but in 1983. Captain 1st Rank Kolton did not coordinate the program, but rather it was coordinated by Hero of the Soviet Union, Rear Admiral L. M. Zhiltsov. There were no questions connected with the research of the rescue chamber, since the government's experimental program was provided for by section 4.5.8 which contains the following: "Verifying the rescue chamber by straight settings of actual surfacing. The order of the conducted experiments will be determined in coordination with the decisions of the Navy and MCII No. 702/41/03855 from 25 August 1983." Captain 1st Rank Kolton had no part in the coordination of the government's experimental plans for the submarine, he did not take part in conducting these experiments, and it is not understood why he attaches himself to this part [of the ship's development]. Maybe the respected Kolton has, as in the song known to most: "something happened with his memory, he began to remember everything that did not happen to himself."

I. B. Kolton's claim that no experiments were carried out on the previously developed rescue chamber does not agree with the facts. In the stage when the technical projects were worked out on the submarine *Komsomolets*, the following construction experiments were conducted:

■ a scale model of the rescue chamber was prepared, its surfacing was conducted from a maximum depth of submersion and with operational parameters that characterized its steady surfacing.

■ preparation of a dummy model of a surfacing chamber and of a fairwater fin [sail] of the submarine and conduct of experiments on the separation of the rescue chamber and its release from the fairwater fin with a significant list and trim angle.

■ model work was conducted on the equipment of the rescue chamber and with actual verification including the stationing of personnel and measurement of the time.

The information from retired Captain 1st Rank Kolton concerning the circumstance of forming the decision about the transfer of tests to a period of experimental operation does not coincide with the facts. In December 1983, the government's test on the submarine ended, but a series of experiments conducted with the chamber were not required by the Navy. It was necessary to immediately form a combined decision about the continuation of these experiments on December 28, 1983. Therefore, when the program of the experimental operation of the submarine *Komsomolets* was created, in my personal opinion, including the experimental construction work conducted earlier, there had been anticipated that verification of an actual separation and surfacing of the rescue chamber would be conducted during a short cruise of the submarine at a depth of 50 meters. The program was agreed upon by all the interested organizations and confirmed on June 1, 1984. Incidentally, as far as I remember, the Permanent State Acceptance Commission of the Navy Ships refused to take part in the coordination of this program.

Kolton has no basis to maintain that the study of criminal acts concerning the disaster of the *Komsomolets* showed that there was some connection between the construction of the rescue chamber and the death of the seamen. The attempt by Kolton to connect the facts of the spontaneous separation and the flooding of the rescue chamber during the period of factory testing with the established program of the government's tests failed. The chamber would not have sunk, if the crew had not breached so thoroughly the operating instructions.

A few words about the testing of the rescue chamber as proposed by retired Captain 1st Rank Kolton. To conduct similar tests, the submarine had to be on the bottom at a maximum depth with a highly large list and trim. A manipulation control system for conducting the operation of chamber separation from the submarine with an automatic control program would have to be developed, prepared, and put into the rescue chamber before hand. For this, one must bear in mind:

- a similar list and trim (significantly greater than 15 degrees) does not guarantee the reliable and safe workings of the nuclear reactor and all of the main energy components;
- there is no guarantee that after the submarine is lying on the bottom, it will not slip down to a deeper depth, significantly exceeding the maximum depth or even not overturn, which will lead to its sinking;
- there is no guarantee that after the separation of the rescue chamber, the submarine can rise to the surface as a result of sticking to the bottom and the low effectiveness of blowing the main tanks at a great depth or due to the large initial angular list or trim; and
- the water-tight integrity of the pressure hull of the submarine, after the separation of the rescue chamber, must be secured by the lower lid of the chamber exit hatch; otherwise, given the most unfavorable circumstances in terms of weather and currents, there is a chance the hatch may be "torn off" and then the submarine could flood.

It follows to add to this that the Navy does not have a [deep] proving ground for submarines and they have to search for them outside the limits of our territorial waters, 1,000 kilometers from the base. In addition, there existed, at the time, the need for the Navy to provide secret deep-water tests by fully excluding the possibility of generating similar accidents. From this story, it follows that not one sensible person suggested there was arguable value in risking the crew or the submarine by conducting similar tests. In response to this "foolhardy bravado," we recognized that only a few representatives, who sit in the main apparatus of the government party and who do not partake in the tests or answering for them, would suggest this. Despite his article, Kolton does not represent the only advocate in the country for creating a highly reliable, low noise, and superior submarine Navy, and he is not surrounded by innumerable unscrupulous individuals, rushing only to "push death technology out into the water."

I would like to ask this advocate for the Russian Submarine Navy one question: Why did the commission, during the signing and then during the affirmation of the acceptance of the submarine *Komsomolets*, not demand from the First Institute of the Navy, the presentation of a "Guide to Combat Use of Technical Resources (RBITS)," the basic document for damage control, and from the Head Navy Control, documentation regarding the operation and repair including the creation of a technical crew, as stipulated by the technical design of the submarine? The absence of a technical crew is one the basic reasons a fire broke out aboard the submarine. The absence of RBITS is one of the main reasons that the fire in compartment seven ended in a tragedy. By not making such demands, the Permanent State Acceptance Commission contributed to the tragedy of the submarine *Komsomolets*.

24.

Conclusions

In conclusion, we need to examine the "numerous design imperfections" revealed in the investigation of the accident aboard the submarine *Komsomolets*. Despite the fact that the Navy's top brass wielded accusations of "numerous imperfections" wildly like a Neanderthal club, they never were officially presented to the designer. Nor did the State Commission officially present them. Therefore, we will have to use unofficial materials.

A list of "design imperfections" was signed by naval deputy commander in chief Vice Admiral V. V. Zaytsev, and it is called "Submarine Design Peculiarities that, in the Navy's Opinion, Influenced the Advent and Development of Large and Fast-Developing Fires and Hindered Ship Damage Control." It is presented in its entirety in Appendix Two of this book. We will limit ourselves for the moment only to the conclusions based on the results of analyzing this list.

None of the "design peculiarities" could have caused the accident and the loss of the submarine.

The "consequences" indicated by the authors do not reflect the actual circumstances of the accident, and they are directed at justifying the inactivity of the submarine's leadership in ship damage control and at covering up the mistakes it made.

Certain items of the "Design Peculiarities" may be used in design development as a way to determine the possibilities for improving equipment and finding new technical concepts that would increase ship survivability and reduce the probability of incorrect actions by personnel.

You can agree or disagree with these conclusions. But if the highly placed authors of the Navy's remarks believe that all of these "design peculiarities" caused the accident and loss of the submarine *Komsomolets,* and if they do nothing to prohibit patrol duty by submarines having such "peculiarities," then what should we call them—criminals or liars? There is no third choice in this case. It would be permissible to ask: How can the Navy allow such submarines to operate? Won't there be more fires, won't more ships sink, and won't more people die?

19. *Komsomolets'* superstructure over Compartment Two

The State Commission left unaddressed many pieces of equipment and devices having deficiencies that were discussed in the examination of the circumstances of the accident aboard the submarine *Komsomolets:*

■ the self-contained emergency buoy failed to operate after the submarine's loss (see figure 19);

■ the sunken submarine locator failed to operate;

■ the inflating system of the PSN-20 life rafts failed to work completely, "by the book";

■ the survival suits and diving suits are hard to use;

■ the face masks of the IDA-59 apparatus are uncomfortable and unreliable.

We should also add to this list the "Listvennitsa" loudspeaker communication system, although it has already been discussed.

These are all different items of equipment, but there is one common trait that unites them. All of these items of equipment were designed on the basis of specifications of the Navy's institutes, and under their observation and leadership. The Navy accepted this equipment as armament and as supply items. The questions that arise in this connection are: Aren't there a little too many negative remarks regarding equipment for which the Navy bears responsibility, and is there, in fact, "something rotten in Denmark"? And could it be that concern for the "cleanliness of the uniform" has overshadowed concern for creating reliable equipment? Now this is something to think about.

Now a few words about measures to increase fire protection to submarines and exclude accidents aboard them. These measures were developed on the basis of an examination of the circumstances of the accident aboard the submarine *Komsomolets*, and have been accepted for implementation.

A joint decision of the USSR Ministry of Shipbuilding Industry and the naval leadership foresees development of a large number of measures directed at: raising the fire safety and survivability of submarines, developing documentation, and designing crew training equipment. As for the degree to which these measures will be implemented and by when, and how much they will help to increase the survivability of ships and improve crew training, time will tell. However, many years will pass before there can be any discussion of results.

In August 1990 the USSR Council of Ministers published a decree on the results of the examination of the circumstances behind the accident aboard the submarine *Komsomolets*, which was drafted by the naval leadership. It contains measures for creating training centers and for improving ship basing and technical maintenance conditions, it foresees fulfillment of a large number of scientific research and experimental design projects, and it does not overlook the social sphere either.

But there is one thing that raises questions: The deadline for fulfilling measures to organize training centers, to improve submarine basing and technical maintenance conditions, and to improve measures in the social sphere, had been extended to the year 2000. Most of the funds for scientific research and experimental design work (up to 75 percent) were to be spent on projects having nothing to do with the fire safety of submarines, their survivability, or with designing individual protective and rescue equipment for submariners. Nor is

optimism raised by the nonspecific nature of measures to create training centers and establish submarine basing and technical maintenance conditions. The
planned purchase of fifty thousand survival suits abroad evoked bewilderment
in light of the cheerful assertions by Vice Admiral R. L. Dymov, chief of the
Navy's search and rescue service, that series production of Russian-made survival suits would begin in 1991.[1]

Naval commander in chief, Fleet Admiral V. N. Chernavin, said nothing about these issues in his interview with the journal *Morskoy Sbornik* (No. 12,
1990). The tone of the statements is optimistic and confident. This immediately brings to mind Vice Admiral V. V. Zaytsev's "classical" pronouncement:
"Confident reports prior to 1635 indicate that ship damage control efforts were
proceeding according to plan, that the situation aboard the submarine was being monitored, and that entry of water into the pressure hull was not noted."

The "secret" stamp applied to decisions makes it very easy to produce
such "confident" reports. But as to what awaited after "1635," time has told.

And in conclusion it would be somewhat interesting to compare the
position of specialists of the U.S. Navy with the position of specialists of our
country's Navy regarding the accident rate aboard ship. Here is what is said
about this in an article written by the "troubadour" of the Navy's leadership,
Captain 1st Rank S. I. Bystrov, editor of the naval department of the newspaper *Krasnaya Zvezda*.[2]

> Late last year specialists of the U.S. Navy came up with pro-
> posals which in their opinion could help to reduce the accident
> rate. Principal among them are: raising the theoretical level of
> personnel training, improving the practical skills of servicemen
> in maintaining combat activity, introducing computerized train-
> ers into the training process, and intensifying naval supervision
> over construction and repair of warships. The priority with which
> these proposals are listed deserves attention: The problems of
> improving personnel skills are addressed by three of them. And
> this is in the professional American Navy.

What can we say about these proposals? The adherence to principles
and high civic-mindedness of specialists of the U.S. Navy in the performance
of their duty evoke respect. It is immediately evident that people are working,
rather than looking for others to blame. And now let's listen to our own specialists: "Our compulsory-service seamen have not permitted as many accidents as
American professionals. And what the Americans put in last place regarding

influence upon the accident rate—the reliability of equipment—is in first place in our country."

What fine recruits we have! They have certainly tweaked the noses of those celebrated American professionals. Naturally, with such fine men, only the equipment can be to blame. But the finest man of all is Captain 1st Rank S. I. Bystrov. How expertly he plays up to our generals and admirals who oppose a professional army! And industry is not forgotten either. He also has some "good things to say" about it. Though somewhat condescendingly, of course, in passing: "And by the way, there can be no argument when it comes to recognizing the services of our industry." Indeed, this is the damning of the designers and shipbuilders with faint praise.

Appealing to all "not to shift blame on anyone, but to objectively analyze all of it and implement effective, economically supported and rooted measures," with army straightforwardness, Bystrov proposes the sequence in which this "objectivity" should be exercised: "First of all, perfecting the design, technical reliability, and quality of our ships, making damage control equipment and rescue resources effective, and upgrading the quality of personnel training."

How appropriate it is to repeat Bystrov's pronouncement here, though in somewhat amended form. The order in which he lists the problems deserves attention: Those of upgrading equipment quality are addressed by three of them.

Captain 1st Rank (Retired) V. A. Boyko expressed the naval leadership's position more clearly: "Let's build sufficiently viable submarines with full crew rescue support at the level of the best world accomplishments. And after that we can talk about the mistakes of personnel."[3] A well-known admonition is apparently true: "A wise person learns from other's mistakes, while a fool has no desire to learn from his own."

Let submariners understand me correctly: Equipment, and especially military equipment, has to undergo constant improvement, regardless of accidents or any other circumstances. But the main objective today should be to raise the level of crew combat and occupational training, to improve the quality of ship technical maintenance, and to solve all problems associated with these objectives. Here lies the fundamental difference between the leadership of the military-industrial complex and, in Captain 1st Rank Bystrov's terminology, "one of the interested parties that is unfortunately opposed to the Navy."

Roll Call of Sailors Lost on the Submarine *Komsomolets*

Apanasyevich, Igor Olegovich; Senior Seaman, Steering Signaler

Avanesov, Oleg Grigoryevich; Captain 2nd Rank, Senior Assistant Commander of the submarine

Babenko, Valentin Ivanovich; Captain 2nd Rank, Commander of the Electro-mechanical Combat Section

Bondar, Sergie Stefonovich; Warrant Officer, Turbine Technician

Brodovsky, Yuri Analtolyevich; Warrant Officer, Hydroacoustic Technician

Bukhnikashvili, Nadari Otariyevich; Senior Seaman, Hold Machinist

Burkulakov, Talant Amitzhanovich; Captain 1st Rank, Head of the Political Department of the Division

Chernikov, Sergei Ivanovich; Warrant Officer, Chem—Technician

Filippov, Roman Konstantinovich; Seaman, Electrician

Golovchenko, Segrei Petrovich; Senior 2nd, Cook—Instructor

Grundul, Alexei Alexandrovich; Seaman, Torpedoist

Ispenkov, Anatoly Matvyevich; Captain 3rd Rank, Commander of the Electro-technical Division

Kapusta, Yuri Fedorovich; Warrant Officer, Head of the Secret Section

Kolotilin, Vladimir Vasilivich; Warrant Officer, Technician of the Range Control Group

Kovalev, Gennadiy Vyachyeslavovich; Warrant Officer, Technician of the Combat Communications Section

Krasnobayev, Alexander Vitalyevich; Warrant Officer, Computer Technician

Krasnov, Sergei Yuryevich; Seaman, Radio Meterist

Kulapin, Vladimir Yuryevich; Seaman, Hold Machinist

Maksimchuk, Yuri Ivanovich; Captain 3rd Rank, Assistant Commander of the Sub-Political Section

Manyakin, Sergie Petrovich; Division Captain 3rd Rank, Commander of Navigation

Markov, Sergei Yevgenyevich; Senior Lt. Engineer of the Electro-technical Group

Mikhalev, Andrea Vyachyeslavovich; Seaman, Hold Machinist

Molchanov, Igor Alexandrovich; Lt. Commander of Mine-Torpedo Combat Section

Nakhalov, Sergei Vasilyevich; Warrant Officer, Senior Commander of Radio Technicians

Naumenko, Yevgeni Vladimirovich; Captain Lt. Commander of Computer Group

Nezhutin, Sergei Alexandrovich; Captain Lt. , Commander of the Range Control Group

Shinkunas, Stasis Klemyensovich; Senior Seaman, Radiometerist

Shostak, Alexandr Alexanderovich; Lt. Engineer of the Range Control Group

Smirnov, Mikhail Antolyevich; Captain Lt., Commander of the Navigating Combat Section

Speranski, Igor Leonidovich; Captain Lt. Engineer Hydroacoustics Group

Sykhanov, Valeri Ivanovich; Seaman, Cook Instructor

Tkach, Vladimir Vlasovich; Senior Warrant Officer, Senior Command of Steering Signalists

Tkachev, Vitali Fedorovich; Seaman, Steering Signaler

Valyavin, Mikhail Nikolievich; Warrant Officer, Turbine Group Technician

Vanin, Yevgeni Alexyevich; Captain 1st Rank, Commander of the Submarine

Vershilo, Yevgeni Edmundovich; Senior Seaman, Electrician

Volkov, Nikoli Alexyevich; Captain Lt. Commander of the Electrotechnician Group

Volodin, Alexander Vasilyvich; Captain 3rd Rank of Combat Communication Section

Yelenik, Mikhail Anatolyevich; Warrant Officer, Senior Cook—Instructor

Yudin, Vyacheslav Alexandrovich; Captain 3rd Rank, Commander of the Division Damage Control

Zamogilnyi, Sergei Vasilivich; Warrant Officer, Senior Commander of the Electro-technical Group

Zimin, Vadim Vladimirovich; Lt. Engineer, Combat Communications Section

Appendix II—

"Design Peculiarities" of the Submarine *Komsomolets*

The Navy's Main Directorate for Operation and Repair (MD, O&R), prepared a list entitled "Submarine Design Peculiarities That, in the Navy's Opinion, Influenced the Advent and Development of Large and Fast-Developing Fires and Hindered Ship Damage Control," This appendix presents twenty items in that list and the consequences the Soviet Navy associated with the "peculiarity." Each peculiarity is then followed by a set of observations made by Designer Romanov in response to the Navy's opinion.

Peculiarity 1

"Placement of three oil tanks, an oil-separating unit, reserves of GPD (thirty units), and regeneration resources (ten cans) in compartment seven, which contains a large amount of electrical equipment (power panels), the absence of an oil-cleaning system, and presence of a large number of openings communicating with the outside. Distribution panels in power compartments are not protected from the influence of oil vapor. The requirements of the TPPL-75, Articles 11.4.2, 11.4.14, 11.4.15, 11.4.16, 11.4.18, and 11.4.19 regarding the location of electrical equipment, and of Article 11.4.26 requiring installation of resources for removing oil vapor from air at the locations of electrical equipment, are not satisfied.

The consequences:

This resulted in a decrease in fire and explosion safety, saturation with oil vapor, and the advent and rapid development of the fire."

The designer's observations and response

a. There were forty-nine alternating current distribution panels, nine direct current distribution panels, four alternating current main distribution panels, and one direct current main distribution panel—that is, sixty-three distribution panels—within the electric power system of the submarine *Komsomolets*. The presence of four distribution panels and one section of the main distribution panel in compartment seven cannot be said to be "a large amount," given an average density of 10.5 distribution panels per compartment (distribution panels are not located in the reactor compartment). Such placement of panels is characteristic of all of the Navy's submarines, and it is not a peculiarity of the submarine *Komsomolets*.

b. For practical purposes there was only one tank containing turbine oil in compartment seven of the submarine, and not three—a 9 m³ reserve oil tank, because the 7 m³ dirty oil tank is not filled with oil, and it is used only to replace oil in the (GTZA) main turbo gear unit (in this case the reserve tank is dried out completely), and the 0.8 m³ emergency oil drain tank does not connect with compartment seven (instruction K-902-022 TO). The reserve and dirty oil tanks are equipped with ventilation, oil traps, and shut-offs making it possible to disconnect these tanks from compartment seven in the event of fire (instruction K-902-032 TO). The temperature of oil in the reserve tank did not exceed a figure between +3 and +5 degrees Celsius during the cruise under normal operating conditions, which precluded any evolution of oil vapor from it. The oil reserve's location in the aft compartment is not a peculiarity of the submarine *Komsomolets*. Nor is location of the oil separating unit and of reserves of damage control and regenerating resources in compartment seven a peculiarity. There are no restrictions on their location in aft compartments. Regenerating reserves must be located in each compartment according to naval requirements. Tests carried out by the State Commission Working Group proved the GPD resources to be highly fire- and explosion-safe. As for the overall amount of equipment, compartment seven aboard the *Komsomolets* has less than any of the others. This is obviously why compartment seven was loaded with reserves of food and supplies before the ship's cruise, even though the design does not foresee their storage in this compartment.

c. The assertions of the MD, O&R that compartment seven contained a large number of openings connecting with the outside is inconsistent with reality. There are significantly fewer such openings aboard the *Komsomolets* than in other submarines of the Navy. In particular, there are fifty-three openings in the pressure hull in the aft compartment of a certain third-generation submarine with a compartment seven of the same size as that in the *Komsomolets*. The number of openings is even greater in other submarines in which the aft compartments are larger. There were only thirty-eight openings in the pressure hull in compartment seven of the submarine *Komsomolets*.

d. The assertion of the MD, O&R that the distribution panels aboard the submarine *Komsomolets* were not protected from the influence of oil vapor is inconsistent with fact. Power production equipment (the GTZA in compartment six and TTsNA in compartment five) generating free vapor from hot oil (temperatures up to 70 degrees Celsius) was supplied with self-contained units for removing oil vapor from air. In addition, the air of power compartments was cleaned of oil vapor by compartment air-conditioning equipment containing FK-U cassette filters rated for oil vapor absorption. The equipment in compartment seven did not produce any free hot oil vapor, making it unnecessary to install a self-contained oil cleaning unit. This is why the compartment air-conditioning equipment containing the indicated cassette filters was used to remove oil vapor from air in compartment seven. This system for removing oil vapor from the air also is used aboard other submarines of the Navy, and the *Komsomolets* is not unique in this. Five years of the submarine's operation demonstrated the effectiveness of the system for removing oil vapor from the air of compartments. In all of the time that the *Komsomolets* was in operation, not a single case of oil getting on equipment in any compartment was ever documented. It should be noted that such a combination of the functions of the air-conditioning and cleaning system is to be expanded as a measure to increase the fire safety of the Navy's submarines (decision No. S-13/1788, September 22, 1989, of the USSR Ministry of Shipbuilding Industry and the Navy, item nine in the attachment).

e. The complaints of the MD, O&R that the designers failed to satisfy the requirements of the TPPL-75 [Submarine Design Requirements] are wrong. These TPPL were published by the Navy in 1976 without coordinating them with industry. The detail design of the submarine *Komsomolets* had already been approved by this time (1972), and the shop drawings were, for practical purposes, finished. No decisions were made regarding the procedure and time of introduction of the TPPL-75. Thus, the requirements in TPPL-75 were not introduced on any submarine of the Navy. In 1981 the "Basic Technical Requirements" OTT-6.1.1-81 became the standard for future submarines. The submarine *Komsomolets* was designed in accordance with specifications approved in 1966, and the TPPL-67 submarine design requirements, developed by the Navy. As far as the essence of the question is concerned, all requirements of Articles 11.4.2, 11.4.14, 11.4.15, 11.4.16, 11.4.18, 11.4.19, and 11.4.26 of the TPPL-75 were satisfied in the submarine *Komsomolets*, with the exception of requirements on using [special KMZh] cable in emergency electric power networks. Because such cable was difficult to manufacture, it was not used aboard any submarine.

f. The "consequences" of imagined peculiarities of the submarine *Komsomolets* conjured up by the authors are also inconsistent with fact. The high fire and explosion safety of this ship was confirmed by a hands-on inspection of its condition during the period from October 11–20, 1983, by an expert commission appointed by the Navy. The fire and explosion safety of compartment seven diminished as a result of the unauthorized storage of provisions and supplies in it and the uncontrolled delivery of oxygen into the compartment, which went unnoticed because of a faulty oxygen gas analyzer. An elevated oxygen concentration in the compartment (estimated at up to 30 percent) led to the advent and intensive development of fire. As far as saturation of the compartment with oil vapor is concerned, calculations carried out by the Central Scientific Research Institute named after A. N. Krylov and the Naval Institute Number One demonstrated that it is impossible for oil vapor to reach even the lower concentration limit of ignition when the temperature in the compartment is as high as 70 degrees Celsius (the actual temperature was around 20 degrees Celsius) and when air cleaning units are not working.

These many facts allow us to say that all of the complaints MD, O&R presented in this first "peculiarity" are unjustified, and are inconsistent with real circumstances on the *Komsomolets* as well as all its contemporary and later USSR submarine designs.

Peculiarity 2

"The design precluded airtightness of compartments six and seven when the shafting was operating because of the presence of transit oil feed and drain lines of the main propulsion unit and a gap in the shafting's bulkhead gland. The requirements of items X-75 and 11.6.4 of the TPPL-67 and TPPL-75, respectively, regarding the airtightness of bulkheads when shafting is operating under normal conditions and at elevated pressure were not satisfied.

Recommendations of the design office regarding the use of the submarine's equipment in emergency situations, 21.GGK-E-478-82, do not foresee closure of valves on oil pipelines when sealing compartment seven. In addition, the design office did not draw up instructions, to be included in the operating documents, on testing the airtightness of intercompartment submarine bulkheads with a vacuum of 100 m Hg (see Article 201, RBZh-PL-82).

The consequences:

This led to an increase and spread of pressure and a fire in compartment six, as well as gas contamination of compartments two, three, and five."

The designer's observations and response

a. The assertion of the MD, O&R that the design did not provide for the isolation of compartments six and seven when the shafting is operating is inconsistent with fact, as is the assertion that there is some sort of "gap in the bulkhead gland." The shafting of the submarine *Komsomolets* is designed in full correspondence with Article X-75 of the TPPL-67, which contains no requirement regarding the airtightness of bulkheads when shafting is operating at elevated pressure, as is asserted by the authors of the remark. The shafting was designed on the basis of standard plans, and it contains no "design peculiarities" in comparison with other submarines as far as both the main thrust-bearing (GUP) lubricating system and the bulkhead gland are concerned.

b. The reference of the MD, O&R to the requirements of the TPPL-75 is wrong for the reasons set forth in the designer's conclusion regarding item 1. As far as the essence of the issue is concerned, the bulkhead between compartments six and seven was airtight aboard the submarine *Komsomolets* when the shafting was operating under normal conditions and at elevated pressure (within normal conditions). The authors of the remark incorrectly interpret the meaning of the requirements of Article 11.6.4 of the TPPL-75 regarding elevated pressure. The article discusses only elevated pressure under normal operating conditions, and nothing else. There are neither requirements in the article on the airtightness of the operating shafting under emergency conditions, nor are there any references to the magnitude of the corresponding elevated pressure.

c. The attempt to criticize the "Recommendations" 21.GGK-E-478-82 drawn up by the designer is wrong, because they were not intended for use by submarine personnel. The recommendations were drawn up in response to an assignment from the Naval Institute No. 1 specially to serve as the basis upon which this institute was to draw up the "Manual on Combat Use of Technical Resources" (RBITS)—one of the fundamental documents of the set of submarine damage control documents. However, the RBITS never was developed or written by the Naval Institute No. 1 because the Navy's Main Directorate for Operation and Repair did not plan or support its development for the *Komsomolets* in time.

The assertions of the MD, O&R that the "Recommendations" lack instructions on closing valves on oil pipelines are misleading and inconsistent with fact. Closure of these valves is not foreseen in the general section on sealing the bulkheads, because this affects submarine power and must be carried out on the basis of a decision by the control room (Article 89, RBZh-PL-82). In the event of fire in compartment seven, the "Recommendations" (items

3.3 and 3.20) provide instructions on de-energizing (that is, shutting down) the oil pumps of the lubricating system of the main turbogear unit (GTZA) and shutting down the unit itself. The instructions on servicing the GTZA oil system do make reference to closing valves on the oil pipeline when oil pumps are shut down in order to seal the bulkhead between compartments six and seven (instruction K-902-022 TO, items 2.3.1 and 2.5.4).

    d. The complaint of the MD, O&R that the absence of instructions on testing the airtightness of the submarine's intercompartment bulkheads with a 100 mm Hg vacuum is unjustified. The designer's operating and design documents do not foresee testing a submarine's intercompartment bulkheads for air-tightness with a 100 mm Hg vacuum, and there is nothing in Article 201 of the RBZh-PL-82 that says that such a test must be conducted on the basis of the designer's documentation. No other article or instruction makes such testing an official requirement.

    e. The "consequences" conjured by the authors are inconsistent with fact. The rise in pressure and the fire in compartment six were the result of the failure of the attack center to satisfy the requirements of articles 89 and 121 of the RBZh-PL-82 concerning shut-down of the main turbogear unit, the disconnection of the high-pressure air mains entering the distressed compartment, and the bleeding overboard the air reserve from the emergency cofferdam of the high-pressure air main located in compartment seven. The fire and rise in pressure in compartment six were not the result of any non-existent peculiarities in the design of the shafting. The lack of a RBITS contributed to this situation. The assertions that any shaft design peculiarities resulted in gas contamination of compartments two, three, and five are simply absurd, because the shafting is not associated with these compartments in any way. Compartments two, three, and five were contaminated with gas through unclosed mains because the personnel failed to satisfy the requirements of Articles 89 and 90 of the RBZh-PL-82.

Peculiarity 3

    "The design does not allow for sealing of the bulkhead between compartments five and six from the direction of compartment five due to the absence of valves in compartment five on the system for supplying vapor to the gasket in the equipment that removes the vapor-air mixture from TTsNA No. 1, 2.

    The consequences:

    This resulted in gas contamination of compartment five, an increase in pressure in it and subsequent ignition of oil vapor, and the death of people in the compartment due to burns."

The designer's observations and response

a. The design does not provide for sealing off the pipeline of the system removing vapor-air mixture from the gaskets of the turbocirculation pumps from the direction of compartment five, which was indeed a mistake of the designer.

b. The "consequences" presented by the MD, O&R are inconsistent with the facts:

i. The personnel had not closed the clinket gates on the line carrying spent vapor from the turbocirculation pumps (300 mm diameter). This, in practice, excluded the influence of the suction system pipeline (50 mm diameter or one thirty-sixth of the area of the 300 mm line) on the entry of gas into compartment five through the gaskets of the turbocirculation pumps.

ii. The high rate of growth of pressure in compartment five in the initial period of the accident and confinement of the deflagration to just the upper part of the compartment's central passage permit the assertion that oil vapor or products of incomplete combustion may have entered compartment five, not through the suction system leading from the gaskets of the turbocirculation pumps, which is located along the sides of the compartment, but out of the oil tank supplying these pumps when combustion products from compartment seven were blown through the tank into the oil separation line, which had not been reset in its initial position after the separation system was last operated. Products of incomplete combustion may have entered compartment six through the pressure-equalizing valve between compartments five and six, which is constantly open under normal operation. The turbocirculation pump oil tank vents and the pressure equalizing valve are located in the upper part of the central passage. Eventually, these sources of hot gases were closed by the submarine's personnel, which for practical purposes stopped the growth of pressure in compartment five. It has been established (as discussed in great detail in the chapter, "Fire in compartment five") that the flare-up in the fifth compartment occurred as a result of personnel not carrying out the instructions concerning the operation of the oil separation system. After the separation of the oil, the personnel did not return the system to the initial position (they did not close the valve to the main system), the result of which caused smoky gas to enter into the TTsNA oil tanks unimpeded. This led to the heating and the frothing of oil in the tanks and the consequent dispersal of oil and oil vapor in the compartment. At the oil pump, the oil vapor and the scattered oil were ignited. A high concentration of oxygen in the compartment sharply enhanced the force of the flare-up on the personnel of the compartment.

iii. The assertion of the MD, O&R that the failure to include a method to isolate this pipeline from the direction of compartment five by the designer led to the death of personnel due to burns appears to be an attempt at obfuscation. The personnel of compartment five (Warrant Officer S. S. Bondar and Seaman V. Y. Kulapin) did not die of burns, but as a result of carbon monoxide poisoning through their ShDA equipment. This unfortunately was due to mistakes made by the attack center and the compartment five commander. Air supply to the medium-pressure air main was stopped at the direction of the attack center without notifying personnel wearing ShDA masks and using air from the medium-pressure air system. The commander of compartment five failed to monitor operation of the stationary breathing system, which supplied air to ShDA equipment from the high- or medium-pressure air system. After the entire air reserve in cofferdam No. 4, located in compartment seven, was bled away as a result of the fire, and the supply of air to the medium-pressure air line was cut off, poisoned air from compartment seven began entering compartment five's stationary breathing system through one of the high- or medium-pressure air pipelines and then into the ShDA equipment. Warrant Officer Bondar and Seaman Kulapin, who were connected up to ShDA equipment, were poisoned by carbon monoxide. Because of delays in evacuating the victims, the poisoning was irreversible.

Peculiarity 4

"The design did not provide for remote delivery of a fire extinguisher from the LOKh system into the distressed compartment by the attack center (the requirements of Article X1-37 of the TPPL-67, Article 12.2.34 of the TPPL-75, and Article 1.5.6.25 of the OTT6.1.1-81 were not satisfied).

The consequences:

This made it impossible to use the fire extinguisher from the LOKh station in compartment seven to put out the fire, and it may have led to unjustified delay in delivering the fire extinguisher from compartment six into compartment seven, had the roving watchstander been in compartment four or five."

The designer's observations and response

a. The detailed design for the submarine *Komsomolets* was drawn up with a LOKh system that could be started remotely from the attack center in accordance with requirements of the specifications and the TPPL-67. Later on, citing insufficient reliability of remotely controlled electromagnetic valves, decision No. S-13/002834, 17 October 1975, of the USSR Ministry of Shipbuilding Industry and the Navy prescribed replacement of these valves aboard all submarines by manually controlled fittings: this is what was done on the *Komsomolets*. The OST [A11-Union Standard] on designing the LOKh firefighting system was corrected on the basis of that decision. A manually initiated LOKh system is used on most submarines, and therefore the assertion of the authors of the remark that this was a peculiarity of the submarine *Komsomolets* is inconsistent with fact.

b. It should be noted that the USSR Ministry of Shipbuilding Industry and the Navy ordered the designers (on the basis of decision No. 1/02095, August 4, 1987) to complete design developments in support of introducing remotely initiated LOKh systems aboard submarines. This decision was based on the results of developing a new remotely controlled valve for the LOKh system. In this case, for unknown reasons, the Navy decided not to install the system in the submarine *Komsomolets*, and it did not foresee completion of these developments for this ship. Consequently, it is wrong for the Navy's MD, O&R to lodge any complaints about the absence of a remotely started LOKh system aboard the submarine *Komsomolets*.

c. The reference of the MD, O&R to requirements set forth in TPPL-75 is wrong for the reasons set forth in the conclusion regarding item 1. The same can also be said for the requirements of the OTT6.1.1-81. As for the essence of the issue, the requirements of Article 12.2.34 of the TPPL-75 and Article 1.5.6.22 of the OTT6.1 1-81 have to do with remote starting of the LOKh system (remote control), and not with remote delivery of the fire extinguisher by the attack center, as the authors of the remark assert. Moreover, the requirements of the OTT6.1.1-81, which were issued in place of the TPPL-75, allow starting of the LOKh system both from the attack center remotely and from the compartments, including manually.

Peculiarity 5

"The submarine design did not foresee a system with the necessary freon reserve for fast recharging of any LOKh station to provide for repeated delivery of freon to a distressed compartment in the presence of large fires in order to create a fire-quenching concentration. In addition, the operating documents (instructions on operating the LOKh system) say nothing about the loss of fire extinguishing properties when high pressure is present in a distressed compartment. Other resources capable of extinguishing a fire at elevated pressure are not foreseen by the submarine's design.

The consequences:

A fire-quenching concentration of freon could not be created in compartments six and seven, and the fire could not be put out. The submarine lacks resources for extinguishing a fire at compartment pressures exceeding 2 kg/cm^2."

The designer's observations and response

a. The LOKh system in the submarine *Komsomolets* was developed in full correspondence with naval requirements OTT MO 6.1.17-79, Part II, and OST V5.5059-81, which do not foresee installation of tanks containing a reserve of freon. The complaints of the MD, O&R can be viewed only as a proposal for development.

b. None of the Navy's submarines has containers with a freon reserve; thus, this is also not a peculiarity of the submarine *Komsomolets*.

c. It is unsuitable to place reserve freon containers aboard submarines because attempts to recharge stations in an emergency situation could only aggravate the emergency situation aboard the ship.

d. The instructions on operating the LOKh system were developed for the submarine *Komsomolets* in accordance with standard instructions coordinated with the Navy, which say nothing about the fire extinguishing characteristics of freon. Nor is anything said in the operating instructions of LOKh systems in other submarines of the Navy. It does not make any sense to introduce this information into LOKh system operations, because the instructions are not part of the set of submarine damage control documents. Information on the fire-extinguishing characteristics of freon and on the range of uses of the LOKh system should be contained in the RBZh-PL-82, which is the principal submarine damage control document, in attachment No. 3, "Firefighting Resources." And who was the author of the RBZh-PL-82? The Soviet Navy was the author.

e. There are no other resources in the country today that are highly effective in extinguishing fires in situations where the pressure is elevated. Experimental design work aimed at creating such resources was in its initial stage at that time. Consequently, any discussion of the absence of these resources aboard the submarine *Komsomolets* as being a peculiarity is totally misleading and pointless.

f. The assertions of the MD, O&R that a fire-extinguishing concentration of freon could not be created in compartments six and seven because of the absence of freon reserves aboard the submarine are unfounded. Freon had not, in fact, been delivered to compartment seven, and its delivery into compartment six did not begin until after the fire went out.

Peculiarity 6

"The design does not foresee protection of electric circuits between synchro transmitters and synchro receivers of the 'Korund' system from short-circuit currents (the requirements of Article VII-7 of the TPPL-67, Article 8.2.7 of the TPPL-75, and Articles 1.3.3.1 and 1.3.3.6 of the OTT6.l.l-81 were violated).

The consequences:

This resulted in a fire in the GKP, which complicated leadership of submarine damage control efforts."

The designer's observations and response

a. Protection of electric circuits between synchro transmitters and synchro receivers of the "Korund" system from short-circuit currents is not required, as is confirmed by experiments carried out by the developers of the "Korund" system. Such protection is absent from all submarines of the Navy that have the "Korund" system; hence, this also is not a peculiarity of the submarine *Komsomolets*.

b. Analysis of the interrogation of the personnel of the *Komsomolets* by the State Commission indicates that the "Korund" caught fire, not in the vicinity of the synchro circuits but in the power supply units of the "Korund," which are located inside the stand of the "Vektor" subsystem. The power supply system circuit of the "Korund" was fully protected against shorts. Once again, the assertion of the authors that the designer failed to satisfy Article VII-7 of the TPPL-67 is inconsistent with fact.

c. The cause of the fire in the "Korund" console and its consequences were presented sufficiently objectively in the conclusion written by Vice Admiral V. V. Zaytsev, the naval deputy commander in chief and the chief of the Main Directorate for Operation and Repair, in response to the "Analysis" written by Vice Admiral Y. D. Chernov:

> At 1122 the transformer block servicing the "Korund" system's rudder position indicators caught fire in the control room. Compartment three filled with gas, and so the attack center was compelled to carry out the subsequent submarine damage control actions while wearing individual protective equipment. Knowing the situation, and having made certain that rudder control failed,

the control room was obligated to have given the command to de-energize the "Korund." This was not done, however.

In light of the above, the so-called "consequences" of this conjured peculiarity of the submarine *Komsomolets* have no real basis.

d. The requirements of the TPPL-75 and the OTT6.1.1-81 do not apply to the submarine *Komsomolets* for the reasons set forth in observation "e" to Peculiarity 1. As for the essence of Article 8.2.7 of the TPPL-75 and Articles 1.3.3.1 and 1.3.3.6 of the OTT6.1.1-81, all that can be said is that the requirements of these articles have not been accepted by industry even for designing submarines of the future, because they are unrealistic (as regards mistakes by personnel) and the requirements for operating conditions (pressure) are unsubstantiated.

Peculiarity 7

"The design does not provide for complete de-energizing of electrical equipment in a distressed compartment by switching apparatus. For example, in order to de-energize compartment seven, according to recommendations on using technical resources in emergency situations, 21.GGK-E-478-82, cables must be disconnected at GRShch 02 (compartment five), at ShchTG 1 (compartment six), and at APPM-413V (compartment four), which is practically impossible to do.

The consequences:

It is impossible in a major emergency situation to completely de-energize a submarine compartment, which is why the accident occurred and why a fire arose in compartment four."

The designer's observations and response

a. All power lines of the electric power system are de-energized by a switching apparatus. The only lines it doesn't de-energize are the control, blocking, and monitoring circuits. These are the circuits to which the "Recommendations" refer. The electric power systems of all submarines of the Navy are built on the basis of this principle, such that this is not a peculiarity of just the submarine *Komsomolets*. Introduction of switching apparatus into control circuits unjustifiably complicates the circuits and reduces the reliability of a submarine's electric power system as a whole.

b. Complete de-energization of compartment seven requires, besides disconnecting electrical equipment with switching apparatus, additional disconnection of: one cable in compartment two (two strands), two cables in compartment four (ten strands), two cables in compartment five (three strands), and three cables in compartment six (three strands). The labor consumed by this operation does not exceed two to five minutes, and it does not present any difficulties to trained personnel. The cables in the submarine *Komsomolets* were not disconnected, not because it was a major emergency situation as the authors of the remark assert, but only because the personnel did not know what had to be disconnected due to the absence of the RBITS, and because they never practiced this operation in ship damage control training. During the accident the personnel did not even make an attempt to disconnect the cables.

c. The assertion of the MD, O&R that development of the accident was a consequence of incomplete de-energization is unfounded, because this could in no way have affected the fire in compartments six and seven. This led only to a short flash in the TsNPK No. 1 pump starting station (and not to the fire in compartment four, as the authors of the remark assert), after which the TsNPK pump continued to work in its prescribed mode. Even after the circuit breaker tripped in the RShchNo.12 distribution panel, which is located in compartment seven, the electric power system of the submarine remained serviceable, and continued to function until the end of the tragedy.

Peculiarity 8

"The Kingston-less design of the MBT sharply reduces the longitudinal stability of a submarine when it is not in trim and when the sea is disturbed. The requirement of Article 12.2.2 of the TPPL-75 was not satisfied: 'Ballast tanks of the middle group and, as a rule, part of the tanks of the fore and aft groups must have Kingston valves, and mandatorily, second vent valve shut-offs.'

The consequences:

This resulted in the flooding of MBT No. 8, 9, and 10 and disturbance of their integrity, as a result of which the submarine lost buoyancy and longitudinal stability."

The designer's observations and response

a. Most submarines of the Navy are designed without the Kingston valves, and this is not a peculiarity of the submarine *Komsomolets*.

b. The TPPL-67, in accordance with which the submarine *Komsomolets* was designed, does not contain a requirement of mandatory installation of Kingston valves in main ballast tanks. For the reasons set forth in observation "e" regarding Peculiarity 1, the requirements of the TPPL-75 do not apply to the submarine *Komsomolets*. Even as written, Article 12.2.2 of the TPPL-75 did not contain a mandatory requirement of installing Kingston valves in the end groups of main ballast tanks, as is reflected in the text of the article cited by the MD, O&R. The new OTT6.1.1-81, Article 1.5.6.11 published by the Navy contains no requirements for installing Kingston valves in ballast tanks. Here as well, the complaints of the MD, O&R indicating that the absence of Kingston valves from the main ballast tanks violates requirements are groundless.

c. The line of reasoning of the MD, O&R suggesting that the design of main ballast tanks without Kingston valves sharply reduces the longitudinal stability of a submarine if it is not in trim and if the sea is disturbed is essentially nonsense. A submarine does not go out of trim on its own, but as a result of a loss of buoyancy reserve when the end compartments or ballast tanks fill up; in this case, the submarine's longitudinal stability also decreases regardless of the design of the main ballast tanks and the sea state. Reduction of longitudinal stability manifests itself in Kingston-less submarines to a somewhat greater degree than on submarines equipped with Kingston valves; however, the ability submarines have for blowing ballast tanks makes it possible to completely exclude the influence of the lack of Kingston valves on ship buoyancy and stability. In addition, sea state begins to affect the buoyancy reserve of a submarine (and not its longitudinal stability, as the authors of the remark assert) at a sea state of five to six points or more. At the time of the accident of the submarine *Komsomolets,* the sea state was around two to three points, and its influence upon the ship's buoyancy reserve was negligible.

d. The "consequences" developed by the MD, O&R are inconsistent with the real circumstances. The submarine surfaced with its starboard main ballast tanks No. 5 and 10 not blown. Under the particular circumstances of the accident, the port tank No. 10 would have lost its integrity and would have filled with water regardless of design. There are no grounds for asserting that tanks No. 8 and 9 lost their integrity and filled with water. The submarine sank as a result of the flooding of compartment seven and the partial flooding of compartment six. This flooding occurred with absolutely no effort to control it attempted by the personnel.

Peculiarity 9

"The design of the VVD [high pressure air] system does not permit blowing of the corresponding MBT by what is left of the air reserve when one of the VVD cofferdams ruptures. Blowing the MBT using the VZY [external air] system when on the surface is possible, but its effectiveness is extremely low, and it leads to a large loss of air reserve through blown tanks (see Act No. 6/8, May 26, 1989, on the results of testing the effectiveness of blowing the aft group of MBT using the VZY system).

The consequences:

This led to the impossibility of blowing the aft group of MBT using cofferdam No. 2 during the accident. As a result of the system's low effectiveness and a large loss of air through the blown MBT No. 7, the possible blowing of the aft MBT by the VZY would not have positive results in preserving longitudinal stability."

The designer's observations and response

a. The high-pressure air system aboard the submarine *Komsomolets* was built in accordance with OST V5.5017-79, and it is similar in its structure to the same systems of other submarines of the Navy. The assertion of the MD, O&R that this system is unique to the *Komsomolets* is inconsistent with fact.

b. Neither is the assertion that it is impossible to blow the corresponding main ballast tanks when one of the cofferdams ruptures using the remaining high-pressure air reserve accurate. When any one of the cofferdams fails, the high-pressure air system provides for surfacing of the submarine and subsequent blowing of previously unblown main ballast tanks through the blowing line using air from the outboard air main [VZY] with the assistance of a diver. The assertion that the effectiveness of blowing the main ballast tanks using the outboard air system when surfaced is extremely low, and that it results in considerable loss of air reserve through the blown tanks, is based on technical ignorance, on an ignorance of the elementary laws of physics. Act No. 6/8, May 26, 1989, to which the authors of the remark refer, has not been furnished to workers of industry, and it is not known who took part in the tests. In this connection it is impossible to offer any kind of conclusion regarding this act.

Field trials conducted November 2–3, 1989, aboard a certain submarine with the participation of representatives from the designer, from the Naval Institute No. 1, from the Naval Academy, and from the Northern Fleet's 1st Submarine Flotilla confirm the high effectiveness of blowing the main ballast tanks using the outboard air system, and the high effectiveness of blowing any tank regardless of the physical state of neighboring tanks.

c. The "consequences" formulated by the MD, O&R are deliberately misleading:

i. The personnel of the *Komsomolets* made no attempts during the accident to blow the main ballast tanks with air from cofferdam No. 2 of the high-pressure air system through the outside air main because of their poor knowledge of the ship's systems.

ii. Main ballast tanks can be blown with outboard air from high-pressure air cofferdam No. 2 by way of a special main connecting the No. 1 and 2 high-pressure air cofferdams. Because of the absence of the RBITS, the personnel had not practiced this variant of blowing the tanks.

iii. If the aft group of main ballast tanks had been blown with outboard air when the port tank No. 7 was flooded, only one-eighth of the expended air would have been used unproductively. To say that the system's effectiveness is low and that there would supposedly be a greater loss of air through the blown starboard tank is simply not rational.

Peculiarity 10

"The design does not foresee a system aboard the submarine for computerized documentation of events pertaining to calculation of stability and unsinkability, or an automated system to produce recommendations to the leadership regarding damage control in major emergency situations. In addition to this, the submarine lacks instruments to monitor the submarine's static attitude in a disturbed sea (violation of the requirements of Articles 9.2.5, 5.2.4 of the TPPL-75, and Articles 1.1.2.7, 5.2.2.8 of the OTT6.1.1-81).

The consequences:

1. An objective picture of the course of events in the accident situation could not be obtained.

2. The absence of a computer reduces the effectiveness of damage control and increases the time it takes to reach decisions in complex emergency situations.

3. The means of objectively monitoring change in the submarine's attitude are lacking, making it impossible for the GKP to correctly predict the submarine's behavior when water enters a compartment and the MBT."

The designer's observations and response

a. Automated systems for solving unsinkability problems and for issuing damage control recommendations are absent from all submarines and surface ships of the Soviet Navy. Instruments monitoring static attitude are absent as well. Moreover, we have still not developed the concepts of creating these systems, and we have not conducted exploratory research on the design of such instruments. The Navy has not issued the specifications for their design. All of the discussion concerning absence of these automated systems and instruments aboard the submarine *Komsomolets* are seemingly directed at consciously and deliberately misleading public opinion.

b. The requirements of the TPPL-75 and OTT6.1.1-81 do not apply to the submarine *Komsomolets* for the reasons set forth in observation "e" regarding item 1 of the "peculiarities," and any reference to them is wrong. As far as the essence of the issue is concerned, Article 5.2.4 of the TPPL-75 and Article 5.2.2.8 OTT6.1.1-81, which present the requirements for designing the systems and instruments, have not been accepted by industry even for the design of submarines in the future. Article 9.2.5 of the TPPL-75 and Article 1.1.2.7 of the OTT6.1.1-81 have no relationship to the issue under discussion.

c. As for the "consequences," the following needs to be said:

The attack center of the *Komsomolets* did nothing to study the objective information on the course of events in the accident situation. It neither monitored the change in the ship's attitude, nor did it carry out any kind of calculations on change in its buoyancy and stability. All of this could have been done without a computer or special instruments. As a result of the attack center's inaction, the loss of stability was a surprise to it. Given such an attitude, no computers could have helped; the authors of the remark are concerned not with clarifying the true causes of the tragedy but only with finding plausible "evidence" in an effort to conceal and justify the poor occupational training of the crew of the submarine *Komsomolets*, which was indeed the sole cause of the tragedy.

Peculiarity 11

"The design does not foresee a system for monitoring the filling (flooding) of the submarine's MBT.

The consequences:

This made it impossible to establish the causes of listing, or to monitor filling of MBT No. 8, 9, and 10 when their airtightness was disturbed."

The designer's observations and response

a. The TPPL and OTT contain no requirements to install systems aboard submarines for monitoring the filling of the main ballast tanks. The remark of MD, O&R that such a system is a necessity is groundless. Not a single submarine of the Soviet Navy has a system for monitoring the filling of main ballast tanks. Hence, the absence of such a system from the *Komsomolets* is certainty not a peculiarity of this submarine. Certain classes of submarines have systems that indicate completion of blowing of main ballast tanks. However, tank batch-blowing systems only were introduced in submarines of more recent classes, and the need for installing systems indicating the completion of blowing disappeared.

b. About the "consequences": The attack center could have clarified the causes of listing during the repeat blowing of the end main ballast tanks, which was done at 1134, by visually observing the tanks from the bridge. This clarification was not done. The cause of listing could have been clarified and filling of the ballast tanks could have been subsequently monitored by periodically introducing batches of air into the tanks through the diver tank blowing lines. This was not done either. In light of the above, it is clear that these "consequences" are wrong, and that they reflect a lack of understanding of both the ship systems and the facts of the matter.

Peculiarity 12

"Use of RAVA rubberized metal hoses, which have low resistance to temperature effects (around 150 degrees Celsius), in the outboard water system. Absence of a device in the outboard system preventing entry of water into a compartment as a result of rupture of RAVA hoses (the requirements of Article VII-7 of the TPPL-67, Article 8.2.7 of the TPPL-75, and Articles 1.3.3.1 and 1.3.3.6 of the OTT6.1.1-B1 were violated). In addition, there is nothing in the technical documents indicating to the personnel that RAVA hoses have low resistance to temperature effects.

The consequences:

RAVA hoses ruptured in response to fire and the elevated temperature in the compartment, which led to uncontrolled flooding of the compartment and loss of the submarine's longitudinal stability and buoyancy."

The designer's observations and response

a. There are no requirements of any kind in the TPPL and OTT on heat resistance of articles used aboard submarines. RAVA-reinforced hoses are guaranteed to remain serviceable at a temperature of 150 degrees Celsius for thirty minutes and at full working pressure, which are rather high characteristics for rubber articles.

b. The assertion that there are no devices in the outboard water system preventing entry of water into a compartment as a result of rupture of RAVA hoses is inconsistent with fact. There is a remotely controlled Kingston valve at the intake of the cooling line of the stern-tube gland, and a check valve in the drain line, which can isolate a damaged RAVA hose.

c. RAVA hoses are used aboard all submarines built in recent years, and their use aboard the *Komsomolets* is not unique to this submarine.

d. The assertion that the requirements of Article VII-7 of the TPPL-67 were violated is inconsistent with reality. The requirements of the TPPL-75 and the OTT6.1.1-81 do not apply to the submarine *Komsomolets* for the reasons set forth in the conclusion regarding item 1 of the "peculiarities." As for the essence of the issue, Article 8.2.7 of the TPPL-75 and Articles 1.3.3.1 and 1.3.3.6 of the OTT6.6.1-81 have not even been accepted for submarines of the future, because they are unrealistic (as regards mistakes of the personnel) and because of the requirements on operating conditions (pressure) are unsubstantiated.

e. The heat resistance characteristics of RAVA hoses are presented in documents given to the personnel based on K-909-045-ED1 (items 1049 and 1333).

f. As for the "consequences":

i. The operator at the main propulsion unit console did not fulfill requirements of Articles 90 and 91 of the RBZh-PL-82 with regard to sealing off the distressed compartment, and he did not close the remotely controlled Kingston valve of the stern-tube gland's cooling system, which does not affect the submarine's propulsion. This lack of action resulted in entry of water into compartment seven following rupture of the RAVA hose in response to the fire. The heat resistance of the RAVA hose has no relevance to this.

ii. Because of the absence of the RBITS, this measure was not practiced by the ship's personnel in firefighting exercises.

iii. The "consequences" conjured by the MD, O&R are inconsistent with the actual circumstances of the accident.

Peculiarity 13

"Low reliability of the electric power system and its components, especially of series AM and AM-M circuit breakers, the gap of which between the main contact securing pins is not checked during manufacture.

The submarine lacks a program supporting the reliability of technical resources (the requirements of Article 2.3 of the OTT6.1.1-81 and Article 6.2.5 of the TPPL-75 were violated).

The consequences:

The low reliability of circuit breakers has resulted in emergencies aboard submarines on several occasions. Sixteen fires occurred aboard second-generation submarines in the period from 1971 to 1985 due to shorts in automatic AM and AM-M circuit breakers. Because of the absence of such a program, it is impossible to organize high reliability maintenance of technical resources during operation."

The designer's observations and response

a. The assertion that the reliability of electric power equipment in systems in the submarine *Komsomolets* is low is not justified by any facts, and is inconsistent with the reality of the ship's operations. Not a single failure of the electric power system as a whole or of its components was ever documented in over five years of operation. According to the Elektrosila Association, the gap between the pins securing the main poles of series AM and AM-M circuit breakers is checked for its correspondence with shop drawings. The results are entered on the data card of each circuit breaker.

b. The requirements of the TPPL-75 and OTT6.1.1-81 do not apply to the submarine *Komsomolets* for the reasons set forth in observation "e" regarding item 1 of the "peculiarities."

c. As for the essence of the reliability issue:

i. The requirements regarding reliability of particular systems and of the submarine as a whole were satisfied by the designer by issuing specifications on new equipment with high reliability indicators, and with the large volume of experimental design work carried out by the equipment manufacturer, including manufacture of experimental models of this equipment. The requirements of the OST and GOST on designing these systems and devices were fulfilled by the designer during the planning of these systems and devices. All of this made it possible to guarantee high comprehensive reliability indicators in the specifications on the submarine *Komsomolets*.

ii. The high comprehensive indicators of the reliability of the systems, equipment, and the ship as a whole were confirmed by bench tests on experimental models of new equipment. The bench test included testing for failure-free operation of this equipment throughout the entire time of continuous operation established by the specifications, and experimental operation of the submarine on the basis of a special program, to include a fully independent cruise. A log was developed and a spare set of equipment not used aboard other classes of submarines was delivered in order to keep the submarine's reliability high. The high reliability of equipment designed on the basis of the designer's specifications and of the submarine as a whole manifested itself during the accident, in the course of which all equipment and systems operated without failure until the last moment, and all safety and blocking systems foreseen by the design worked, which ensured automatic accident-free shut-down of equipment of the main propulsion unit, including the reactor and the main turbogear unit.

iii. The designer drew up the following basic documents on the reliability of the submarine *Komsomolets*:

- design reliability justification K-020-556
- specific features of base support K-020-073
- equipment reliability indicators K-030-640
- technical crew calculations and justification K-030-631
- recommendations for developing the RBITS 21.GGK-E-478-82

iv. In accordance with the standard program for supporting submarine reliability No. 004-65-013, the Navy should have developed a specific program, with the designer's participation, to support reliability during operation of the *Komsomolets*. The program was not developed, and responsibility for this failure is borne by the Navy's Main Directorate for Operation and Repair—the author of this remark, who apparently is trying to dump the responsibility upon the designer.

c. About the "consequences":

i. Leaving aside the thoughts of these authors of the remark regarding electrical equipment of second-generation submarines as being irrelevant to the accident aboard the submarine *Komsomolets*, we need to say that in five years of operation of the *Komsomolets*, no negative remarks were ever made regarding the work of series AM and AM-M circuit breakers. During the accident these circuit breakers provided for automatic disconnection of damaged networks, distribution panels, and damaged electrical equipment, and ensured trouble-free operation of the electric power system until the submarine's loss.

ii. However, the Navy's MD, O&R did fail to carry out the following basic measures to support high reliability of technical resources during operation of the submarine *Komsomolets*:

- A reliability support program was not created.
- A set of repair documents for planned preventive inspections and repairs to be carried out between cruises was not developed.
- Basing [ashore support] of the submarine in accordance with requirements of document K-020-073 was not provided for.
- A technical crew was not organized for the submarine.
- The operating cycle governing use of the submarine foreseen by the specifications was not maintained, as a result of which the ship set off on its cruise with equipment and systems whose useful lifespan had already been expended (automatic systems, outboard fittings, gas analyzers).

iii. In light of the above, the thoughts of MD, O&R regarding the absence of any kind of "program," which made it impossible to maintain "high reliability of technical resources" aboard the submarine *Komsomolets*, is indeed correct, but it is their very own responsibility and not that of the designer.

Peculiarity 14

"Flammable materials that are not heat resistant were used to trim [fit-out or finish] compartment seven (glue, thermal insulation, etc.); Article V-4 of the TPPL-67, Article 3.5.10 of the TPPL-75, and Article 5.2.3.8 of the OTT6.1.1-81 were violated.

The consequences:

This resulted in swift development of the fire and an increase in the temperature in the compartment to 800 degrees Celsius."

The designer's observations and response

a. Materials corresponding to OST V5.9025-80 and the "Statute on Selection of Nonmetallic Structural Materials for Submarines" No. 74-0450-06-78 were used to fit-out compartments of the submarine *Komsomolets*, including compartment seven. They are all permitted for use in submarines. There were simply no other alternative materials that had been permitted for use in submarines. These materials are used to fit-out the compartments of all submarines of the Navy, such that this is not a peculiarity of the *Komsomolets*.

b. The assertion that Article V-4 of the TPPL-67 was violated is inconsistent with fact. As for the TPPL-75 and OTT6.1.1-81, these requirements do not apply to the submarine *Komsomolets* for the reasons set forth in observation "e" regarding item 1 of the "peculiarities." As for the essence of the issue: Article 5.2.3.8 of the OTT6.1.1-81, which was published to replace the TPPL-75, states: "Structural, heat, and sound-insulating and finishing materials...must be only nonflammable or fire-retardant." This requirement was satisfied to a realistic extent aboard the submarine *Komsomolets*.

c. The assertion that the materials used to fit-out compartment seven resulted in "swift development of the fire and an increase in the temperature in the compartment to 800 degrees Celsius" is absurd. According to calculations, when there is a fire in the compartment, when the initial oxygen concentration in the atmosphere is nominal, and when air does not enter from without, the average compartment-wide temperature would be around 200 degrees Celsius. Intensive development of the fire (and not swift, as the authors of the remark assert) was the consequence of the high oxygen concentration in the compartment atmosphere due to its uncontrolled entry. Further entry of air into compartment six out of the high-pressure air system due to incorrect actions taken by the submarine's command led to development of the fire and the increase in temperature in the compartment to 800 to 900 degrees Celsius (according to calculations) at a compartment pressure of 13 kg/cm^2.

Peculiarity 15

"The SDS [stationary breathing] system is not equipped with the necessary protection from entry of contaminated air from a damaged compartment under high pressure into the ShDA [emergency breathing] system when the airtightness of VSD [medium pressure air] and SDS pipelines is disturbed (Article 8.2.7 of the TPPL-75, Article VII-7 of the TPPL-67, and Article 1.3.3.6 of the OTT6.1.1-81 were violated).

The consequences:

This led to poisoning of personnel in compartments five and two connected up to ShDA."

The designer's observations and response

a. The stationary breathing system (SDS) of the submarine *Komsomolets* was developed in full correspondence with guidelines RD V5.5536-82, coordinated with the Navy. Such systems were developed for all submarines according to the same principle, and it is not a peculiarity of the submarine *Komsomolets*.

b. The SDS system excludes the possibility of entry of contaminated air from a damaged compartment at high pressure into hose-type breathing apparatus even when the integrity of medium-pressure air [VSD] and SDS lines is disturbed, because the SDS system is self-contained in each compartment, and the pressure in the medium-pressure air system is considerably higher than it could be in a damaged compartment.

c. The requirements of Article VII-7 of the TPPL-67 are satisfied to their full extent in the submarine *Komsomolets*. The requirements of the TPPL-75 and OTT6.1.1-81 do not apply to the submarine *Komsomolets* for the reasons set forth in observation "e" regarding item 1 of the "peculiarities." The essence of the issue: Article 8.2.7 of the TPPL-75 and Article 1.3.3.6 of the OTT6.1.1-81 have not been accepted by industry even for designing submarines of the future, because they are unrealistic (as regards mistakes by personnel).

d. As for the "consequences":

i. Personnel of compartment two were poisoned as a result of the incorrect actions of the commander of this compartment, who connected the SDS to the medium-pressure air system according to the back-up procedure, and then the submarine's command, which disconnected the high- and medium-pressure mains without warning the personnel of compartment two of this.

ii. Personnel in compartment five were poisoned because the commander of this compartment failed to monitor operation of the SDS system, which was receiving air from the damaged cofferdam No. 1 of the high-pressure air main, and the incorrect actions of the attack center, on the instructions of which air was cut off to the medium-pressure air system without the personnel of the compartments being notified.

e. Hence, the assertion of the MD, O&R that the absence of any kind of "necessary protection" resulted in the poisoning of the personnel is inconsistent with fact. It should be noted that among the measures to raise the reliability of personnel life-support resources in emergency situations, which were developed as a result of the accident, there are no measures for improving the SDS system.

Peculiarity 16

"The number of ship's personnel [crew] calculated by the central design office serving as the designer was insufficient to service equipment under normal conditions, and absolutely not enough to carry out submarine damage control in times of accident.

The consequences:

Damage control was made difficult, and it was impossible to fulfill all of the requirements of the guidelines regarding damage control."

The designer's observations and response

a. According to the detail design, the crew of the submarine *Komsomolets* should have consisted of forty-one persons, in which case the number of personnel in BCh-5 should have been nineteen officers and warrant officers. Without the consent of industry, the Navy increased the crew to fifty-seven (sixteen additional) persons by its Directive No. 730/2/00395 dated April 23, 1982; in this case, the number of personnel in BCh-5 was increased by only one person. Apparently, the Navy (specifically the MD, O&R) felt that this number was fully sufficient for this department, which maintains technical resources and carries out submarine damage control. This same directive introduced the position of watch mechanical engineer, which was not justified by any rationale or documentation, but which reduced the number of BCh-5 personnel serving watch in the compartments.

b. Later, four of the ten warrant officers of BCh-5 were replaced by compulsory-service seamen on the basis of naval directives; this significantly reduced the potential ability of the BCh-5 department in terms of both the technical maintenance of materiel and in ship damage control. The still later addition of one officer and two seamen to BCh-5 could not compensate for the weakening suffered by the earlier mass replacement of warrant officers.

c. It follows from these later modifications of the crew structure that the potential of BCh-5 was reduced, and the number of personnel became "insufficient," not because the designer incorrectly calculated the size of the crew, but because the Navy unjustifiably replaced warrant officers by compulsory-service seamen and reduced the number of BCh-5 personnel serving watch without grounds.

d. The assertion of the MD, O&R regarding an insufficient number of personnel is not reinforced by any kind of calculations. Were the qualifications of the specialists adequate, the increase that was made in the crew size, eventually to sixty-four persons, would have been more than enough to maintain the submarine under normal operating conditions. Analysis of the personnel's actions during the accident showed that most of the crew did not participate in ship damage control, and that the burden of this fight was carried by only a few persons.

e. The submarine *Komsomolets* set off on its cruise without the full complement of personnel in the damage control division of BCh-5 (and Warrant Officer Y. P. Podgornov had not been certified for independent control). The lack of a full complement further weakened the principal division of BCh-5, which was responsible for damage control. The requirement of Article 173 of the RBZh-PL-82, which prohibits a submarine from going to sea undermanned, was violated.

f. About the "consequences":

Analysis of damage control efforts aboard the submarine *Komsomolets* shows that:

i. The submarine's leadership used the commander of the damage control division for duties inconsistent with the prescriptions of Article 45, RBZh-PL-82, as a result of which neither the buoyancy and stability of the ship, nor the expenditure of high-pressure air, nor pressure in the compartments was monitored, and competent actions were not taken in submarine damage control.

ii. Captain 1st Rank Y. A. Vanin's crew did not have sufficient knowledge of the matériel of the submarine, and its combat training level was very low in regard to ship damage control; during the accident the submarine's attack center displayed passiveness in ship damage control efforts, and certain decisions that it did make were, as a rule, incompetent.

iii. The attempt by the MD, O&R to transfer the blame for the outcome of the accident onto the designer appears to be directed at obfuscating the low occupational and combat readiness of Captain 1st Rank Vanin's crew.

Peculiarity 17

"Low reliability of the 'Listvennitsa' ship GGS [loudspeaker communications] and battery-free telephone communication. Breakdown (short-circuiting) of the corresponding cables in one of the compartments resulted in loss of internal ship communication (the requirements of Article 5.3.5 of the TPPL-75. Article 5.2.4.2 of the OTT6.1.1-B1 was violated) .

The consequences:

Absence of communication made efficient leadership of submarine damage control practically impossible."

The designer's observations and response

a. The "Listvennitsa" loudspeaker communication system (GGS) is now installed aboard all submarines of the Soviet Navy; hence, this is not a peculiarity of the submarine *Komsomolets.*

b. The "Listvennitsa" loudspeaker communication is installed as a requirement of the Navy's Main Communications Directorate in spite of the opinion of the designer, who pointed out its shortcomings in comparison with the previously used "Kashtan" loudspeaker communication system. Without going into the technical details of the matter, I must say that the entire responsibility for the low reliability of the "Listvennitsa" loudspeaker communication system lies with the Navy's Main Communications Directorate, which issued the specifications, financed and monitored the development, and accepted the loudspeaker system for the Navy.

c. The assertion of the MD, O&R that the breakdown (short-circuiting) of the corresponding cables in one of the compartments led to loss of communication via the battery-free telephone system is inconsistent with fact. There are full grounds for believing that telephone communication between compartment five and the attack center was lost due to the incompetent use of this system (i.e., the distressed compartments were not disconnected at the switchboards).

d. The assertion of the MD, O&R that loss of communication made efficient leadership of submarine damage control practically impossible is inconsistent with fact, because all of the necessary and fundamental decisions and actions relating to ship damage control should have been carried out by the personnel of compartment three, which is the compartment containing the attack center. This assertion by the MD, O&R is only an excuse for the lack of response by the submarine's command in the damage control effort.

Peculiarity 18

"The design does not foresee a system for relieving pressure from the distressed compartment in major accident situations (the requirements of Article 12.2.9 of the TPPL-75 were not fulfilled).

The consequences:

This led to a fire in compartments six and five and gas contamination of compartments two and three."

The designer's observations and response

a. Navy guidelines on designing submarines do not contain requirements on developing a special system for relieving pressure from a distressed compartment. Not a single submarine of the Navy has such a system, and therefore its absence from the *Komsomolets* is not peculiar to the ship.

b. Article 12.2.9 of the non-applied TPPL-75 does discuss the relief of pressure by compressors during normal submarine operating conditions, which has nothing in common with the remarks here. Therefore, the reference to it, even for a ship to which it applies, is irrelevant and technically inappropriate.

c. In accordance with Article 275 of the RBZh-PL-82, the responsibility of developing recommendations on relieving pressure in each compartment of a surfaced and a submerged submarine of each class is assigned to the naval formations (organizational commands). These recommendations were obviously not drawn up, and obviously they were not studied by the personnel of the *Komsomolets* during submarine damage control exercises. The absence of the RBITS from the ship also contributed to this failure.

d. The assertion of the MD, O&R that the absence of a system for relieving pressure from distressed compartments led to the fires in compartments six and five and gas contamination of compartments two and three is inconsistent with the reality of the situation. The fire and gas contamination of the compartments was caused by the failure of the submarine's command to fulfill the requirements of articles 89 and 121, and the failure of the personnel to fulfill articles 90 and 91 of the RBZh-PL-82 regarding sealing off compartments, disconnecting high-pressure air and hydraulic system pipelines passing through the distressed compartment, and bleeding air reserves overboard from the damaged cofferdam No. 4 of the high-pressure air system. The absence of the RBITS and the failure of the naval command to fulfill the requirements of Article 275 of the RBZh-PL-82 concerning development of recommendations on relieving pressure from compartments also played a negative role.

Peculiarity 19

"The VVD [high pressure air], VZY [external air], and VSD [medium pressure air] systems do not correspond in full volume to the requirements on maintaining viability of technical resources (Article 5.3.5 of the TPPL-7, articles 5.2.4.5,2, 1.3.3.1 of the 0TT6.1.1-81).

The consequences:

Loss of airtightness of the air systems led to swift development of a compartment-wide fire, a rise in pressure in compartments seven and six, and of a temperature to 800 degrees Celsius."

The designer's observations and response

a. The assertion of the authors of the remark that the high- and medium-pressure air and outboard air systems do not correspond "in full volume" to the requirements of maintaining the viability of technical resources is groundless and unspecific. These systems were built in full correspondence with OST V5.5057-79, and they satisfy all requirements of the Navy. The air systems of the submarine *Komsomolets* do not differ from the systems of other third-generation submarines, and they are in no way "unique."

b. The requirements of the TPPL-75 and the OTT6.1.1-81 do not apply to the submarine *Komsomolets* for the reasons already set forth in paragraph "e" of the response to the first "peculiarity." That said, the essence of the issue is as follows: The requirements of Article 5.3.5 of the TPPL-75 and Article 5.2.4.2 of the OTT6.1.1-81 concerning system back-up had been fully realized in the *Komsomolets*, while the requirements of Article 1.3.3.1 of the OTT6.1.1-81 were not accepted by industry even to design submarines of the future because they are unrealistic (as regards mistakes by personnel).

c. The assertion by the MD, O&R that swift development of a compartment-wide fire occurred because the high-pressure air, the medium-pressure air, and the outboard air systems somehow "do not correspond" to requirements of the Navy does not reflect the actual events of the tragedy:

> *i.* In the initial stage of the accident there was neither a swiftly developing nor a compartment-wide fire.
>
> *ii.* An intense local fire was a consequence of the elevated oxygen concentration in compartment seven due to uncontrolled delivery of oxygen into this compartment. Failure of the control room to fulfill the requirements of articles 89 and 121 of the RBZh-PL-82, and the incorrect decision to blow the aft group of main ballast tanks with air from the damaged cofferdam, caused the rupture of the emergency blow pipe and, hence, the bleeding of air from it into compartment seven. This resulted in the loss of integrity of high- and medium-pressure air as well as the outboard air system pipelines, the bleeding of air out of high-pressure air cofferdams No. 1, 3, and 4, and the transformation of a local fire into a compartment-wide fire. These

assertions (number 19) of MD, O&R effectively obfuscate the inappropriate actions of the attack center of the submarine *Komsomolets*.

Peculiarity 20

"Valves of the emergency compartment pumping system are not equipped with manual control from adjacent compartments (the requirements of Article 12.2.21 of the TPPL-75 were violated).

The consequences:

This made it impossible to use the pumping system to relieve pressure from the distressed compartments."

The designer's observations and response

a. The emergency pumping system aboard the submarine *Komsomolets* was built in accordance with the OST, and it did not differ in any way from similar systems aboard other submarines. The assertion of the MD, O&R that the design of the emergency pumping system is a "peculiarity" of the *Komsomolets* is inconsistent with fact.

b. The requirements of the TPPL-75 do not apply to the submarine *Komsomolets* for the reasons set forth in the observation "e" regarding item 1 of the "peculiarities." However, the essence of the issue is as follows: Article 12.2.21 of the TPPL-75 states that the compartment pumping valves must be equipped with manual control from adjacent compartments. Aboard the *Komsomolets*, these valves had manual and hydraulic drives. The electrohydromanipulater that controls the opening and closing of the compartment pumping valve is located in the adjacent compartment, and it provides for manual control out of the adjacent compartment, as is required by Article 12.2.21 of the TPPL-75. Thus, the assertion of MD, O&R that the design of the *Komsomolets* did not fulfill this article is contrary to reality.

c. As stated, the "consequences" could obfuscate the inaction of the attack center of the submarine *Komsomolets* in containing the accident and fighting for the ship's survival. The decision to relieve pressure was made by the submarine's command at 1150, that is, at a time when the hydraulic system was disconnected such that control over ship systems in the distressed compartments was lost and the pressure in the compartments had attained 13 kg/cm². Under these conditions the pumping valve could be opened only by hand inside the distressed compartment, which would be unrealistic. It should be noted that the RBZh-PL-82 says nothing about the preliminary opening of this valve in case of fire. Considering that this valve is designed as a check and stop valve, it would have been reasonable to include a statement to this effect. The absence of the RBITS and failure of the naval command to fulfill the requirements of Article 275 of the RBZh-PL-82 regarding the development of recommendations on relieving pressure from distressed compartments also contributed to this failure.

Notes

Introduction

1. *Krasnaya Zvezda*, August 8, 1989.
2. *Sovetskiy Voin*, No. 1, 1990.
3. *Rodina*, No. 4, 1990.
4. Rear Admiral L. L. Belyshev, deputy chief of the Naval Main Shipbuilding Directorate, the journal *Morskoy Sbornik*, No. 6, 1989.
5. *Sobesednik*, No. 30, 1990.

Chapter 1

1. *Krasnaya Zvezda*, August 8, 1989.
2. *Smena*, July 29, 1989.
3. *Krasnaya Zvezda*, March 15, 1990.
4. Bringing a crew up to the first line means officially confirming the readiness of a submarine crew for independent navigation and patrol duty. This is preceded by a theoretical course attended by the crew in the training center, its training under a program of shore training between cruises, and study of submarine materials, instructions in manuals on operation of combat and technical resources of the ship and the organization of ship service, together with test cruises at sea and the passage of special tests, including in combat training and in organization of ship damage control.
5. *Krasnaya Zvezda*, April 15, 1989.
6. *Sovetskaya Rossiya*, April 26, 1990.

7. *Smena*, July 29, 1989.
8. *Krasnaya Zvezda*, October 7, 1989.

Chapter 2
1. *Leningradskaya Pravda*, July 16, 1989.

Chapter 3
1. *Izvestiya*, January 15, 1990.

Chapter 4
1. LOKh—an inert gas fire-extinguishing system aboard submarines. Freon is used as the fire extinguisher. Each compartment of a submarine contains a station of the LOKh system, from which a fire extinguisher can be delivered into that or adjacent compartments. The system is used to put out large fires at any stage of their development. The command "Deliver LOKh to compartment seven" means deliver the gas fire extinguisher to compartment seven to put out a fire.
2. "Listvennitsa"—name given to the internal ship loudspeaker communication system installed aboard contemporary Soviet submarines, including the *Komsomolets*.

Chapter 5
1. Line of defense—in an emergency, the attack center designates a line of defense—that is, it indicates the transverse bulkheads of the compartments that separate the zone of distress from the rest of the ship. At these lines of defense, the personnel seal off the bulkheads and plug the main pipelines passing into the damaged compartment. Constant monitoring of the airtightness of bulkheads and pipelines, the temperature of the bulkhead, and pressure in the distressed compartment are established at the lines of defense.
2. A quickly dismountable rack-and-pinion device is used to close bulkhead doors aboard submarines. In this case, the reference is to the rack-and-pinion ring, which had to be turned until the recesses in this ring lined up with teeth on the door, after which the door could be opened.
3. VPL—air-foam fire-extinguishing system. In this case, the reference is to the liquid that forms after the foam settles. For greater detail about the system, see endnote 35.
4. IDA-59—self-contained breathing apparatus. To connect an unconscious person up to an IDA-59 means securing the mask over the victim's face,

opening the oxygen bottle delivery valve, and verifying that the victim is breathing. For greater detail on the IDA-59, see note 2 of Chapter 13.

5. *Sovetskaya Rossiya*, April 26, 1990.

6. *Morskoy Sbornik*, No. 6, 1989; No. 2, 1990.

Chapter 6

1. *Krasnaya Zvezda*, 8 August 1989.

2. Here and subsequently, pressures are indicated in the values of a technical system of units (the meter-kilogram-force-second system of units), because all pressure measuring instruments aboard the submarine *Komsomolets* were graduated on the basis of this system.

Chapter 7

1. *Krasnaya Zvezda*, October 7, 1989.

2. *Izvestiya*, January 15, 1990.

3. *Krasnaya Zvezda*, May 13, 1989.

4. *Na Strazhe Zapolyarya*, April 25, 1989.

5. *Sovetskaya Rocciya*, April 16, 1989.

6. *Na Strazhe Zapolyarya*, April 28 1989.

Chapter 8

1. SDS—ship stationary breathing system. Provides air for breathing to hose-type breathing apparatus (see above). Charging the SDS system means supplying air to it from the high- or medium-pressure air lines.

2. ShDA—hose-type breathing apparatus. It is intended for breathing by personnel in a smoky compartment atmosphere. Air for breathing is supplied from the ship's high- and medium-pressure air lines through a stationary breathing system. It permits limited movement of personnel connected to ShDA apparatus. "Connect up to the ShDA" means donning the face mask or starting to breathe air from the stationary breathing system.

3. IP—the IP-6 self-contained breathing protective mask. Possesses an independent breathing support system. Used to protect respiratory organs from poisoned air at normal atmospheric pressure. To be "connected up to an IP" means wearing the IP-6 self-contained breathing protective mask.

Chapter 9

1. VPL system—air-foam fire-extinguishing system. Used aboard submarines to extinguish small local fires. A typical system consists of two air-foam emulsion preparing stations located in the end compartments, a line pass-

ing through all compartments, and hoses bearing dispensers (sprayers) located in all compartments. The air-foam emulsion is delivered by air at a pressure of 15 kg/cm². One of the system's stations is permanently connected to the line, that is, the VPL system is always ready for immediate use. When a damage control alarm is announced, the status of the stations of the VPL system is kept under constant observation. When the air-foam emulsion of the station connected to the line is used up, it is recharged. At this time the other of the system's stations standing in reserve is connected to the line. Stations are recharged and connected to the line during a damage control alarm without orders from the attack center.

2. TsVK—here, the digital computer system room. The TsVK room aboard the submarine *Komsomolets* is located in compartment three, next to the control room.

Chapter 12

1. When sending a radio message, a submarine must receive a message (an acknowledgement) from the addressee indicating that it had been received and correctly understood (decoded). The entry "no acknowledgement" means that messages confirming receipt of the distress signals by the addressee had not arrived.

Chapter 13

1. SIZ—individual protective equipment, collective name of equipment used to protect the breathing organs of an individual from environmental effects. Regarding ShDA, see endnote 32.

2. IDA—IDA-59 self-contained breathing apparatus. Has a self-contained breathing support system. Used for underwater work and for work in compartments with high pressure and a poisoned atmosphere.

3. VSK—rescue chamber. Aboard the submarine *Komsomolets* it was intended for the rescue of all personnel from a depth exceeding the submarine's maximum diving depth. It was equipped with limited life-support resources, and it had its own electric lighting.

Chapter 14

1. PDU—portable breathing device. Intended for short-term (around 10 minutes) protection of the personnel's respiratory organs in a smoke-filled compartment. Small in size. Each crewmember is obligated to always have a PDU with him when aboard a submarine.

2. SPS documents—secret Soviet Navy documents.

3. PGA-VPM—portable instrument for measuring the concentration of carbon monoxide in the atmosphere of compartments. Measurements are taken with indicator tubes for different concentrations of carbon monoxide through which compartment air is pumped.

Chapter 15
1. RDO—radio message. All radio messages from a submarine are numbered.

Chapter 17
1. RSP-30 mm—signal cartridges launched with a flare gun.

Chapter 18
1. Regenerating cartridges—chemical substances used aboard submarines to regenerate air (restore its percent concentration of oxygen and carbon dioxide) in compartments. Made in the form of flat wafers contained in metallic soldered rectangular cans. The submarine *Komsomolets* had only an emergency reserve of regenerating cartridges.
2. *Morskoy Sbornik*, No. 6, 1989.
3. *Izvestiya*, January 15, 1990.

Chapter 19
1. *Izvestiya*, January 15, 1990.
2. *Podvodnik Zapolyarya*, April 20, 1989.

Chapter 20
1. *Krasnaya Zvezda*, April 19, 1989.
2. From a report submitted by B. S. Taubin to USSR People's Deputy A. F. Yemelyanenkov.

Chapter 21
1. The newspaper *Krasnaya Zvezda*, April 19, 1989; the journal *Sovetskiy Voin*, No. 1, 1990.
2. *Komsomolskaya Pravda*, December 17, 1989.
3. *Morskoy Sbornik*, No. 7, 1990.
4. *Izvestiya*, January 15, 1990.
5. *Krasnaya Zvezda*, April 21, 1989.

Chapter 23
1. *Sovetskaya Rossiya, Leningradskaya Pravda*, etc.

2. *Sovetskiy Voin*, No. 1, 1990.

3. *Sovetskaya Rossiya*, April 26, 1990.

4. Ibid.

5. *Sovetskaya Rossiya*, April 26, 1990.

6. *Pravda*, May 12, 1989.

7. *Sovetskiy Voin*, No. 1, 1990.

8. *Morskoy Sbornik*, No. 2, 1990.

Chapter 24

1. *Izvestiya*, September 3, 1990.

2. *Krasnaya Zvezda*, March 15, 1990.

3. *Smena*, April 15, 1990.

Glossary

acceptance trials. Test of a ship to determine it meets the performance and technical standards established by the State

Aleksey Khlobystov. Soviet submarine tender/repair ship

"Anis." Specialized retractable submarine antenna

attack center. The area of the control room where the periscope stations and other equipment necessary to plan and control ship operations are located

AZ. Safety rods in the ship's nuclear reactor

AZ GTZA. Emergency safety system of the main turbogear unit

ballast tanks. The floodable tanks around the hull that are flooded to submerge the ship and blown "dry" to increase buoyancy and surface the ship. The tanks are grouped to permit control of the transverse and longitudinal trim and stability of the ship.

BBR system. Emergency cooling system for the submarine's nuclear reactor

BCh-1. Designation given to the navigation department on a Soviet submarine

BCh-3. Designation of mine-torpedo combat section on a Soviet submarine

BCh-5. Designation given to the engineering department of a Soviet submarine

Bukhta. Radar system including the retractable mast that supports the radar antenna

cofferdam. Plenum for the storage of high-pressure air (air bank)

conning hatch. Access hatch above the control room

DG. Diesel generator

gas generators. Devices that use powder fuel (similar to rocket fuel) to rapidly produce gas for evacuating MBT in an emergency

GEU. Main propulsion unit

GGS. General nomenclature for the submarine's loudspeaker communication system

"Gibel lineynogo korablya *Novorossiysk*." The Sinking of the Battleship *Novorossiysk*

GKP. Main command post

Gosstandart. State Committee for Standards

GUP. Main thrust bearing

GTZA. Main turbogear unit

hermitization. Ensuring the gas-tight integrity of a system such as the LOKh tanks

IDA-59. Self-contained breathing apparatus

IDA-59 CGP. Oxygen regeneration cartridges

IP-6. self-contained breathing protective tank

"Ivolga." Radio antenna located near the bridge area

KAS-150. Air-dropped rescue containers

KIL-164. Soviet ocean salvage ship

Kingston valves. Valves used to close sea access to cooling systems or flood ports at the bottom of submarine ballast tanks that otherwise are open to sea. Without Kingston valves, the tank requires a positive pressure to avoid flooding. In heavy seas, that air can escape from an open flood port, so the Kingston valve, while an added complication, can reduce the potential of losing buoyancy in heavy seas or if the tank is vented unintentionally.

KISGO. Compartment Readiness Command and Information System installed in contemporary Soviet/Russian submarines

KO. Volume compensator of the reactor cooling system

"Kora." Specialized retractable submarine antenna

"kor. R." A non-standard term used by the crew of the *Komsomolets* that apparently means "on the reactor shell"

Korund. The rudder control system

KP. Control panel

KR. Shim rods in the ship's nuclear reactor

LAS-5M. Emergency inflatable life raft

"Listvennitsa." A replacement to the dependable "Kashtan" internal ship loudspeaker communication system installed aboard submarines. *Komsomolets* had the new system despite protests from the designers.

LOKh. A fire-extinguishing system aboard submarines, which uses an inert gas (in this case freon) to starve the fire of oxygen.

longitudinal equilibrium. End-to-end (bow-to-stern) stability

MBT. Main ballast tank

Mir. A Soviet deep water submersible apparatus

"Molybden" Console. Remote console to monitor temperature, operate equipment such as hydraulic pumps, and blow main ballast tanks.

Morskoy Sbornik. Soviet/Russian Naval journal published bi-monthly

Mstislav Keldish. A Soviet science-research vessel

oil separator. Equipment to separate contaminants such as water from oil

Onega Panel. Remote console of the Onega system that can monitor the insulation resistance of equipment throughout the ship

OST. All-Union [Soviet] Standard, used to promulgate details to ensure the standardization of technical systems

OTT. Document of the basic technical requirements for submarines

PDU. Short-term portable breathing device (about 10 months)

PGA-VPM. Portable instrument for measuring the concentration of carbon monoxide in the atmosphere of compartments

"Prichal." Portable radio sets intended to allow communication between compartments in an emergency

PSN-20. inflatable life rafts carried outside the pressure hull on the rescue chamber, which were designed for twenty persons.

RAVA. Rubberized metal hoses used in cooler systems

RBITS. Manual on Combat Use of Technical Resources

RBZh-PL-82. Manual of Submarine Damage Control

RDO. Radio message

Regenerating cartridges. Chemical substances used aboard submarines to regenerate air (restore its percent concentration of oxygen and carbon dioxide) in compartments

RShchN. An electrical distribution panel

RSP. 30 mm. signal cartridges launched with a flare gun

SDS. Ship stationary breathing system

ShDA. Stationary Emergency Breathing System to which the crew can attach a hose to breathe when the air in the compartment is fouled

"Shtil" system. System which supported the reactor's emergency shielding system

Signal Number 6. Coded message (signal) that a submarine is in distress

"Sintez." Specialized retractable submarine antenna

"Sinus." Power supply system for the submarine's automatic equipment control system

SIZ. Collective name of equipment used to protect the breathing organs of an individual from a hazardous environment

SPS documents. Secret naval documents

State Commission Working Group. Representatives of the Soviet Navy and the Ministry of Shipbuilding Industry appointed to determine the causes of the loss of *Komsomolets*

"Tayna gibeli linkora *Novorossiysk*." The Mystery of the Sinking of the Battleship *Novorossiysk*

TPPL. Series of documents that specify submarine design requirements as promulgated by the Soviet Navy

TsKB. Design bureau

TsP. Control room of the submarine where the ship systems are monitored and controlled

TsVK. The digital computer system room located in compartment three, next to the control room aboard *Komsomolets*.

TTsNA. Turbopump units

"Udovl." Term used on the *Komsomolets* that indicates the satisfactory condition of the members of the damage control party

UKV Komar. Radio transponder and identification beacon

VMF. Soviet naval authority responsible for the completeness and authenticity of ship's logs

VPL. Air-foam fire extinguisher system

VPR. Reversible 400 Hz converter

VSD. Medium pressure air system

VSK. The rescue chamber located above the control room and in the sail/fairwater

VVD. High-pressure air tanks

VVD-200. High-pressure (200 kg/cm^2) air system used to blow ballast tanks to increase buoyancy

VVD-400. Emergency high-pressure air system

VZY. Air main for systems external to the ship

Index

259

About the Author

D. A. Romanov, a retired Soviet submarine designer, was the Assistant Chief Designer for the *Komsomolets*. While he has lost the support of the Russian Navy, he is still very respected for his expertise and courage by his peers in the submarine design community. He lives in St. Petersburg, Russia.

About the Editor

K. J. Moore is the founder and president of the Cortana Corporation, a high-technology applications firm concerned with submarine development. While on duty with the U.S. Navy, he served on board submarines in the positions of weapons officer, engineering officer, and operations officer. For the Navy and in private industry, he has held analytical assignments that involved the study of Soviet and Western submarines and submarine tactics. He also has managed major research efforts under the DARPA (Defense Advanced Research Projects Agency) submarine technology program (SUBTECH) that included investigations into the feasibility and design of automated damage control. Mr. Moore has made more than a dozen visits to the former Soviet Union and has met personally with leaders of the now Russian submarine design bureaus and related organizations. It was during one of these visits that he was introduced to D. A. Romanov.

About the Translator

Jonathan Evans Acus was born and raised in Cincinnati, Ohio, where he began to study Russian at Princeton High. He received his degree in Russian Language from Clarion University of Pennsylvania in 1987. He went on to do graduate work in Russian Linguistics at the University of Iowa and the Pushkin Institute in Moscow, Russia. He worked as an interpreter at the U.S. Consulate in St. Petersburg, Russia, from 1992 to 1994, and he worked as a translator at Cortana Corporation in 1996. He has worked in the IT field for the Harris Corporation for the past nine years. Jonathan resides in Leesburg, Virginia, with his wife Norma and his two children, Christopher and Sophia.